NOT QUITE HEALED

NOT QUITE HEALED

*40 Truths for Male Survivors of
Childhood Sexual Abuse*

CECIL MURPHEY & GARY ROE

Not Quite Healed: 40 Truths for Male Survivors of Childhood Sexual Abuse
© 2013 by Cecil Murphey and Gary Roe

Published by Kregel Publications, a division of Kregel, Inc., P.O. Box 2607, Grand Rapids, MI 49501.

The authors and publisher are not engaged in rendering medical or psychological services, and this book is not intended as a guide to diagnose or treat medical or psychological problems. If you require medical, psychological, or other expert assistance, please seek the services of your own physician or certified counselor.

Any persons identified in this book have granted permission for their stories to be told. The text clarifies where names have been changed, per the individual's request.

Scripture taken from the Holy Bible, New Living Translation, copyright © 1996, 2004, 2007 by Tyndale House Foundation. Used by permission of Tyndale House Publishers, Inc., Carol Stream, Illinois 60188. All rights reserved.

ISBN 978-0-8254-4270-4

Printed in the United States of America
13 14 15 16 17 / 5 4 3 2 1

— Contents —

— *1* —

SHOULDN'T I BE HEALED BY NOW?

MY NAME IS CECIL MURPHEY, ALTHOUGH EVERYONE CALLS ME CEC.

In the fall of 1985, I began to face my sexual and physical assaults. I'm still in the process. I'm closer to total victory, but I'm not quite healed.

Someone could counter with, "You're a slow learner" or "You haven't followed Jesus closely enough."

I don't try to answer such charges. I've moved as rapidly as I know how and don't feel I have to justify anything. After more than twenty years, when I talk about my healing, I say, "I'm almost healed."

Almost.

I wish I could say that I'm totally healed; but that would be a lie. This much I can say: I'm as straightforward and transparent as I'm capable of being. In the recovery process, I've searched relentlessly for total healing. I don't know if that labels me quick or slow, truly open or slightly self-deceived.

Some men heal quicker than others do—we know that. But I challenge the statement of anyone who boasts of total healing from sexual abuse in eight months or a year. Or even ten years.

I write this because I watched a once-famous and highly respected minister being interviewed on TV. He had previously admitted having a long-term sexual relationship with another man, and when the story came out, his church fired him. He also said a few words about being sexually abused as a child.

His admission of childhood abuse put him with the rest of us who have faced our pain and reached toward victory. That day I applauded him.

Less than a year after he had been publicly exposed, the man did an interview on national TV. These aren't his exact words, but he said something like this to the interviewer: "I'm free, totally free." He paused and smiled.

When pushed by the interviewer, he said, "I have no desires toward men." He went on for another sentence or two, saying he had been delivered from every evil desire.

His words sounded wonderful.

I didn't believe him.

I don't think he intentionally lied. Instead, I would say that it's what he wants to be true. I don't believe he's fully healed.

I wrote the previous paragraph without hesitation because I'm a survivor of childhood sexual abuse, and I've worked for several years with other former victims of sexual molestation. All of us who struggle with our past speak of a process—a long, long process. It's also an ongoing battle.

I understand the man's desire for instantaneous healing or quick deliverance. I'm sure we'd all like to have the pain wiped away and never be troubled again.

I absolutely affirm that God can produce such a miracle. I don't know of any, but I still think that's possible. As I listened to that man, I *wanted* to believe him. But his words didn't have what someone called "the ring of truth."

I'm sorry for him. If he's totally healed, he has no struggles to face. That's a positive factor, but it's also a negative one. As I point out later, battling for victory strengthens us and enables us to hold up our experiences for others who go through the same combat.

I'd like to be wrong about that man. If he's not fully delivered, he'll probably be miserable and exhausted from pushing back and denying his emotions or he'll slip and return to his old ways.

◆　◆　◆

A few months ago I participated in a seminar in which one of the plenary speakers was a pastor who spoke of his abuse and that it had once made him afraid to allow anyone to get close. He said God had healed him.

As I listened, this thought raced through my brain: *he's still not going to let people get close.* Then I thought perhaps I was being judgmental and silently chastised myself.

A few weeks later, another survivor and I had coffee together. He had also attended that plenary session. Without my saying a word, my friend referred to that pastor. "He shouldn't have been up there speaking," he said. "He's not healed enough himself."

How did both of us—independently—come to that same conclusion? I can't give you three reasons or any concrete analysis. Yet both of us sensed he spoke more about his *hopes* than his *reality.*

That's a major reason Gary and I wrote this book. Gary hasn't struggled openly about his abuse as long as I have, but I believe he has healed sufficiently to help me coauthor this book. His words, for lack of a better phrase, have the right tone. When he talks, I sense he's speaking from experience and understanding, and not from yearning for what he doesn't yet have.

✦ ✦ ✦

I understand the desire for complete emotional healing. In fact, after two years of facing my abuse, I often heard myself saying, "I should be healed by now." When I spoke those words, I didn't understand the pervasiveness of molestation. I wanted to be completely free from my past abuse and to have the memories wiped away.

It doesn't work that way. It *is* a process—and the word *process* means that it doesn't happen quickly. Or as I said in one seminar, healing from abuse is a process and not an event.

First, we need to realize that sexuality involves our total selves—mind, body, emotions, and spirit. God created us that way, and sexuality is a powerful force in our lives for good or for evil.

Second, our abuse took place in secret, and it happened when we were young and innocent. We lived with our hidden anguish for years. I turned fifty before my memories flooded over me and forced me to learn to cope with my painful childhood. Gary was in his mid forties before flashbacks revealed the abusive childhood he had endured.

Here's a statement I've adapted from VOICE Today,[1] an organization that works with survivors of sexual molestation:

> A victim of murder feels no more pain;
> A victim of childhood sexual abuse feels pain
> for the rest of his life.

Anyone may challenge that last phrase, "for the rest of his life," but I believe it's true. Terrible things were done to us, and it takes a long time—years, the rest of our lives—to work through the process and to undo the damage. *All our lives* is accurate because the damage is deep, painful, and we lived with our wounds a long, long time.

Deep. Painful. Those two words express why this is such a long journey. A major reason is that we continue to uncover layers of our inner lives tainted by the abuse.

MY NAME IS GARY ROE.

Sexual abuse was one of the cards I was dealt growing up. As a result, I have certain struggles or handicaps. I'm convinced that learning to deal with those handicaps and to heal is a lifelong process.

Not only is healing an ongoing process, but it demands courage to survive the barrages of hurt, sorrow, and self-accusation. The more we trudge forward, the stronger we become. The scars are subterranean and insidious, but there *is* healing.

At the beginning we may assume full healing is imminent—which I did—because we're unaware how severely we've been damaged or don't realize that our wounds have been festering for years.

For many, the abuse itself took place during a short period of time. It could have been a one-time assault or something that happened repeat-

---

1. See www.VoiceToday.org.

edly for three or four years. Regardless of whether once or forty-six times, the molestation worked like an undetected virus that invaded our souls, went systemic, and infected every part of our psyche. Among other things, abuse destroys our ability to see ourselves as we are.

At our core, we're sexual creatures, male and female. This is part of being created in the image of God. When others abuse us sexually, they touch us at the center of our being. Everything becomes skewed and produces a ripple effect that spreads through our entire personhood. The abuse alters the way we view ourselves, others, God, and life itself.

Here are two verses that help me understand this: "Run from sexual sin! No other sin so clearly affects the body as this one does. For sexual immorality is a sin against your own body. Don't you realize that your body is the temple of the Holy Spirit, who lives in you and was given to you by God? You do not belong to yourself" (1 Corinthians 6:18–19).

As I read Paul's words, I noticed his point that sexual sin is different from other transgressions because it has more pervasive, lasting effects than other failures.

How could healing not be difficult, excruciating, and time-consuming? We need to fight, not just for ourselves, but also for our families and all the others around us who've been touched by the abuse we endured.

When my flashbacks began to come, I told God that I wouldn't survive unless the purpose was bigger than myself. I wanted the war to be about more than myself and my survival. I hated the abuse, and I detested the idea that other boys—right now—are being molested by predators.

"I want to become a warrior against abuse," I told God, and invited him to use me in the war to fight such an insidious evil. The bigger picture of contending for other kids who couldn't stand up for themselves became a major driving force behind my desire to heal.

I saw not only my own life but also the lives of other victims and survivors in the balance. I was determined to do what I, as one person, could do to make the public aware and to reach out to other survivors.

That's one reason I've written this book with Cec. It's why I'm still relentlessly sifting through behavioral patterns and ways of thinking that are victim inspired and fear focused. I'm determined to become a victorious warrior. I won't give up. I will fight. And in fighting this evil, I will learn, and I will heal.

Our own healing must become *the* primary focus for us, or we'll continue to follow the same dysfunctional patterns we've been stuck in for years. We have to make a conscious choice to let go of fear and be open so that God's love and compassion can motivate us. We need to experience that love and compassion ourselves before we can spread it to others.

But I want to be clear: true, deep healing *is* spiritual warfare. Sometimes our learned and long-established behavior is our enemy. We have to fight our natural resistance. It's hard work but well worth it, not just for us, but also for everyone we love and care about.

Abuse causes most of us to end up with little self-esteem (although some become braggarts or bullies to cover it). We were overpowered, and control often remains a big issue—fighting for it or surrendering to those who threaten us by their words or presence.

Because someone we trusted betrayed us, many of us are unable or slow to believe others. We may freeze when someone unexpectedly touches us. Some of us slide into substance abuse to deaden the pain. Sexual dysfunction of some kind is common.

This isn't an exhaustive list, but I mention these because they're symptoms of long-term issues. Even to be aware of them isn't a cure, but it's like a doctor analyzing our symptoms and prescribing the medicine.

I'm not quite healed,
but I am being healed.

— 2 —

WHY AM I *STILL* NOT HEALED?

CEC

Some days most of us ask the question: "Why am I *still* not healed? I've been on this journey for five years."

Other days we examine our lives and remember where we started. In those self-reflective times, we admit we've come a long way. A friend said to me, "In the moments when you tell yourself that you ought to be farther down the road, you're probably healed more than you know."

Maybe he was correct, but I'm still unhappy. I want to be totally, completely, fully healed.

Why not? Why not?

I keep discovering the insidious results of the sexual abuse. It's a good thing I didn't see everything in the beginning, or it would most likely have overwhelmed and immobilized me. God *is* healing me, and I'm grateful. In my worst moments, it seems as if the healing takes place one day at a time, or perhaps even slower—one small step a year.

I've jokingly said, "If I'd known in the beginning that this would be such a hard, painful journey, I probably wouldn't have started."

In my early days of grappling with the issue, I felt that way because the feelings were too intense—and too brutal. But now I add, "I'm glad I struggled and fought. It's been worth reexperiencing the pain to discover the grace of God in many unexpected places."

◆　◆　◆

Both Gary and I tend to be overly responsible and take on burdens that belong to others. If something is wrong, our old way of thinking was, "It's obviously my fault." In childhood, we took on the blame for the situation. That's an exaggeration, but we grew up with that unspoken denunciation burned into our psyches.

Perhaps some of that was exacerbated by both of us becoming pastors—we were the servants, the official problem fixers, and we felt we were accountable to guide parishioners toward wholeness. Our motivation wasn't healthy, but people often rewarded us for our conscientiousness and kindness.

This isn't blaming church members; it's an attempt to be candid about my misconceptions about being a church leader. In retrospect, I realize I had so many wrong assumptions. I tried to love people and do kind things for them—and that was genuine—but sometimes for the wrong reasons. Although unconscious of the truth, I served them because I wanted their acceptance and love. That wasn't my only reason, but it was significant.

Here's what I've learned from my healing in progress: we try to make up for whatever we didn't get in childhood by expecting other people to provide for those unmet needs.

GARY

I was afraid—afraid of what other people thought, afraid they wouldn't like me. Or worse, I feared their anger. I also worried that if I didn't do whatever I could to make them happy, like many others in my life, they'd abandon me. If I performed well, their response would get me what I needed.

So why didn't it work? Why didn't I get what I wanted and needed?

CEC

I say it somewhat differently. I needed to be loved. I needed to be wanted and to feel I was worthwhile or significant to others. I became so enmeshed in taking care of others that I had few thoughts about taking care of myself.

Both of us learned that we didn't satisfy those deep yearnings by trying to heal other people. Fixing them didn't fix us. We remained needy. Nobody came along to repair our inner damage.

And as long as I have such overpowering needs, I know I'm not healed. At least not completely. That's why I think of myself as a work in progress.

Here is a statement of the same stark reality from Gary: "I didn't get what I needed from my mother. She gave birth to me. She's the only human person from whom I could have that basic, symbiotic relationship—and I didn't get it."

Symbiotic relationship is a term we use to express the depth of relationship between mothers and their children. A mother gives her children life and they depend on her to keep them alive. It becomes an emotional dependence during childhood. When children don't have that intimate relationship—and Gary and I are living examples—we're bereft of a special, caring connection.

Both our mothers are dead.

GARY

She's gone, and with her is gone forever the chance that my mother-love needs would be met.

I'm embarrassed to admit this, but I went through most of my life looking for the mother-love that I never received. It was subterranean, and I couldn't stop the unrelenting search. I now realize that I felt unloved and unlovable because my mother failed to provide the first, most basic emotional needs in my life.

This void showed up when I sensed someone I loved had started to pull away—I felt abandoned, just as I had been by my mother. The sense of rejection devastated me. I desperately tried to repair the damage—to fix the problem, to stop the rejection—as my soul screamed, "Please don't leave me!"

It was like a recurring nightmare. After each person emotionally abandoned me (and I usually contributed to it), an inner voice whispered, "You're unlovable." In retrospect, I can say that with each abandonment,

I was being deserted when I wanted to be loved. Each time was a reminder of my original unfilled need for mother-love.

That's the insidious nature of sexual molestation. Sexual abuse is the gift that keeps on giving. We end up profoundly confused about how to receive love from others and how to offer it to others. We often chase others away while pleading for them to stay.

Consider this example. A spouse comes home with shocking news: "I'm having an affair." (She may not say it that directly.) This happens to many men. For those of us who have been sexually abused, it's more than the breakup of a relationship—it's the end of a relationship with a person we trusted. And most of us have little trust stored up.

"The trust has been broken once again," we say. "We're rejected by the most important individuals in our lives." The old fears and deprivations of childhood flash into our hearts. Abandoned. Unloved. Unworthy of being loved.

The primal cry breaks through and becomes a piercing scream.

◆   ◆   ◆

Here are statements I can make about my life. I think they apply to many of us:

+ My yearning for unconditional mother-love can be met only by God. My mother gave me birth, and no human can replace her. Although I can get most of my needs met through other people, I can only get my primal-cry-for-unconditional-mother-love from my mother. She's no longer available.
+ I'm determined to stop looking to other people to meet that basic, unconditional mother-love need. They aren't our mothers, and they can't satisfy that craving. No human can. Only God.
+ My fear of being deserted, along with any defensive self-protection I attempt, comes from not feeling loved. I know I'm loved by many individuals, and I could make a list of their

names. I'm grateful, but their love isn't enough. They can'tsatisfy my primal cry. Only God can.

+ I can't give to others what I never had. I've tried to love unconditionally, and I do the best I know how. Unless I allow God to meet my most basic need, I'll be forever hampered in giving and receiving love.

+ Only when I allow God to meet my need for unconditional love will I begin to understand others for who they are and be able to love them as they are. Until then, unconsciously, I'll keep trying to get from them what I missed in my childhood.

CEC

We can make sexual abuse an idol—even an idol of disdain. We can elevate what happened to us and empower it with responsibility for everything that happens in our lives. Molestation can define us and control how we react to any situation.

What happened to us affects every relationship we have—even when we're not aware. Most of us acknowledge that we're shaped by the events in our lives. Molestation is probably the saddest, most devastating experience. That's especially true if we think of our respective ages when the abuse occurred.

There are positive answers for each of us. The more we heal, the more we acknowledge that we are worthwhile and lovable.

Both Gary and I have come a long way from the beginnings of despair and abandonment. If we pause and look at our progress, we might be amazed at what God has already done for us.

Almost every morning, I lie in bed for a few minutes and count the good things in my life before I get up. Each night, Gary replays memories of the ways God has used him that day. Even at the worst of times, he can remind himself, *I'm healthier than I used to be.*

More healing has to take place—and it will. I'm not quite healed, but I'm getting closer.

And closer.

What is happening in my life illustrates what I believe takes place in the lives of most survivors. The effects of our trauma continue to manifest themselves. There will always be people and events that trigger our abuse meters and send us reeling.

But we keep on.

Healing is a lifelong journey. To see it as anything else sets us up for disappointment and discouragement.

Gary and I and many, many other men have committed ourselves to pursue healing until the day we leave this life.

A friend of Gary's says, "Don't give up before the miracle happens." To this Gary adds, "I'm in the middle of the battle, and I thank God it's the middle and not a final end of defeat."

I am not quite healed;
I am a healing-in-progress.

3

WHY WAS I VICTIMIZED?

CEC

"Why me? Why did that person choose *me*?" I can't tell the number of times an anguished man has asked that question. It usually comes in the midst of deep pain and often through many tears.

Every situation is individual, but there are several common factors to tell why they chose us.

We were needy kids. Those four words probably sum up everything, but I'll break it down.

We didn't feel loved by our parents (or the parental figures in our lives). That doesn't mean they didn't love us; it means that we didn't feel that parental love.

Like all children, we were born with the need to be loved and nurtured—that's basic to any kind of emotional health. All of us were born with "skin hunger," which becomes satisfied by being held, kissed, and patted. Those are normal needs, and most loving parents don't need anyone to tell them to kiss their children.

One anonymous person wrote this on my blog: "Skin hunger and same-sex attraction are hard to tell apart. I'm pretty sure I'm gay, and I enjoy sex with guys, but often what I want is for a dad figure to hold me, or even just look at me. . . ."[1]

That's sad, but he understands the need for healthy human touch. His words, *a dad figure*, trace back to our basic yearning to be held, stroked, or patted by our parents during our early years.

Too many of us don't receive that loving touch.

---

1. www.menshatteringthesilence.blogspot.com

We also yearn for the right words, spoken in soft tones. Each of us needs to feel we're special to our parents. This doesn't mean we're the only ones they love, but we want to believe those parents brought us into the world and showered us with love. Discipline is part of that, of course, but most of all we need to hear those magic words, "I love you." I'm not sure any of us hear them often enough.

I can speak for myself and say that not once in my childhood did I ever hear either of my parents say those words to me. Did they feel loving toward me? Possibly—and that's my way of giving my parents (especially Dad) grace.

About six months before my dad died, I visited and finally got alone with him. I talked for quite a while, and I said quite clearly, "One thing I've wanted is to know you loved me."

He didn't reply. Even though I asked, he didn't say the words. I felt then, as I still do today, more than thirty years later, that the word *love* wasn't a word in his speaking vocabulary.

I'll try it the other way. *If* I had felt loved and wanted, and *if* my parents had assured me of their love by their words and satisfying my skin hunger and ministering to those needs of the young, I would probably not have been victimized.

We needy kids carry an invisible sign on our forehead that perpetrators sense. They gravitate toward unfulfilled and disadvantaged children. That doesn't put the blame on us, and I'm not trying to make parents feel defensive.

Think about those who molested us. They were people we knew—call them authority figures or people we should have been able to trust. For most of us, the abuse didn't take place because some stranger in the park grabbed us and held us down.

We wanted to trust; we needed someone who made us feel wanted. Loved. Even exceptional.

My male perp used to tell me I was special and said many, many nice things to me. He invited me into his room and fed me snacks. I ate those snacks while I sat on his lap.

Think again of what I mentioned above:

1. His words affirmed me (special).
2. He treated me as special (invited me into his room).
3. He gave me gifts (food in this case).
4. He held me (on his lap).

None of those actions are in themselves evil. As a kid, I'd sit on anyone's lap who wanted to hold me. So few adults held me that I gravitated toward those who extended their arms.

Those four things I've mentioned (and there may be more) were the preliminary steps. Because I didn't resist, my molester took the next step. His holding led to brushing my hair with his hand, stroking my face, and telling me what soft skin I had.

He knew what he was doing. He sensed my need and manipulated me to satisfy his evil craving.

+   +   +

After I had written the above words, I read an article in *USA Today* about profiling serial molesters. This call for profiling came out in late 2011, after a sexual-abuse scandal broke out with charges against coach Jerry Sandusky at Pennsylvania State University. Donna Leinwand Leger interviewed psychologist Michael Seto, director of forensic rehabilitation research at the Royal Ottawa Health Care Group in Canada.

Here are excerpts from that article:

+ "Serial child molesters seek out vulnerable children and cultivate relationships with them."
+ "They are not picking children at random."
+ "They are seeking out children who will be more receptive to their approach—children who may be socially cut off, impoverished, lacking a father figure."[2]

2. Donna Leinwand Leger, "Predator Profiles Mere Sketches," *USA Today*, November 16, 2011, 6A.

Experts have a name for what those predators do by giving gifts, having outings, sleepovers, and other ways to have physical contact with their prey. They call it *grooming*. That is, the predator gains a child's trust and ultimately gets him or her accustomed to sexual behavior. "When the grooming starts, the child may like the attention. They like the individual. The children are oftentimes very conflicted," said Ryan Hall, a forensic psychiatrist in private practice in Lake Mary, Florida.[3]

◆   ◆   ◆

I once sat with a small group of therapists, and we discussed this topic. One of them made a statement something like this: "Most of the boys I've treated were driven by an intense need for affection. They received no attention or love at home, so they were easy targets."

Another man said, "When a man prepares to molest a boy, he shows extreme interest in everything the boy says or does. It's not true interest, but that's how the child perceives it. His feigned interest makes the boy receptive."

"The abuse itself is often accepted in silence," a woman said, "because the boy feels he's receiving affection or has an attachment to the older person who has exploited the boy's needs."

"I've treated four perpetrators," another stated. "All four, in some way, said they were able to recognize vulnerable children who are easily abused." He pointed out that those children feel isolated, don't like themselves, feel insecure, and are pushed aside or ignored by their families. He went on to say that predators "who take advantage gradually accustom the targeted child to increasing physical contact in such a way that the child feels he willingly chooses it."

As I listened to them, I realized that sexual molestation is less a single act so much as it's a process—a gradual process—that leads to abuse.

---

3. Quoted in ibid.

GARY

We were needy kids. The fact is, all kids are needy. We come out of the womb completely dependent on those around us. We cannot meet our own needs. We can't communicate verbally yet. All we can do is lie there and cry or scream when necessary. We are born vulnerable.

If our parents or other parental figures meet our needs, it makes the difference. But if our love-from-our-parents needs aren't met, we may survive, but we have a love hunger. We start with a deficit in life, and predators not only sense our vulnerability, but they take advantage of it.

In my case, the lack of feeling loved by parents increased my susceptibility and left me unprotected. An elderly man knew this—in the way that only predators seem to know—and he took advantage of my neediness.

One therapist I worked with pointed out that I was probably a naturally sensitive, quiet kid. I was also defenseless. And the molester was a grandfatherly figure, certainly someone a boy should be able to trust. My parents left me unprotected, and I became an easy victim.

Like Cec, I don't remember hearing the words "I love you" in my home. I have a feeling my mother may have said them from time to time but, based on her actions, my heart could not accept her words as being real. There is no doubt that feeling unloved set me up for all kinds of lies and dysfunction.

A wonderful family took me in to live with them during my high school years after my dad died. One thing really struck me almost immediately. Every night before bed, both parents said to each one of their kids, "I love you. I'm proud of you."

The first time I heard them say this, I was shocked. The words also hurt.

Hearing them speak as they did to their children touched a long-forgotten hunger buried deep within me. As I lay in bed that night, I thought about their words and the way they hugged their children.

An unbelievable sadness came over me. I'm not sure I made a direct connection between what those children received and I didn't. But one thing did happen: I started to cry. I didn't know that I was grieving over what I didn't get from my own family, and I had no idea yet the horrors that I received instead of that love. All I knew was that it hurt, and that it hurt bad.

Not long afterward, my new mom said those two powerful sentences to me: "I love you. I'm so proud of you."

That night I went to bed shocked because I'd heard them, and I was overwhelmed with a lightness, a joyfulness I hadn't known before. That night I was fully at peace when I drifted off to sleep.

Even so, I couldn't fully "hear" or receive those words. Although I knew she meant them, my heart was too wounded. *If she only knew who I really was*, I thought, *she wouldn't talk that way*. After being raised in what I call a cloak-and-dagger environment full of deception and double messages, it was hard to adjust to love and approval, even though it was what I had longed for. Over time, I began to relax, and a sense of security set in.

When I went to college, however, that sense of security slowly dissipated, but it returned whenever I was in the presence of that family again.

Looking back, I can see how powerful the presence of safe people can be. The warmth and love I received from them were probably the first healing awareness I received for my woundedness.

Because of my adopted family, I've learned the power of words and touch. I try to tell my daughters that I love them and I'm proud of them every chance I get, and I hug them.

Even today, I regularly receive phone calls from my foster mom. I don't think I've ever heard from her or seen her in person when she didn't say something like, "We love you. We're so proud of you."

I've healed enough that I can finally believe their words.

We might not have gotten that affirmation and affection growing up. It's still out there, though. God makes safe, loving people available in our lives to meet some of our previously unmet needs.

Sometimes we have to seek them; sometimes we only have to be open to them. That brings us back to the fact that we have to engage in our own healing and make it our priority. We surround ourselves with safe people and listen to what they have to say to us.

Most likely, it will be some version of "I love you, and I'm proud of you."

Cec

Many of us once-abused kids ask the question, "Why me?" and we often come up with reasonable answers—or so they seem to us. Too often, however, they're the responses our violators have given us. And we accepted them without question. Why wouldn't we?

+ "You were such a wonderful child, and you wanted me to do it."
+ "You kept hanging on to me, and I did it to make you feel better."
+ "You were such a lonely kid, and I felt sorry for you."
+ "You said you liked it, or I wouldn't have touched you."

Those answers have some truth in them, except we need to remind ourselves:

+ We were children.
+ We trusted them to take care of us, not to victimize us.
+ We were lonely and felt unloved. What they gave us wasn't love; it was abuse.
+ We didn't know how to refuse an adult, especially someone who had been "nice" to us. They were bigger and more powerful.
+ We did like it—even though somewhere inside, we knew it was wrong. They stimulated our penises, and we naturally responded to touch. That's how God made the human body. But they didn't have the right to do that.
+ They were hypocrites. They tried to make us think they were doing this because of their love for us; instead, they molested us, doing that to meet their addictive craving.

♦ They didn't know how to define love. We have trouble defining the word, but this much we know: love never hurts or destroys another.

GARY

Christy, a good friend, is fond of relating a conversation she and I had a number of years ago. Emotionally, she was miserable and just beginning to tackle the issue of horrendous sexual abuse in her background. Her marriage was struggling. Her young daughter had just been diagnosed with a life-threatening disease. She wondered where God was and how he could possibly care about her. The pain was overwhelming.

In the midst of this time, she recalls coming to me and saying, "Gary, Why? Why? Why me?"

"Why not you?" I replied.

My answer became a turning point for her. She described something breaking inside her that day. She began the process of accepting what happened and learning to move past it.

Christy is now a successful counselor in private practice. Many seek her services because of her expertise and effectiveness.

Her past and how she healed from it (and is still healing) are powerful weapons in her arsenal. Because she has gone through the pain and recovery, she can help others heal.

When I said to Christy, "Why not you?" I was still unaware I had been sexually abused (my flashbacks started several years later). Christy is now using her healing experience to help me heal. Just yesterday, in the midst of a conversation about my current difficulties, she said, "You once said to me, 'Why not you?' Now it's my turn. Gary, why not you?"

I've been thinking about that ever since she said it.

Indeed, why not me?

Do I believe that horrible, unthinkable, evil sexual abuse skewed my world? Yes. Did the molestation profoundly affect my relationships and present me with a lifelong handicap that others don't have? Yes. Do I honestly believe God turned (or can turn) my ugly life into something beautiful? Yes.

At my best moments, I can see this clearly in my life. In my worst moments, I live in the denial that is so familiar to me.

Do I dare emotionally acknowledge what happened to me? Do I dare fully accept it, raise my arms and shout, "Why not me?"

Most of us survivors have asked or probably should ask, "Why me?" It's a natural and appropriate question. Too many of us either don't ask or we assume the answer is something like this: "I deserved it," or "I was bad," or "I wasn't worth anything better."

For most survivors, asking the why-me question is one stage we have to go through. It is a stage along the path to healing.

Cec says it's not a question he ever asked. "It didn't occur to me. By the time I began to heal, I was mature enough to realize the reason didn't matter. I had been a victimized child, and an adult was responsible."

We all heal in different ways and at a different pace. If you're still asking the question, that's all right. Sooner or later, God will bring you to "Why not me?" And from there you say, "I didn't deserve that kind of childhood."

Once I accept those statements, I'm in the process of healing. I can release the pain of childhood, and I can move forward in peace and healing.

Each day I face a choice: I continue to allow my perpetrators to victimize me by letting their words and deeds control my mind and heart, or I consciously choose to give my life and will to Christ's loving care.

"It was not my fault."

"It was not my fault."

"It was not my fault."

I may have to say those words fifty times a day (and they are true), before I can convince myself that I truly was an innocent victim who was hurt and molested by someone who had no regard for me, for my rights, or for my life.

Never forget you were a child. An adult or older person spoke the right words, but they deceived you. It was not your fault.

I was a needy, innocent child;
someone took advantage of me.
I wasn't bad;
something bad was done to me.

4

WHERE WAS GOD?

GARY

Horrible, unthinkable things have happened to us. We were violated at the core of our beings, and our lives forever altered and skewed. We couldn't protect ourselves. We couldn't stop it. Ultimately, most, if not all of us, ask the question, "Where was God?"

I heard a long time ago that we tend to respond to God as if he were like our earthly fathers. Intellectually, that made sense to me. Since I was operating mainly from a base of denial, however, I could not really grasp that my human father instructed my understanding of my heavenly Father.

Recently, I met with a friend and fellow survivor who challenged me again about this. He talked about his own experience. He said, "I made God into someone who gives me what I deserve. I deserved to be alone, abused, ashamed, screwed up. I constructed a God based on my experience and background."

As he sat across the table telling me this over coffee, it sank in a little deeper. I had done that too. I still do it sometimes. I believe we all do.

I've done more thinking about this issue lately. I lived and thought exactly what my friend did. I constructed my idea of God based on what had happened to me and my experience as a child. Since we only really know what we've experienced, this makes sense. How could I do anything else?

✦ ✦ ✦

I loved my father. He was a good dad. By good, I mean that I think he did a remarkable job based on where he came from and his own background.

I knew my dad loved me. He was a big guy. When I was with him, I felt secure and protected. He had a warm smile. He loved jokes and had a marvelous sense of humor. I always wanted him to wrap me in a big bear hug, but I don't remember his ever doing that.

He was a hard worker. He never finished high school, but chose to start his own business. He made it a success. He worked long hours and took good care of his employees. He considered their welfare his personal responsibility. His auto salvage yard seemed more like a family than a business.

When he was home, he was usually tired and emotionally unavailable. His marriage with my mom wasn't good, and our home was often an emotional war zone. Things cycled from screaming and yelling to stone cold silence and back again.

I don't remember his talking with me very much. But he attended all my activities—every baseball game and every swim competition. Though he continually complained about money (he came from a very impoverished background), he was clearly committed to doing whatever was needed to give me every opportunity to succeed.

Looking back, I respect him more and more. I can see his affection for me in many ways. I liked him and enjoyed being with him. But he didn't stand up for me. I don't believe he knew the abuse was going on back there from the time I was about three or four until six years of age. But why didn't he know? My abusers were family members. I'm convinced my dad didn't know, yet how could he have been so blind? Or was it a chosen blindness?

Because he did not know or was oblivious to it, he didn't protect me. I think he was afraid of my mom. Though he was big and a man's man, I believe down deep he was insecure. My mom was a small woman with a hard, domineering personality in the home. She controlled things, and he allowed her to rule our home. After an interchange between them, he often retreated into the master bedroom, shut the door, and turned on the TV. It seemed to me that he didn't know what to do with her. He would withdraw, pull inside himself, and not talk much at home for days. Though he was at every event I participated in, I don't remember doing much with him.

I vividly remember one scene that repeated itself every night. During my elementary school years, I had swim team practice for several hours in the afternoons. Mom sat in the bleachers, watched practice, and made notes in a notebook. Dad arrived by the time practice ended, and the three of us went to eat at a local cafeteria.

We sat down, and after Mom ate her entrée, she pulled out the notebook. She read aloud every mistake I made during the swimming practice that day. She badgered me about what I needed to change and insisted I must become better. Dad just sat there. I don't remember his ever saying a word.

They finally split up. After the divorce, and when my mom was out of the picture, I lived alone with my dad. Things got better. He began to come out of his shell and engage. He was broken, but happier. Just when I was beginning to experience some of what I had longed for, he dropped dead of a heart attack. He left me. I was alone.

I'm not saying this to run down either parent. I'm writing this to illustrate how these experiences powerfully affected my view of God and my relationship with him.

If I'm honest about how I really felt about God in my heart (and in my most depressed moments, occasionally I still feel this way), I would say something like this:

> God is there, sometimes. Sometimes he's not.
> He values hard work and is busy about his own business.
> He has the power to intervene but mostly chooses to stay quiet.
> Although God could protect me, I can't really trust him to do that.
> God is unpredictable, and I don't know if I can really count on him.
> He might pull back, distance himself from me, or even leave.
> God is strong, but I see him as weak in his willingness to protect and guide me.

> Though present sometimes, God withholds himself, and I
> wonder if he really loves me. He's distracted, unavailable.

All this adds up to a clear conclusion: As a child, I couldn't trust God to come through for me. I wasn't convinced he loved me. I had to seek for that primal-cry love in someone else. I had to take care of myself, meet my own needs, and figure life out on my own.

I've been honest here because that's how I responded during my childhood. I now accept this warped view of my heavenly Father as the largest, most crucial component of my denial.

I believe that the most important and fundamental relationship we have in life is our relationship with God. What we decide about that relationship determines how our other relationships go. If I'm in denial about God and that primary relationship, a ripple effect of denial will permeate every relationship of my life. It leads to a life of frustration, anxiety, and depression.

Because of what happened to me and the relational patterns of my earthly father, I didn't see God for who he truly is.

So where was God when that was happening to me? He not only was there, but he was involved, loving and protecting me in the midst of that hell. God finally rescued me from that environment and filled my life with solid, safe people outside my family who stepped in time and time again.

If I want to be honest about what should have happened, I should be dead, or at least I should be catatonic and institutionalized. The fact that I'm here and doing as well as I am is a miracle—actually, more like thousands of miracles along the way.

My emotions may still go crazy when I say such things. But my emotions are not trustworthy indicators of what is really happening. Remember that I operate from a deep base of denial. I do not see things for what they are. My feelings are not facts, and too often they're not based on fact. They are simply my feelings.

As I begin to live more in reality, I face a disturbing truth: In my fantasies, I constructed a god based on my background and experience. Natural. Inevitable. Automatic. But not true.

It reminds me of the movie *The Matrix*. In the story, the character Morpheus (which means "transformation") seeks and meets a character named Neo (meaning "new"), who unknowingly lives in the Matrix (a computer-generated reality that he believes is his life). Neo has an inkling that his life is a sham, and Morpheus offers him a chance to experience reality for what it is. Neo decides to take the risk, knowing that once he does, he can never go back.

Morpheus introduces him to the "desert of the real." The truth is shocking, and Neo begins to freak out. He finds that he has been a captive all his life, his mind controlled by machines as he lived in the computer-generated, untrue world of the Matrix. Reality is that he is now at war against the machines and their agenda to keep him trapped in the Matrix. He doesn't like this new world. It terrifies him. But he has no choice but to engage in this battle. It's reality.

Before he can do that, however, Neo has to allow others to help him heal from the effects of living his life inside the Matrix. It takes time. As Neo heals, he enters into training, learning about how to live in the desert of the real. His mind becomes more his own, and he triumphs as the hero of the story. He becomes a warrior against the evil that trapped him and that still holds most people captive.

As he lives more in reality, the Matrix has less and less hold on him. Finally, he is able to reenter the Matrix, but he doesn't operate according to its rules. His life mission is to expose the Matrix and bring it down.

I understand that film because I lived in a world of my own construction for decades. The abuse was not my fault. To some degree, I had to construct that world to survive. Actually, I believe we all live in our little imagined world to some degree. Some of us just spend more time there than others.

Part of healing is discovering the depth of our own personal Matrix, and coming to the conclusion that we no longer choose to live there. We get to engage in the desert of the real. This is coming out of the darkness and into the light. As we do, we'll trust God more. As we trust more, he reveals more of his goodness.

I matter to God—
the one who has the power to heal me.

— 5 —

I AM AN ARTICHOKE.

CEC

People often use the image of peeling an onion to describe dealing with issues one layer at a time. For me, that metaphor breaks down because when the peeling stops, there's nothing left. By contrast, I think of the artichoke, especially in the area of male sexual abuse.

The artichoke has tiny thorns at the tip of each leaf. Think of that as a danger signal—a warning of pain if we proceed. The best way to handle the thorny problem is to snip off the thorns and keep going.

We peel off the leaves one at a time and eat them. With my metaphor, it means we face our issues one at a time. When all the leaves are gone, we are left with only the heart—the most delicious part.

This illustration is a good way for me to understand sexual abuse. We start by facing the abuse. It's thorny, threatening, and painful. From there, if we're willing to move forward, we face the effects—we pull off one leaf at a time. We chew on a leaf until we're ready to swallow it and move on to the next.

The problem with abuse is that we rarely know or understand the effects. We struggle with the obvious issues (Gary and I talk about many of them in this book) and feel we've done it. We've arrived. Healed. We're free.

Not quite.

We discover there are more leaves we have to pull away. If only it were that easy. Of course, all metaphors break down at some point. We don't grasp the other issues, especially in our first days of healing. We focus on the issues of which we've become aware. It usually takes time before we realize that there are more—many more—problems and deeper concerns we have to face.

Let's call it another level and leave the picture of the artichoke. Healing from abuse means that we're always digging, digging, digging deeper. We continue to move from one level to the next—getting down into the nonconscious parts of ourselves. If we probe below the surface, we discover things about ourselves that might come as great shocks. Our deeper selves want to save us from pain, so they go to great lengths to hide dangerous truths. It takes a great deal of concerted effort, honesty, and time to move into the lower levels of our subterranean territory.

Let's change the picture again. I like the image of a spiral. It keeps coming around, and we see the same thing but from a different point on the spiral.

I want to explain what I mean by telling you how the spiral has worked in my life. One of the effects of sexual abuse is that a man feels a lack of self-worth. He may not say, "I'm nothing and worth nothing," yet his emotions reinforce that message. They make him feel he's useless and no good.

On that I speak from experience. Only now, years later, can I articulate it, but my inability to express it didn't make the issue less significant.

I felt useless. Worthless. Not as good as other boys. I had three brothers (one older), and they all seemed handy with tools. When I tried to use a wrench, Dad or one of my brothers laughed or snatched it away so I didn't mess up anything. In a family where working with our hands was of high value, it's easy to see why I failed each time.

My father was a hard worker—and drove himself five days a week; he stayed drunk most of the other two. He laid heavy demands on us. He assigned us chores even when we were quite small. Because I was the oldest of the three youngest children, I felt responsible to see that we accomplished everything he told us to do.

I'm not sure how it happened, but I became designated as the good kid who did his share and usually a little more. Chuck, the baby, did his chores if I kept at him and checked on him frequently. My younger brother, Mel, avoided work as much as possible and rarely did the work Dad laid out for him.

I faced a choice almost every day until I was twelve or thirteen: I could leave Mel's chores undone (which I sometimes did), or I could cover up and do them for him (my usual response) so that Dad didn't yell at me. Sometimes he beat me even if Mel was the one who didn't do his assigned tasks.

Trying to tell Dad about Mel being irresponsible did no good. I received the blame, and Dad yelled at me and beat me anyway. "You lazy wart," he said. I was never clear on what the "wart" part meant, but I got the message. I must have absorbed those words because they've stayed with me ever since.

Think of the combination: I had little self-esteem, and the most important man in my life, my father, called me lazy. I wasn't aware of my response to that verbal and physical abuse for another forty years. It reinforced my lack of self-esteem. It showed itself by a compulsive, frenetic push to deny my laziness.

Here's how my life has evolved. I worked hard. I don't say this to brag, but to point out my drivenness. Feeling tired proved to me that I was lazy. During high school, except for having a place to stay and having my mother wash my clothes, I fully supported myself. I ate my meals away from home. I also carried a B+ average and was never able to move beyond that because I wasn't good at ROTC, in which I earned a straight C every semester.

I became aware of being driven only after I finished two grad school programs—and earned top grades in both. I also studied at both grad schools *at the same time.* In January, I received an MA in education with honors, and in June I received a Master of Divinity magna cum laude. I was also a part-time pastor of a small church where I preached Sunday morning, taught Sunday school, and worked with the young people on Sunday and Wednesday evenings.

This isn't bragging; this is exposing the blatant effects of my childhood abuse. This is the confession of a man who was driven to achieve to prove that he wasn't lazy or worthless. And because he didn't believe he was worth anything, he tried harder.

I began to write a year after I earned the double masters' degrees. I was enrolled in a PhD program, and by then I had become a full-time pastor. I had enough sense to drop out of the doctoral program (and endured a lot of self-loathing for being lazy).

When I was still a full-time pastor, I preached twice in the morning, taught Sunday school between the two services, and conducted a Bible study at night. I also visited prospects one or two nights a week. I wrote twenty-five books before I left the pastorate to write full time.

I was driven. This was the same issue that began with a sense of worthlessness. The frenetic behavior hid the truth from myself because I stayed too busy for serious self-examination.

The relentless need to prove myself pushed me, although I had no awareness of what compelled me. It felt normal and natural. In reality, I was still proving to Dad and to the world that I wasn't slothful and inadequate.

At the time of this writing, I have published 130 books. Some people admire me for doing so much, and in the past that would have nudged the self-esteem meter up slightly—and temporarily. I had to keep getting accolades for my achievements.

As strange as that is, people sometimes referred to my amazing amount of energy. "I'd like to bottle that energy up and sell it," the writer Suzanne Stewart used to say.

I didn't know what she meant. Truly I didn't. I didn't believe I had as much energy as other people. I chided myself. If I didn't sleep so much, I told myself, I probably could get more done.

Insidious. Evil.

I was a driven man for most of my life.

The spiral had shown itself in three ways. First, I felt worthless. Second, I felt lazy. Third, I tried to overcome the laziness by overachieving.

One day, it hit me: I wasn't lazy. (At the time, I hadn't yet dealt with my sexual or physical abuse.) I raced into the room where my wife, Shirley, sat, and I yelled, "I'm not lazy!"

She stared at me, a quizzical look on her face. "Whoever said you were?"

"Dad did. All the time." After I said those words, something happened inside me. That moment of enlightenment became the first crack in the wall of worthlessness that had enslaved me.

My insight didn't end the problem, but the awareness slowly made the truth known to me. Knowing the truth about myself is not the same as living the truth about myself. But self-awareness was the first step, and more would follow.

I still work hard, but less often do I feel the *compulsion* to prove my worth to anyone. A heavily self-disciplined lifestyle has been so ingrained in me; I don't want to be different. The spiral has moved into a realm of awareness. The compulsion to prove my worth may return in some virulent form, but I'm now emotionally and spiritually equipped to face whatever form it morphs into.

I like who I am, and I'm grateful for the energy God has given me. I continue to work long hours, but the motivation is different. I'm free from the tyranny of the voice that whispers, "You're lazy."

Instead I say, "God gave me the gifts of high-level energy and self-discipline, and I do everything quickly. I'm extremely blessed."

GARY

I felt small, worthless, and never good enough. I developed an insatiable desire to prove myself. I also had tremendous pressure from one of my perpetrators to excel, achieve, and outperform all the other kids. *Maybe if I perform well enough, I can please them and they won't hurt me again*, I thought.

To an extent, my attitude worked. The abuse stopped when I started school at age six. I assume the continued rape was too risky. But at the time, I thought I'd somehow performed well enough to earn a reprieve. I did well and earned straight A's—I went through grade school without a single B. Even more significant within the school than my academic achievement was the fact that I joined a swim team, and by age ten, even though I was small, I was ranked in the top ten in the nation.

As a swimmer, I piled up trophies and medals. Life became a

competition. I received praise from my primary perpetrator, and that fueled my yearning to achieve even more. But with each success, the bar was raised higher. I didn't know it, but I had stepped onto a treadmill of never-ending, ever-escalating self-expectations.

I still felt worthless, small, and never good enough. I had no sense of satisfaction despite my accomplishments. I didn't know it, but I was desperately searching for love and safety. Constantly I sought the approval of others. I did anything to please important people in my life and was overjoyed when they praised me.

When I was ten, our swim coach led us in a sort of mantra after an extremely long, exhausting workout. "What do you do when you hit the wall?" he yelled.

"We go over it!" we screamed in response.

Those words became my motto for life. Driven. Obsessed. Compelled to win. As a kid in school, I believed approval and love would be my rewards.

For that to happen, I had to be the best. When I didn't think that was possible, I just didn't try. I found a way to quit certain activities like taking piano lessons. That driven approval-seeking continued through high school, college, and seminary. I graduated co-valedictorian of my high school class, third in my class in college, and second in my class at seminary. I continued to swim well, routinely competing against guys a foot taller, and still ended up nationally ranked every year in college. I was recently elected to my college's athletic hall of fame.

But none of that rewarded me with what I most needed.

After completing seminary, I went to Japan as a church-planting missionary. I attacked the language, completing the normal two-year course load in a year and a half. When we moved to our ministry station, I worked nonstop. I pushed myself to the limit, fighting headaches and what became chronic fatigue. (As I had yet to learn, my mind pushed until my body rebelled.) Every three months or so, I collapsed for two or three days. I berated myself for being so weak, and I kept on.

I couldn't pace myself; I didn't know how to rest. Fun was nonexistent.

Only work and performance counted. If I wasn't working, I grew restless. My only form of entertainment was watching movies to distract myself.

Often, it felt as if I were going to implode.

After five years in Japan, I returned to the States and pastored two churches over the next fourteen years. During that time, my wife and I adopted three girls (sisters, aged six, nine, and eleven) from Colombia, South America. It was like having grown triplets overnight. Our lives changed dramatically, and my stress level exploded off the scale.

I couldn't outrun the pressures. I couldn't even keep up with them.

During all of that, the huge, yet so-far-unknown shadow of abuse hung over me. I didn't know it was there because I had been running from it all my life.

One day I stopped. I simply couldn't run any longer. My tank registered empty.

That's when the flashbacks started. I didn't want to believe what I was seeing and experiencing. I was shocked, confused, and terrified. Yet I knew they were true. Memory gaps began to fill in. Certain events in my past and in my family started to make sense—horrible, terrible sense. I saw the effects of the abuse in every nook and cranny of my behavior and thinking.

That was my spiral at work. The issues hadn't changed, but they hit me in different ways.

Or to use Cec's other metaphor, I discovered the thorns of the artichoke, and they were painful beyond description. As I allowed myself to feel the pain, however, I also experienced relief.

I had been a victim. It hadn't been my fault.

If it wasn't my fault, that meant I could change. I could heal. I could choose a different path.

Life could be different.

Gary Roe could be different. Another turn of the spiral.

Like Cec, I still labor long hours. At present, I work full-time as a hospice chaplain, serve as a part-time pastor, and cooperate with Cec on writing projects. At times the abuse still drives me. But the motivation for my work is slowly changing. I'm making progress—and it is a process.

God is gracious with me; I need to be more gracious with myself.

Because I'm being healed,
I continue to gain new insights into my behavior.

MORE LESSONS FROM THE ARTICHOKE.

Cec

I was nearly through the first draft of this book when I plucked another leaf from the artichoke. I faced something about myself that I had heard many times before. That doesn't mean I had learned it.

Here's an aphorism I wrote three years earlier, and it continues to come up in my life: no matter how many times I hear something, I will deny what I'm not prepared to accept.

I've also learned that the incident that provokes the insight—an insight enough to make us change—may appear quite insignificant when compared with the enormity of the issue. That's when people may say to us, "You overreacted." Perhaps we did, but we weren't responding to *that* incident as much as to the hidden meaning it triggered.

Triggers is one of those buzzwords that refers to jolting reminders of traumatic events. They're often overwhelming emotions much like the ones we felt at the time of the abuse. They can be smells, sounds, places, or seeing a picture of the abuser. Some triggers are more subtle. If our abuse happened when we felt lonely, rejected, or sad, those feelings often produce anxiety.

◆ ◆ ◆

Here's my story and I don't want to point an accusing finger at my friend. This is about me and not about someone else's actions or motives.

A friend of longstanding returned my phone call yesterday. The first sentences out of his mouth were angry and loud. We've known each other for years, and he'd never spoken to me like that.

He jumped me about something and screamed at me for making the phone call—and I apologized. He admitted that I hadn't known how he felt and he hadn't told me, but he didn't apologize for yelling at me.

We briefly discussed the purpose of my call, and I concluded the call as quickly as I could. Before I hung up, I apologized again. And he said, if not in actual words, what amounted to, "It's all right. I forgive you."

About twenty minutes later, I realized I was furious, but I couldn't figure out what troubled me. Off and on for the next couple of hours I wrestled with my burgeoning anger.

"What's going on?" I kept asking myself.

Immediately I chided myself and said, "Just get over it. He's a good friend."

But I couldn't get over it.

I went to bed and fell asleep. Two hours later I awakened, and the incident was even stronger on my mind. I lay in bed and pondered what troubled me. I've learned that sometimes I have an emotional reaction and have to move away from the actual incident so I can figure out the cause of my feelings.

As I lay there, I kept thinking of the intense feelings over the incident. Just then, I experienced one of those *aha!* moments. Even though I felt hurt and angry because of what he said and also because he didn't apologize for yelling, those two things were only the triggers that opened up the pain.

I finally admitted I was upset, and soon I figured out three reasons why this was true. First, I apologized *twice* for something that wasn't my fault. Second, it irked me that I apologized because I hadn't known I created a problem by calling him—and it was something I had done seven or eight times during the past year. Third, shouldn't he have apologized for his harsh tone and fuming words?

As I lay in bed and rehearsed as much of the conversation as I could remember, I "heard" the voice of my parents inside my head. Mom would not have shouted as loudly as my friend did, but her words started with a warning: "If you ever . . ." or "I've never been so hurt in all my life as I was when you . . ."

Far worse to me was my dad's voice. He was a man of few words, but the anger I heard in my friend's tone felt exactly like the same violent level my dad used before he "whipped me" as he called it.

Connecting my friend's yelling to my dad's violence was the first blip of insight—a sharp leaf to pull from the artichoke and eat.

But there was another bite I still had to take.

I had apologized during the phone call. *Twice.* I said I was sorry for something that wasn't my fault.

"What goes on inside me that I feel compelled to do that?" As soon as I asked myself the question, I knew the answer. That's how I had responded to Dad. I apologized repeatedly (even when the incident hadn't been my fault). Sometimes—rarely—if I apologized enough, he calmed down and forgot or warned me not to let it happen again.

Three sentences yelled inside my head as I got out of bed and paced our family room.

"I had nothing for which to apologize!"

"I didn't do anything wrong!"

"I apologized twice for something that wasn't my fault!"

As I heard the scream of that third sentence, I realized something— something I had heard before but not accepted.

I became aware that I frequently used to say, "I'm sorry." I apologized whenever anyone directed a negative comment at me or I couldn't do something that others did well. I was sorry for not being mechanical, for not being more athletic, for not having more money. And if I did something that was foolish or unkind, I apologized two, three, or perhaps six times.

My late brother-in-law Carl Boehmke once said to me, "Why are you always apologizing?" I'm sure he said more than that, but those words stuck with me. I was then married, twenty-seven years old, and the father of three children. I was an adult but still not able to face the reality that I didn't have to be able to do everything or accomplish everything others did.

That frequent apologizing may not sound like I was taking responsibility for something that was outside my control, but it was. It meant I had failed to do what was expected of me. I *should have been* more mechanically minded, or more thoughtful, or more sensitive, and the list went on indefinitely.

I didn't stop apologizing after Carl softly rebuked me, but it was the beginning. Those words stayed inside my heart for years. (Obviously, or I wouldn't have remembered them.) The problem is that I never acted on his rebuke or knew what to do about my need to apologize.

Oddly enough, only two weeks before the phone call, my friend of longstanding Tom Scales had gently rebuked me for apologizing for something—again not my fault. I had partnered with another person in a project and the other person messed up badly, and I felt culpable about circumstances over which I had no control. I had become responsible for someone else's failure.

Then it hit me.

Responsible.

That's who I was—the responsible one. That's who I had been most of my life. Every child has a role in the family scheme, and those positions aren't consciously meted out. My position of being the good boy, responsible for my younger brothers, extended beyond our home. When I was in third grade, Mel's first-grade teacher called me down to her class to talk to my younger brother because he had misbehaved.

Even though she hadn't been my teacher, she told me that she knew I was a good student and felt sure I could straighten him out. Good student meant good, responsible boy.

When Mom and Dad filled out their will, they wanted me to be the executor. "I live a thousand miles away," I said. Five of my six siblings were still alive, and I told my parents to ask one of them. They explained their reasonings—one wasn't responsible, one sister was married to a man they didn't like. They insisted I was the only one. That's the first and only time I refused my parents.

Both of them let me know that they were disappointed. And yes, I apologized five or six times, even though I refused.

That's who I was. (I wasn't always good, of course, but my family didn't know of my youthful rebellion because I did those things away from home.)

Like Gary says elsewhere about himself, I felt responsible. That good-boy image followed me through my teen years and into my adult life. I suppose it's natural that I would end up an ordained minister. That's a wonderful place for people who like to feel accountable for everyone. It may not be healthy, but a lot of us are like that.

✦   ✦   ✦

So I took another bite of the artichoke, and my eyes filled with tears. I had been enlightened—I received an invaluable insight—but that was only the beginning. Part of taking that bite was to chew on it by deciding on corrective steps.

We all deal differently with our insights, so I can tell you only what I did (and am doing).

First, I write prayer requests on three-by-five-inch file cards and pray through the list each morning. I wrote the single word *Responsible* on a card. As I prayed for God's help, I also affirmed my new attitude with such statements as:

> I am not responsible for others' actions.
> I am accountable only for myself and for my actions.
> God has called me to love people and not to be an unhealthy caretaker.

GARY

I discover new leaves all the time. Although I know the effects of my abuse went through my entire being, I'm still surprised when I unexpectedly slam into another result of the sexual trauma in my life. Slowly, I'm learning to smile instead of groan. "Ha! Another leaf. Pull it out, and start chewing."

God is with me, and he is sufficient for whatever is still out there or in there. God wants me to grow up, trusting him through this process. God can handle it. I just need to let him.

Someone recently said to me, "God uses you in remarkable ways when you get out of your own way." I smiled, although I'm not fully sure what my friend meant. But I'm now asking myself, *How do I get out of the way?*

This much I figured out. When I find another leaf, I have to pull it out and start chewing. My responsibility is to myself—to help myself discover what I need to do next.

I have a new mantra: "I eat problems for breakfast." By that I mean I don't expect today to be smooth or effortless. Since the beginning, I feel my life has been a war. That's the reality.

Part of my healing means coming out of denial and engaging with my life as it is, not as I would wish it to be. Today, I will most likely have trouble. Problems will surface. I'll handle them as they come, one at a time.

CEC

For both of us, this is a journey of healing, and it's a lifelong process. There'll always be more leaves to pull off and to chew. There still are many times when we feel small, worthless, and not good enough.

Or we're tempted to take responsibility for others. I'm responsible for Cec Murphey, and he's a full-time job. Shakespeare put the words well into the mouth of Polonius:

This above all: to thine own self be true,
And it must follow, as the night the day,
Thou canst not then be false to any man.[1]

It hurts to learn more about myself,
but the pain assures me that I am learning.
And growing.

---

1. William Shakespeare, *Hamlet*, act 1, sc. 3.

— 7 —

I ACTED OUT.

CEC

I recently read a romance novel written in 1932. Quaint, of course, but one thing stood out. At the end of chapter 9, the hero picks up the heroine and carries her into the bedroom. The chapter ends with these words: "He kicked the door closed behind them."

"The next morning" are the first words in chapter 10.

In those days writers were careful not to write about sexual matters, but readers figured out what they meant. Maybe that's why we speak of pre–World War II as the time of innocence.

I mentioned that concept because of a phrase I hear quite often today about men who have been sexually assaulted in childhood. They talk about their change of heart, conversion, counseling, and move on to the changes in their lives.

Once in a while a man admits, "I acted out," and he doesn't go into any detail. I'm certainly not a voyeur; I'm not interested in reading graphic descriptions, but I would like a little more direct honesty.

Here are possible statements he could make:

> I fell into sexual sin.
> I went back into my old ways.
> I was promiscuous.
> I got into porn.
> I had sex with another man.
> I committed a homosexual act.
> I got into a cybersex relationship and finally met her in
>   person.

As repulsive as those statements may sound to some, they're honest. I realize that saying a simple sentence about engaging in sexual acts with someone of the same gender is too difficult for some men to admit. Or they may not feel safe saying those words.

But if a man seeks healing, that's part of the reality if he has "acted out." He needs to learn to speak the truth as candidly as he can. Not to say it straight is a form of denial or at least an attempt to mitigate the seriousness of the activity. Or it may be a statement still wrapped in shame.

I'm certainly not trying to urge survivors to speak openly and publicly until they're ready. But to speak in euphemisms or to use code words isn't being candid.

A number of years ago, a friend wrote to us after a long absence. She said she had "been bad" and didn't want to communicate with us again until she had straightened out.

Been bad? What does that mean? My reaction was to think of several different things, but the most likely was some sexual liaison. She never told us, and we didn't ask—but we wondered.

To say "I acted out" troubles me. Not just because I don't know what the person is trying to say without saying it, but it seems like a secret language to admit to failing without admitting the seriousness of the transgression.

Healing comes from sincerely facing the reality of our painful behavior. The more open we are in our word choices, the more powerful the healing. We can't say "I was mistreated as a child" and expect that to propel us forward. One of the first things we need to be able to say is "I was sexually molested when I was six."

That's being transparent. That also makes us vulnerable because we're facing the ugly reality of our personal shame or failure. That's trampling on our fear. And that's only the beginning.

I've learned that each time I become more transparent, the easier it is to take the next step. Fear becomes a prison that wants to keep us trapped inside. Until we push open the door—with divine help—we'll remain prisoners of failure, guilt, and worthlessness.

Most of us understand that. For a man who has been set free from sexual abuse, the temptation often lures him to reengage. The pull for many is to go back and to behave as they did before the life-changing event that started them toward healing. One way to fortify themselves is to say candidly what they did and face their failures.

Like many other survivors, I struggled with sexual attraction toward men. It tormented me because I didn't understand what was going on and I didn't have anyone in whom to confide. So my battles were inward and silent. I liked women and dated several.

So why these feelings? I asked myself that question countless times. I was sure there was something flawed within my own personality. I had no way to connect those attractions with my abuse.

I became a serious Christian in my early twenties. God set me free. Temptations and attractions were there, but I knew they would be wrong for me. I prayed for strength, and I didn't yield.

In the paragraphs above, I ripped open my heart and risked making this known. Even now, many years later, if I focus on my intense struggles, shame attempts to shackle me. I remind myself, "In Jesus Christ, I am forgiven." I also quote this verse: "He has removed our sins as far from us as the east is from the west" (Psalm 103:12).

Gary

I acted out heterosexually. My father had a heart attack and was in the hospital on life support. I was living with him, and he was my world. He would be dead within a week. I was fifteen years old. I had a girlfriend at the time, and I turned to her for comfort. I was vulnerable, she was willing, and we engaged in sexual intercourse. That was just the beginning.

After my dad died, I needed even more comfort. Whenever we could, we had sex. I was practically living on my own at the time so there were plenty of opportunities. She had also come from an abusive background. Unknown to us, our abusive pasts had driven our relationship to unhealthy, dangerous places.

My behavior was unhealthy and damaging. It was wrong, and I knew it. I felt guilty, but I was needy and gave in repeatedly. Finally, I became so disgusted with myself that I ended the relationship. She didn't understand why.

Now I can see the invisible engine of sexual abuse dragging us to places we really didn't want to go. To this day, I grieve when I think how that false intimacy and my rejection must have affected her. Unknowingly, both of us contributed to the further skewing of our sexuality.

During that time, a wonderful family took me into their home and informally adopted me. I lived with them the last two years of high school and through my college years. I had parents again—this time loving parents—and the accountability to that family removed me from many tempting situations. That loving family provided for the needs in my life that hadn't been met as I was growing up. I like to say it this way: I was rescued in the nick of time.

CEC

Not everyone acts out, and I don't want to suggest they do. We all have our weaknesses, and I urge men to face the realities of their difficulties as they walk down the road toward total healing.

I want to tell you a few true accounts of those who have struggled with acting out.

I was a guest on the Chris Fabry radio show, and one male caller who mumbled his words admitted that he had "fallen back." He wasn't quite able to say what he meant, but he was close. He later sent me an e-mail and asked if he could call me. I gave him permission. He called, and because he knew I had been molested, he spoke clearly and openly.

"I'm going crazy with this," he said. "I don't want to do it again, but I keep going back to my old ways."

"Don't just say 'old ways'—be clear about what you mean. I don't care about details, but I think it's important for you to name the tormenting demons aloud."

He did exactly that, followed by a lengthy pause. I could hear his sniffling so I stayed with the silence.

He told me the story of promiscuous behavior and going to prostitutes. "I finally said it," the man said. "I finally said the words."

I reminded him of the story of the man with demons who called themselves Legion. (A legion was a Roman regiment and sometimes with as many as five thousand troops.) Mark's gospel tells us that Jesus confronted a demonized man in the tombs around the area known as the Gerasenes.

"Then Jesus demanded, 'What is your name?' And he replied, 'My name is Legion, because there are many of us inside this man'" (Mark 5:9). They believed that if a demon's name could be learned, the person gained power over the evil spirit.

Regardless of how we feel about demons today, the principle seems right to me: When I name the demonized part of myself, that's when I begin to exorcise it. We need to know what we face before we can overcome it.

Before the end of the telephone call from the man who had acted out, he said, "I'm not afraid anymore."

✦   ✦   ✦

A woman caller on another radio interview told us her son had been sexually molested when he was ten, and he was now sixteen. She said her husband comforted the boy, and ended with these words: "I was also sexually abused, and I turned out all right."

She went on to say that she and her son have since learned that the husband "acted out" several times. She expressed her son's concern that he would do the same.

I finally asked, "What do you mean by acting out?"

"My husband has . . . you know . . . had sex with several men."

She had named the sin, and I understood her fear. The interviewer must have become uncomfortable, so she interrupted and quoted several Bible verses and assured the woman of God's grace.

The radio host said the right things—but in my opinion, at the wrong time. By rushing in to rescue the woman, she didn't give the caller the opportunity to open up about her concerns. But the woman did name the demon, and that's a positive step.

✦   ✦   ✦

One more story. Fairly early in my own healing, I was part of a small group of men in Louisville, Kentucky, for about a year. One of the men said that he and another member met outside the group and "did some things."

That statement violated an agreement we made in our first meeting—that we wouldn't meet with each other outside the group. Another member said, "What do you mean when you say, 'some things'?"

As the rest of us had assumed, they had engaged in homosexual sex. As I listened to the interchange, I realized the importance of telling the truth. To say "some things" or "acted out" seems like a form of denial or lying by ignoring the seriousness of an act.

✦   ✦   ✦

I relate these illustrations because they happened, and such things take place more often that we like to admit. We fail. We know the right thing to do—but sometimes we're unable to live up to what is right. I hear the same testimonies from members of Alcoholics Anonymous (AA), Narcotics Anonymous, and Sex Addicts Anonymous. This isn't to minimize or excuse our choices, but rather to say we must choose to walk down the paths of integrity and truthfulness.

This chapter isn't meant to condemn, but rather to encourage men who have failed to start over again. God can and will strengthen us.

When we fail, the message remains the same: "If we claim we have no sin, we are only fooling ourselves and not living in the truth. But if we confess our sins to him, he is faithful and just to forgive us our sins and to cleanse us from all wickedness" (1 John 1:8–9).

Years ago, when I worked with AA while a pastor, I learned that some people have to hit bottom more than once. They become sober, and their sobriety might last a month, three years, or five, before something throws them back on another drinking binge.

A long-time sober member said, "Sometimes they have to come back four or five times before it lasts." He smiled and said, "And thank God, many of them come back, and I was one of them. It took me four times to make it."

I hate it when I learn that someone has backslidden, fallen, sinned, acted out, gone backward—however we choose to say it. But I also believe that part of healing comes from straightforward talking and admitting what happened. It's one way for us to face our shame.

To use euphemisms negates the seriousness of the wrong behavior. One way to face the seriousness is to call it by name.

Read these statements below:

> I shot a man.
> I was obsessed by the Internet.
> I went back on God and did evil things.
> I associated with my druggie friends again.

Even a veiled statement is probably better than denial. But why not speak the truth? Why not face the reality? Facing the starkness of reality brings healing and victory.

I encourage men to speak the truth about themselves, even if they have to limit their words to a small group. To do so liberates them, and they no longer have to carry a secret burden of fear that someone will find out. Because they admit and accept their failures, they can move forward.

Earlier in this chapter, I mentioned the man who phoned me and said he had acted out. "I knew better," he said at least three times, "and I prayed for God's help, but I gave in and . . ." Then he told me about an earlier time when he had engaged in sexual activities with men.

I did the one healing thing I could do: I listened without condemning him. That's all he needed—someone to listen and *not* tell him what a terrible failure he was.

I don't know answers to every problem. I don't understand why some of us gain victory almost immediately and for others it takes years. I do know this, however. It's shameful to admit we've failed, especially after we've determined not to repeat our behavior. Even worse is to fail and deny it or try to hide the fact. Facing it each time is a powerful step toward full recovery.

As a mentor of Gary's once said, "It's not what you did, but what you do next that really counts."

If I "acted out," it was sin.

If I failed and I confess it, I am forgiven.

I rely on God to help me overcome the next temptation.

I will avoid using code words for my failure.
I confess my wrongdoing,
ask God to help me not to do it again,
and take more steps down the healing path.

8

I'M ADDICTED TO PORNOGRAPHY.

CEC

Neither Gary nor I have been stimulated by or addicted to pornography. For most of my growing-up years, porn wasn't as easy to see as clicking on a Web site. I would have had to go to an adult bookstore to purchase magazines, books, or films.

With the access of the World Wide Web, we can make only a few clicks and stare at anything we want.

I call it the *new acting out* because it's so easy to log on to sexually explicit sites. It's private, and no one else knows. God knows, of course, but men who use the Net for that purpose are so consumed by lust or desire that they seem unable to think about God.

       ✦   ✦   ✦

I sent e-mails to three men who were at the not-quite-healed stage, and asked if they had had experiences with porn.

This first response comes from a pastor:

> My experience with pornography began before I was ten years old. A relative kept girlie magazines in plain sight in the family living room right next to *Reader's Digest* and *Time* magazine. At night, when everyone else was asleep, my older brother and I sneaked into the living room with our flashlights and grabbed a handful of those magazines and took them back to our bedroom to view the naked playmates.
>
> After looking at the girls, my brother wanted to show me

how people "made love" by climbing on top of me. I learned from that season of our lives that men had sex with each other after looking at nude women in magazines. I was much older when I finally realized that men made love with women too. What I couldn't have known then was that my early exposure to porn and the confusing sexual contact with my older brother were just precursors of the abuse to come. In ensuing years, I would be molested repeatedly by a much older male cousin and seduced by a twenty-six-year-old man when I was only sixteen. Both of them were heavily involved in that type of pornography.

This is from a church leader:

I distinctly remember the intense excitement and fascination I felt the first time I watched hard-core porn between a man and a woman. I was in seventh grade. My friend Jimmy had discovered his father's 8 mm porn flicks. Early one morning, a bunch of us boys gathered at Jimmy's house to watch what no one should ever watch.

Although that happened nearly forty years ago, those images are still planted inside my head.

The real damage of early exposure to pornography occurred inside me later in life after the advent of the Internet. During times of depression or anxiety, it became all too easy to turn off reality by tuning on to a fantasy porn site.

Traveling extensively by myself also became a problem for me because cable porn in hotel rooms was a constant lure.

Another pastor wrote this:

Because my abuse had been homosexual in nature, my acting out with pornography took me only to gay sites. Watching man-on-man pornography was the only kind that elicited that familiar, though awful, feeling of being wanted by someone.

It's difficult for me to admit this, but even though I was married to a beautiful woman who truly loved me, that didn't seem to be enough. The allure of being wanted by a man obsessed me. The sites hooked me.

The problem with watching pornography is found in the law of diminishing returns. Like any addictive substance, after a certain length of time, the doses must become more potent to have the same effect. At times I felt like a heroin addict, because the power of porn pulled me deeper and deeper until I began living it out in my own life.

I say it this way: what you see is what you want, and what you want you will eventually do.

After years of flirting with porn, I acted it out several times, violating my marriage and my own soul. What the porn peddlers won't tell us is that the price of addiction and acting out is more than any soul can pay. I became distraught, even suicidal, at times. Eventually I suffered a nervous breakdown and underwent intense therapy.

Pornography was at least one contributing factor in my abuse at the hands of three different men over thirteen years of my childhood. Pornography was always close at hand. It fed the abusers and served to confuse me about my own sexuality and self-esteem.

A large portion of my recovery has been in reclaiming the innocence stolen from me by pornography and people who used it.

The pastor goes on to say that he's been free of porn for several years, but occasionally he fights the memories and the lure to go back to the tantalizing Web sites.

Like Gary and me, he says he's not quite healed, but he's healthy and has the strength to stand against the temptations.

Here is one post for the blog that came while I was editing this book:

> An addiction to pornography was one of the effects of my early childhood sexual abuse. The women in the pictures were fascinating, though I had no clue why they were unclothed. My brother would "show me" what the women did as we looked at the pictures. The natural result was a strong sexual confusion on my part. For years I thought I *was* a woman.
>
> I now live a heterosexual lifestyle and have been married for three decades. But through these years I have found myself struggling with this addiction. Of course I feel the typical shame and self-loathing after indulging. The more I watch, the more I want to do it. As an adult, the people I see in the pornography still elicit in me the same feelings of being *needed* that I felt as a child.
>
> I have come to understand many things about the roots of my addiction. The primary root is the yearning to *feel* needed. The abuse scarred me deeply and has manifested itself in me at times as an irrational compulsion for gay porn. This is what is called "acting out" for me. I acted out the early homosexual abuse through porn, compulsive masturbation, and a few gay encounters.
>
> Acting out in any way is destructive emotionally and spiritually, but especially to my marriage and to my work. When I sense a temptation to indulge in porn, I try to remember that this feeling is strong, but irrational. The porn will never satisfy me in the deepest way and it can never heal what hurts the most—my broken heart.

* * *

Dann Youle is one of the most courageous men I know. We first met more than a decade ago. Even then, Dann was open about his abuse—in fact, he was far more "fluent" than I was. His transparency encouraged me to be more open. Here's Dann's account of pornography in his life:

> I am a sexual addict. I was sexually abused when I was somewhere between five and seven years old. It happened several times during that period of my childhood.
>
> I buried the abuse for more than twenty-five years of my life. I didn't begin to recall these incidents until I was thirty-four. The biggest consequence of abuse that bore bad fruit in my life was viewing pornography.
>
> As a teenager and at the time of my sexual awakening, I discovered *Playboy* and *Playgirl*. Both grabbed my interest; more than my interest—I couldn't put them away without staring at them for long periods of time.
>
> I had been abused by a close male relative. Even though my dad never abused me, I felt distant from him. He didn't know how to connect meaningfully to me or to express love that I yearned for. I want to add that my dad tried and did the best he could, and he's a good man and a good father. I love him dearly, and if I could go back, I would have never asked to have someone different as my dad.
>
> After I entered puberty, and definitely by the time I was about fifteen, I was well aware that I was very sexual and that I was attracted to the same sex as well as the opposite sex. I felt ashamed and knew it was wrong.
>
> I was raised in a conservative Christian home in the Midwest. Because that was the early 1980s, these things simply weren't open for discussion in most families, and mine was no exception.
>
> There was no Internet, and the TV networks focused on

basic values and mores. Using swear words as acceptable language in TV shows didn't gain popularity and acceptability until sometime in the 1990s. Also, cable TV was just getting popular so I didn't have hundreds of channels to choose from. All that is to say that pornography was pretty much just magazines, erotic stories and books, and adult bookstores.

As a teenager, not knowing why I was so drawn by pornography, and feeling extreme shame, I fed my addiction by buying or shoplifting every porn magazine I could.

I'm the oldest son in my family of origin, so ultimately I got my brother involved in my "game" as well. I believe he was abused by the same relative, although he has no recollection and won't discuss those matters with me.

For a long time I continued to use porn, felt guilty, and believed God didn't love me because I was too bad. This may seem strange, but at the same time, I believed I was called to do some kind of ministry. After I graduated from high school, I enrolled in a Bible college. God was good to me, and I began a closer, more dynamic walk than I'd experienced before. For the college years, I was in a sheltered environment, and everything went well for me. I had less access to porn so it wasn't a strong temptation, but I didn't resolve the deeper issues.

After graduating from college, I moved back to Illinois. I got married and had a family, went to seminary (but didn't finish), and grew in my ministry. I helped others who struggled with their sexual issues.

With support from counseling ministers, pastors, and church leaders, I've been able to minister to many men who have these same issues in their lives.

Then we bought a computer and, although I resisted temptation for several years and stood strongly against porn in my life, the World Wide Web opened up an access to the insidious evil of pornography that I'd not yet experienced.

And I gave in.

And each time, I felt sinful and despised myself.

But out of that addictive experience of trying to help other men who'd been broken by sexual and pornography addiction, promiscuity, and homosexuality, I admitted I needed help myself.

In the fall of 1999, I reentered counseling. During that time, I began to recover my memories of the sexual abuse.

At first when the memories came, I couldn't believe them. *Am I going crazy?* I asked myself. I thought that through the power of a therapist's suggestion and through trying to help others who had been abused and sexually broken, my mind was imagining scenarios that never happened.

As I continued with the counseling and talked to my sister and other trusted friends, it became clear to me that my experience of abuse had really happened.

When the most powerful memory came, I was in a personal quiet time of worship and not focused on the things I was starting to remember. God spoke to me and let me know that even though it was awful, it was real. I also knew that Jesus would go with me through the next phase of healing.

As painful and as frightening as that was, it was the best thing that could have happened to me. It was also the worst. I say it was the worst because I could have never imagined that such an amount of pain could ever exist within me.

However, as I felt that pain, I realized that it was coming up and into the open. As the process continued, I truly released that pain into the wounds of Jesus on the cross, and he was taking the sins committed against me and healing my wounds.

I wish I could say the desire to use pornography went away

and that I never looked at porn again. That would be a lie, though. In fact, for a period of time, and out of the desire to kill the pain and self-medicate, my pornography use became even more pervasive.

God has been faithful and has brought people into my life, "brothers from different mothers," who loved me and gave me faithful, unconditional support. I know what it means to be loved completely without reservation or pretense.

When people tell me they love me, I've learned to believe they really do. I believe God loves me and blesses my life so I can be a blessing to others. I no longer self-condemn if I do slip up; instead, I confess and allow Jesus to love me, heal me, and forgive me on deeper and deeper levels.

I've learned two things about sexual abuse and pornography.

First, pornography is a cheap substitute for real relationships and real love because it's based on the lie that I don't deserve and I can't ever have anything better.

Second, Jesus' love is like no other, and he chooses to love me in so many ways. He reminds me that because I am created in his image, there's no value that any person or world system can place on me that compares to my value in his eyes.

There have been other trials, struggles, and difficulties along the way, but the joys and blessings of this life truly outweigh any difficulty I've encountered.

I'm also a cancer survivor. My wife and I have been blessed with twenty-two years of marriage, we have three amazing children, and I'm currently in seminary pursuing my master's degree in counseling. My heart's desire is to counsel and minister to men who have experienced sexual abuse. I would have never been where I am today without the joy and pain of these trials and temptations. I'm grateful beyond words.

If you read the above words, you can understand why I call Dann Youle a courageous man.

Pornography is a substitute for intimacy.
I choose to strive for the real thing.

9

I STRUGGLE WITH SAME-SEX ATTRACTION.

CEC

In the years I've been dealing with my own abuse and talking with other men, I've seen how shame plays a large role in our tortured lives. Our healing comes as we talk about our issues.

Here's a saying of mine that bears repeating: I know of myself only what I say of myself. That means that when we speak up and tell others the truth about who we are or how we feel, *and they understand our meaning*, we "own" or accept our own words.

Until two years ago I would have said, "Same-sex attraction has never been remotely my issue." Now I say, "I lied to myself because I didn't want it to be true." The attraction doesn't mean acting on the impulse; it simply means the possibility exists for the attraction to become a reality if I acted on it.

In 2010, shortly after I became aware of same-sex attraction, I was at a conference and between sessions I spoke to a good friend. After I mentioned my awareness and how ashamed I felt, he said, "You don't have to act on it."

"I know, and I haven't."

"Neither have I."

I was shocked and stared at him, not sure what to say.

"Didn't you realize I was attracted to you?"

I honestly didn't.

"Didn't you notice the way I fluttered around you?"

I shook my head. (He wasn't a fluttering type so that confused me even more.)

He said he was acutely aware of the attraction, but he had never done anything about it—except struggle with guilt.

That friend can't possibly know how deeply his words touched and encouraged me.

I've finally come to peace about this issue. It reminds me of an e-mail from a good friend, who had been an off-and-on alcoholic for years. "I've been sober for sixteen months. Every day I crave a drink, but I don't give in. And the desire is decreasing—slowly."

◆   ◆   ◆

Here's an e-mail I received from a man who asked me to identify him only as Kiburn; this is his story:

I have one intimate memory with my father. I must have been only three or four years old. I watched while he shaved, with his leather strop (for sharpening his straight razor) hanging from his left arm. He had a shaving brush in a mug and had almost finished.

He looked down at me and asked, "Have you shaved yet today?" I shook my head.

Dad picked me up. "Let's see about that." He ran his freshly shaved face against the grain of my cheek.

"That tickles," I said, and laughed.

"Guess you haven't shaved today."

As well as I can remember, he soaped my face and ran the flat side of his razor over my cheek. He smiled and wiped off the soap and said, "Now you've had your shave."

That's the only time in my entire childhood I remember any tender gesture toward me from my father. This isn't to blame him (although I did for years), but that single experience helps me understand why same-sex attraction was a significant factor in my life.

I needed his physical touch. His embrace. He never hugged me, and I can't recall his ever speaking to me in words that I would have called loving or kind.

✦ ✦ ✦

I resonated with that story because I grew up with a need—a need for male affection. In looking back, I was finally able to put all of this together. I gravitated toward any male who showed me affection. It's obvious to me that Mr. Lee, the pedophile who rented a room from us, fit that description.

In working with survivors, I believe that same-sex attraction is the most shame-based struggle I've encountered. This seems especially true among Christian men because of the ingrained stigma against any homosexual act.

And for some, the attraction implies action. They have moved into gay experiences because they assumed the attraction meant they had to respond to their impulses. But attraction doesn't mean responding to it. The man who fluttered around me said he had never engaged in any homosexual behavior (I believe him), and he doesn't believe he was molested as a child (I take him at his word). "But it's there," he said.

I admired my friend for his courage to tell me.

✦ ✦ ✦

Here are two stories from men who have agreed for us to use their names.

Dave Adams

I was born in a small town in Texas, and my childhood was typical of other children raised in a farming community where wealthy property owners owned the land. Families like ours did the actual work of planting and harvesting the crops. At harvesttime, my parents received a percentage of whatever monies the crops generated. All of us did our part to make ends meet, including taking on part-time jobs. I was no exception.

At age eleven, I had my first job, as a shoe-shine boy at a local barbershop where I worked after school and on Saturdays. It was exciting to earn my own money.

Something changed when a homeless man moved into the back of the shop and the owner made it into a makeshift bedroom. He became quite friendly to me. One day, the shop was closed and I sat down in his room. He sat next to me and fondled me.

For the first time I could remember, I was sexually aroused. It felt good, even though it didn't seem right. During the next few weeks, I grew to enjoy the old man's attention and the accompanying feelings.

I didn't tell anyone about his attraction to me, because I didn't think Christian families were supposed to have "those kinds" of problems. Over time, I reasoned, the confused and unexplained feelings would go away. But my feelings didn't change, and the confusion intensified.

In high school I was introduced to masturbation, and in the words of a then-popular song, I was "hooked on a feeling." In my adult years, I developed feelings of attraction to prepubescent boys. I committed what I believed was the unpardonable sin.

My wrong thoughts developed into wrong actions. I began to repeat what had been done to me as an eleven-year-old kid, who had been ridiculed in the showers after gym class.

Whoever said, "Words will never harm me," had apparently never been in a similar situation.

It has now been almost thirty years since my conviction on charges of lewd and lascivious behavior, and I still wear the label of sexual offender. I served three-and-a-half years in prison, followed by two years of community control and ten years of probation. I lost my career, my personal integrity, and my self-respect. I could well have lost my wife and our two children. That's the bad news.

Now for the good news: Prior to my sentencing, my wife and I attended a series of highly intensive Christian counseling sessions through a local Assemblies of God church. For the first time in my adult life, I learned that I had *not* committed an unpardonable sin. I had become a Christian in second grade, and I recommitted my life to Jesus Christ. I believed he had set me free and that, with his help, I would never molest another boy.

The clouds of doubt and confusion gave way to the "Sonshine" of God's unconditional love and forgiveness. I have kept my vow not to be a repeat offender.

Jim Venice

Jim Venice has shown courage in telling his story of acting on same-sex attraction by becoming part of the homosexual community. The following information comes from a pamphlet containing his written testimony.[1]

Jim's parents married when they were both young, and Jim was their first-born son. His alcoholic father became a convicted felon, and Jim's mother had to raise Jim and his younger brothers. Without any positive male influence, Jim's mother was his hero. He says he became a mama's boy and a sissy. "I was never affirmed in my masculinity. I didn't want to be rough and tough, and I didn't know anything about sports."

Jim played with girls, and they became his friends. He writes about what happened to him at puberty: "The girls that I had played with were becoming attracted to young men. They had crushes on them and talked about their great looks or how cute they were."

He confessed, "I didn't understand what was happening to me. I became attracted to my own sex. I began fantasizing what it would be like to be 'with one of those cute guys.' My fantasies turned to lust, and I began to have a problem with masturbation. I needed help desperately."

Jim underwent a conversion experience when he was twelve years old. He also believed that God had called him into the ministry.

---

1. Adapted by permission. See also "Jim Venice's Testimony: I Am a Brand New Man," Pure Heart Ministries, http://webpages.charter.net/pureheart/About_us/Who_are_we/jims_testimony.htm.

All through high school he was a loner, and the church was "my escape from the world." He also adds, "I never became close enough to anyone to share my private sexual struggles." Like many who suffer from same-sex attraction, Jim said, "I was embarrassed and ashamed. I kept it to myself. . . . I never told a soul." Here's a closer look at his deep inner pain: "I knew what the Bible said about homosexuality and perversion, but I still had my secret problem with fantasizing and masturbation; it became my 'thorn in the flesh' to keep me . . . continually on my knees asking for God's forgiveness. I fasted frequently, praying for deliverance."

Because God didn't deliver him from his sexual dilemma, he decided to marry Debbie. But marriage didn't fix him, and his same-sex attraction didn't go away. "If anything," he stated, "it intensified." After five years of marriage, "I was introduced to homosexual activity." He and Debbie divorced. Jim left all connections with the church and entered into long-term gay relationships. One lasted three years and another almost that long.

The end of Jim's story is that after seven years of being away from the church, in 1996, he returned to God. This time the result was different. He prayed fervently and asked God to forgive him. "There were no divine transformations . . . but when I finished praying, I didn't want to go back to my homosexual lifestyle. I knew it would require a walk of faith, obedience, and self-denial."

Jim became involved with Exodus International,[2] and through their help, his life changed. He came to understand that his attractions weren't the true problem, but rather a symptom of a deeper, God-given, but unmet, human need. "My soul was hungry for life-giving, gender-affirming, nonsexual relationships with men," Jim said. He learned to associate with other men in healthy, nonsexual ways. "That revelation started my journey out of homosexuality. It wasn't a quick fix but rather a long process."

---

2. Exodus International is the world's largest ministry to individuals and families impacted by homosexuality. www.exodusinternational.org

By 2002, Jim and Debbie Venice had remarried and settled down in the St. Louis, Missouri, area where they raised two children and started their own Exodus ministry geared toward those who want to leave the homosexual lifestyle or avoid going into it.

"I can tell you that I am no longer attracted to men, and I'm no longer interested in having sex with men. . . . I am not proud of my past, but I am very proud of our Lord and what he has done in my life."

✦   ✦   ✦

I write a twice-weekly blog for men who have been sexually abused.[3] One of our regular readers sent me the following post called "Same-sex Attraction." I've never read anything as honest as this one by John Joseph:

> Aside from all arguments on either side over the origins and morality of homosexuality, one of the primary remnants of my abuse is a strong sexual attraction to men. I don't consider myself *gay* and I don't live that lifestyle. I am a husband and a father and I choose to live in a loving marriage with my wife of now thirty-two years. Still, this unwanted same-sex attraction (SSA) shows up in my life often and always in the form of compulsion.
>
> I have come to understand a few things about SSA in my life. First, it is an irrational state of mind. I never *decide* to have an attraction to a guy and it is never a romantic thing for me. I don't dream about getting flowers from a man or of being taken to exotic destinations for a getaway with him. For me, SSA is more about feeling insecure or rejected. It happens most often when I am dealing with stress or something uncomfortable in my circumstances.

---

3. www.menshatteringthesilence.blogspot.com

SSA generally starts with a feeling of discomfort in my mind. It is like a pot on the stove with a lid on it. As the water inside heats up, the steam needs an escape valve. If things inside me are heating up, the escape valve can be triggered when I visualize or see an attractive man. I immediately size him up and compare myself with him. If he seems to be bigger, stronger, more successful, or more "together" in his personality I can become attracted. Fantasy takes over and eventually I'm caught up in an irrational state of mind.

The end of this irrational fantasy can be a foray into gay pornography and masturbation, leaving me shamed and depleted. Obviously, SSA is an unhealthy response to life's normal stresses for me. Part of my recovery work is to recognize that it is irrational and to learn how to interrupt the cycle as soon as I recognize it.

Despite my attractions and desires,
I don't have to give in to any wrong impulses.

10

IT'S SAFER TO LIVE BEHIND MY MASK.

GARY

Sometimes I'm amazed at how self-conscious I can be. I talked and behaved in a way that I thought would ensure that people liked me. Because of the abuse, I developed a sensitive antenna, and I constantly gauged what people might think or might feel about me.

I wasn't always correct, but that helped me survive childhood. As a result, I've lived much of my life inside my own head—thinking, posturing, wondering, planning, and controlling situations. Unknowingly, I fashioned a nice, acceptable, and thick mask for myself. Others got to know the mask and seemed pleased with it. Although I wasn't aware of what I was doing, that doesn't excuse me. It means that on some subterranean level I planned it that way—and that's true.

Not only did I not know how to be me (I didn't know who I really was), but I successfully walled myself off from deeper relationships. If I couldn't take off the mask and be myself, I didn't fully engage with others and love them. I was too busy seeking their approval.

My mask was well liked. My mask received the love, or what masqueraded as love, but I went on feeling unloved, because they didn't know who I really was.

CEC

I understand Gary's dilemma, and I also lived that way for a long time. Some survivors never throw away the mask.

For many of us, it's not a matter of dishonest living so much as it's *unconscious* living. Even though Gary was somewhat aware of what he was doing and to some extent the reason behind his choices, his need to be loved, liked, and wanted, overpowered sensible, rational thinking. His mask wearing was still unconscious. He remained unaware of the drive behind his need to hide his true self from others.

The persona he exhibited kept him protected and prevented intruders from violating his personhood—again. It also prevented Gary from being open to true friendship and caring. The walls were thick and heavily guarded.

When Gary asked counselor and friend Joangeli Kasper (who is also a sexual-abuse survivor) about common defense mechanisms, she said, "What I've seen more than anything else is that we learn the art of hiding—hiding in plain sight. There are those of us who think that if we can just make ourselves appear a certain way or behave in a particular manner, we're going to be all right. Acceptable. The path of destruction is that way too. If we can just be bad enough, or mean enough, then maybe people will leave us alone. If I'm hard, nobody can hurt me. It's all a form of hiding."

✦   ✦   ✦

Like Gary, like thousands of other survivors, I also erected walls that kept people from getting too close. Gary and others call it wearing masks, which is an apt description. I referred to it as my protective armor. Either term describes what we did—we insulated ourselves by hiding so that others didn't see the real us. Armor or masks—they became our primary protective devices.

Each of us had a similar purpose for our masks: we didn't want to be hurt or exploited—again.

Perhaps today, we'd call it our default mode. We took on the facade, and in time we were able to convince ourselves that's who we really were—especially if people complimented or admired us.

To change from that default mode isn't always easy, and some give up on the struggle. But as serious Christians, Gary and I believe that with God's help and grace we can change. We can be whole people who don't need to hide behind masks or armor.

As children, we were hurt and emotionally damaged. To cope with life, many of us learned *safe behavior* and how to cope with our damaged souls. The methods we used for survival were significant. Even essential. We needed them to wade through the morass of painful situations and our lack of self-worth. We warded off intruders and possible violators.

As bad as it may sound, they were useful coping devices. They worked, and we survived. Hiding behind a cover provides safety, and we're able to block our pain and show a brave face to others. As Joangeli Kasper said, some of us wear masks that make us seem bad. I've encountered many tough guys who wear such protective armor. But the issue isn't whether we hide our true selves behind a mask of niceness or meanness. Whatever type of mask we use, it is still a masquerade, and a person's default mode may not be healthy. I know too many people who survived by taking unhealthy ways—drugs, promiscuous living, as well as wild or frenzied behavior. They survived childhood, but by the time they became adults, many of them had irreparably ruined their lives.

It's easier to hide behind bad disguises than it is to face reality. Because we survived childhood without allowing our true selves to show, it's natural to continue that way.

If we're determined to heal, one of the things we have to declare to ourselves is, "I no longer need the disguise. I'm facing the reality of who I am. I may doubt at times, but I am acceptable to God right now, as I am and without any mask or armor."

In fact, we've always been acceptable.

The great apostle Paul wrote, "When I was a child, I spoke and thought and reasoned as a child. But when I grew up, I put away childish things" (1 Corinthians 13:11).

That verse has comforted me immensely. It encourages me to realize

I wasn't a hypocrite, deceptive, or trying to live a lie. I was just trying to survive in what seemed like a cold, evil world. Both Gary and I admit that those coping mechanisms saved our lives.

My brothers, whom I believe were also abused, chose alcohol to hide their pain and became alcoholics. That was their choice of mask.

I took a different route, one that was more socially acceptable: I became the good boy and the responsible one in the family. I was the one others in the neighborhood and at school could depend on, the Murphey boy who didn't get into any trouble. I lived with that deception throughout childhood and well into my adult life. Because I wore that disguise so long, I didn't know if it was who I truly was.

It was a facade, but I didn't know or understand that. As a child, I knew I felt different from others kids and was afraid to let them know my pain. Kids can be cruel without being aware of it. In second grade, my friend Ronnie Larsen fell and skinned his knee. He cried, and two other boys in the class laughed at him and called him a sissy.

The lesson I learned from that experience: never cry where others can see you, or they'll label you so you'll never be counted a real boy. That may be a good explanation for the many macho masks we observe. The strong-but-silent stereotype may really be the weak-and-pain-filled man.

Often we *hide* behind one aspect of our personality—and while it's probably a part of who we truly are, it's not a complete picture. Perhaps there's no way to show a total picture. Often a single quality obscures or denies all other aspects of who we are.

Many years ago my friend Dan Somerour mentioned a pastor in our area. I didn't know the minister well, but he seemed friendly and charming.

"He smiles all the time," Dan said. "I don't trust anyone who always smiles." He added, "I wonder who he really is."

Those words stuck with me, and I think Dan was on to something I couldn't perceive. In retrospect, I'm convinced the pastor hid behind the jovial, warm persona. I've done that myself on many occasions.

I don't want to condemn mask wearing because the disguises serve many functions. The obvious one is that they become a hiding place where we're safe from ridicule or sneers. As I think of that always-smiling pastor, I now realize it must have taken a great deal of effort to look happy all the time. I wonder if it tired him to stay focused on being Mr. Happy Face. What did it cost his soul to project the always-pleasant-pastor countenance?

Sometimes masks become social tools that enable us to mingle and move temporarily in certain circles. If I attended an exhibition at an art gallery, I wouldn't be so gauche as to act indifferent or ignorant. I would probably go along with others who raved about a work by giving a satisfactory smile or nod. I certainly wouldn't call attention to the fact that I didn't know the difference between a Monet and a Rembrandt.

Here's another example. Renee lived three doors away from us. Normally she passed our house wearing jeans and flip-flops. But twice I saw her when she went to apply for a job—beautifully made up, her hair cut and styled, she wore a business suit and three-inch heels. That wasn't the "real" Renee, but it was certainly a sensible masquerade. No one would condemn her for putting on the disguise for the interview.

The problem arises when we attempt to become the person behind the mask so that no one can detect any difference between the reality and the role. This is common to most of us, but especially so among us survivors. We need to fit in with our jobs, our neighborhoods, churches, and social organizations. We can think of it as a defense mechanism or camouflage, so others won't see who we really are.

✦   ✦   ✦

A few weeks after I started to heal, I was a full-time writer and no longer the pastor of a church. One afternoon I was running through a park, and I thought about my relationships. Most people liked me because I did kind, caring things for them.

Would they like me if I didn't do those things?

That was unanswerable, of course. I was no longer in a pastoral position or able to find out. But by asking that question, hope filled my heart. I could be kind and loving, or I could push people away. *I had a choice.*

Strange as it may seem, I don't think I realized that fact before. I could choose how I wanted to relate to the world. I guess it's natural not to know what we might have done. After all, I didn't have a choice in childhood when I was abused.

✦ ✦ ✦

After about two years of working through my abuse issues, the state of Georgia offered a free, yearlong program for male survivors of abuse who lived in metro Atlanta. Many of us applied and they selected fifteen of us. We agreed to meet weekly for two-hour sessions for fifty weeks. In one of the first meetings, a man said, "I don't know who I am. I have so many ways I show myself to people, and none of them know who I really am. I don't even know who I am or how I feel about myself."

His comment was an insightful moment for me. It's natural to intentionally disguise who we are to fit in or to avoid confrontation. It's adapting to the situation. But what does it mean to live intentionally behind the mask? And especially what does it mean when we *know* it's a mask? What does it mean not to have any idea who we really are?

Once we're aware of the masquerade, we face an identity problem. No one can truly be everything to everybody. If we use any disguise long enough, we often take on that persona and lose our real selves. We waste so much energy being the good boy, the intellectual, Mr. Universe, or the great athlete that it wears us out.

Perhaps the need to continue to hold the mask in place comes out of our sense of guilt, shame, and uncertainty about our inner selves. We probably don't like who we think we are. Or we think others won't like or love us. Why should they? Something deep inside whispers that we're damaged goods. So we wear disguises that enable us to fit in and protect our inferior nature. In so doing, we become likeable.

The masks hide what we assume are our character flaws. We use the disguise so that no one can probe too deeply or see us too clearly, although we're probably not as successful as we think we are. Others usually sense the mask isn't genuine.

Yet there *is* good news. We can learn; we can change.

For the past four years, I've made a commitment to become as honest as I know how. I want people to know the real me, even though it still hurts a little when they don't like me.

Each month I write an original aphorism below my signature. This is one I used in early 2012: "You may not like who I am, and that's all right. For a long time I didn't like me either."

To my surprise, a number of people commented, "I was the same way."

✦   ✦   ✦

In 2009, I gave the keynote addresses at a writers' conference in Alabama. One pastor came to me later and said, "You are the most transparent person I know."

I smiled and thanked him because he affirmed me for following the path I knew was right for me. Others may have felt I had been too open, but I decided I had to take the risk and be as much the true Cec Murphey as I could.

Here's something I often say to people: "I would rather be disliked for who I am than to be admired for who I'm not. If I have to pretend for you to accept me, you don't really accept me anyway."

GARY

Slowly God began to dissolve the glue that held my mask in place. He used my family, my life situations, counseling, and a few trusted friends to help me discover who I am. I now like the mask less and less.

I can be more present to the people around me. God is healing me. I know that. I feel it, and my friends sense the changes. I keep discovering deeper ways that I tend to hide, but I'm learning to see these as opportunities to grow.

Others may not like who I am,
and that's all right.
For a long time I didn't like me either.

11

WHY DO I FEEL RESPONSIBLE FOR OTHERS?

CEC

Many of us abused males feel as if we're responsible for the welfare and care of others. The more I've thought about it, the more natural it seems.

We were abused as children who weren't mature enough to reason out that we were innocent. On some level most of us knew it was not right, even though we didn't attempt to stop the abuse. It was the *internal* voice, the conscience, the inarticulate part of ourselves that knew something *was* wrong. As children, everything in the world revolves around us. Part of maturing is to realize that the infant game of peek-a-boo is no longer valid. Our perceptions aren't the entire world.

Because we internalized that something was wrong, the most obvious next step was to assume that we caused it. If we caused it, we're not only responsible, but we're also guilty for making it happen.

We each struggle with this issue of responsibility differently. I had my own issues (and they still pop up occasionally).

GARY

One of the results of the sexual abuse in my life is that I often held myself accountable for almost everything.

Why shouldn't I? My perpetrators told me I was the cause for what happened during childhood. They told me I was only getting what I deserved. After all, they were the adults who made the rules and who knew how life worked. If something bad or wrong was happening, it couldn't possibly be their fault. They were in charge, and I was the one who messed up. It had to be me. It was my fault.

I was bad. I felt guilty for allowing the abuse. I heaped further responsibility on myself by saying:

> If I had only . . .
> If I hadn't . . .
> If I could have . . .
> Why didn't I . . . ?

I developed a worldview based on that kind of thinking. In time, I became responsible for everything bad that happened in my life, my family, my marriage, my relationships, and in the church. If someone got angry, I had messed up by my insensitivity or by not acting forcefully enough or acting too forcefully.

As a child, if someone gave me a stern look or seemed confused by what I said, it meant I had done something that person didn't like. If a tragedy happened, I must have played a part in it because of what I did or didn't do. I grew up believing that I was to blame for the feelings and behavior of others.

As a counselor friend said, "The thing that I see repeatedly with sexual-abuse survivors is that they're sure they must have done something wrong for this to have happened to them. When something bad transpires, they assume they've failed to do the proper thing, and many of them spend the rest of their lives trying to be right."

I became a man who desperately tried to control what happened, including the actions of people around me. I usually failed, which made me feel even more guilty, which increased the sense of self-blame.

I'm now mature enough to realize I was trying to protect myself, making sure what happened in childhood didn't happen again. At least that's what I told myself for a long time.

I tried to control with niceness and great performance. "Nice 'em to death" became my motto. Surely if I was nice, warm, or friendly enough, people would like me, more abuse wouldn't take place, and everything would move along fine.

The theory was wonderful; the reality meant a miserable life. I didn't know I was carrying the weight of the abuse around with me.

It may sound ridiculous, but I've recently come to the conclusion that I can't control anyone. I knew this intellectually, but my heart didn't grasp the message. I still kept taking responsibility for everyone else's emotions and actions. I continued to think that if I led better, spoke better, planned better, organized better, counseled better, and met needs better, people would respond well and be happy. Then I would be happy. Finally.

Ridiculous? Of course, but that's how I felt.

My heart is now getting the right message. *I'm responsible for me.* I can only control me—and not even me all the time. I've zero control over what others think, feel, say, and do. In fact, I can't cause anyone to feel anything. Nothing can come out of individuals except what is already inside them. Something I do or say might be the trigger, but I don't cause their reactions. I might push their buttons, but they're still *their* buttons. Their reactions are their own, coming from inside them.

When I was a pastor and a problem arose, it was my responsibility to fix everything. Isn't that what a pastor does? At least that's what I told myself. I got too involved in too many disputes, personal issues, interventions, and difficult situations.

So I failed.

Even so, most people seemed delighted to let me take responsibility for the results. They could then blame me if things didn't work out the way they wanted. I swallowed that blame and opened myself to accept more of the same. No wonder I felt like a failure, even though most people would say I've been successful.

It was a landmark moment when I first verbalized the truth:

It wasn't my fault. I'm not responsible for what happened to me.

I went on to say,

> I'm not responsible for the abuse.
> I was victimized.
> Someone took advantage of me.

I didn't have to become accountable for the abuse because I wasn't the perpetrator or initiator. This was an issue about my abusers:

> It had been their evil actions.
> They manipulated me and made me feel guilty.
> I didn't matter to them—I was a convenient target for a predator.
> I was a child, overpowered by an adult who knew better.
> There was nothing I could have done to help myself.

I reminded myself that I had initially resisted their assaults, but the ensuing violence—the rapes—were harsher and the perpetrators more forceful. They hit me and pinned me down so I could no longer struggle. They convinced me that it was better to shut up and endure.

There was nothing I could have done to protect myself.

Nothing. And if that's true, I'm not responsible, because I was the victim.

It's freeing me to think that way.

The law of boundaries says that people are individuals—separate beings—all created in the image of God. I have property that belongs to me; they have property that belongs to them. My physical and emotional boundaries were violated in heinous ways. It was as if someone had ripped up the fence protecting my being and flung it away, making it easy for anyone to trample my yard, peep into my windows, or invade my house.

Although no one ever said the words to me, I grew up feeling that I didn't belong to myself. I had no boundaries, and others could do with me as they chose. I was powerless to stop them. Now I understand myself better. Like Cec, like thousands of other survivors, I had no one to tell me about boundaries or help me realize that I didn't have to be victimized repeatedly.

But that's changing. It's in process because I'm learning to take charge of my life. I've started to erect my own fences and set my boundaries. I'm taking responsibility for every part of myself, my emotions, and my life. In making that decision, I am also releasing myself from responsibility for all the other problems around me.

Cec has an aphorism that says it well for me, even though it also took him a long time to understand:

> My role is not to solve others' problems.
> My role is to love them while *they* solve *their* problems.

That's a statement of freedom. It's also a boundary statement.

When addressing the issue of my feeling responsible for everything in my life, my counselor once said, "You're just not that big."

I stared at him.

"You're just not that important or powerful, Gary," he continued. "People make their own decisions and have their own emotions. You've got to face your limited ability; they need to be able to face their own issues. You have yours; let them have theirs. Everything is not about you."

Here I am, five years later, still struggling and trying to free myself from the implications of those statements.

Now—finally—I get to decide what I want and what I don't want. It's my decision who comes onto my property. It's my choice whom I let inside and how far. I will no longer allow the abusive behavior of others to rule my emotions and responses. I refuse to hand over control of my heart to another.

I'm responsible for Gary Roe. Taking care of him is a full-time occupation.

The apostle Paul helps me when I focus on the list of things that characterize someone who is growing and maturing. He wrote: "But the Holy Spirit produces this kind of fruit in our lives: love, joy, peace, patience, kindness, goodness, faithfulness, gentleness, and self-control" (Galatians 5:22–23).

The word *fruit* as Paul wrote it makes me think of a cluster of grapes because those nine qualities naturally hang together. They make up the fruit, and it takes the entire cluster to do what's right and to live righteously. Each quality influences the others. I'm far from perfect, but I'm maturing. I'm growing spiritually if these things are evident in my life in increasing measure.

It's interesting to me that the first word in the list is *love* and the last is *self-control*. The more I grow as a Christian, the more able I am to exercise self-control. The more I take responsibility for my life—and only my life—the more I am able to love others. Another way to say it is that the less control over myself that I surrender to others, the more able I am to love them.

In taking self-responsibility, I have to remind myself (sometimes repeatedly) that the problems and difficulties of others aren't my fault. I'm not accountable for what my molester did to me. I don't have to know why he did it or understand his pain. Every molested child is in charge of his own actions. I can't carry their guilt or their shame. I must be diligent in releasing my guilt, and I do that each time I remind myself that God expects me to love and nurture myself. I am my first priority.

My heart didn't grasp that fact immediately. Like the most significant lessons in life, it took time to saturate my being. My behavior wasn't instantly transformed, but I did begin to change. I started with my own declaration of independence that said I would no longer accept accountability for their crimes (and they are crimes).

I'm on a journey. I'm learning. I'm maturing into who I really am and who God wants me to be.

I know—truly know—that God has forgiven me, endowed me with new life, and, most of all, set me free to enjoy my life. "So Christ has truly set us free. Now make sure that you stay free, and don't get tied up again in slavery to the law" (Galatians 5:1). It's my choice whether I live as a slave or as a free man. I get to make that choice daily, moment by moment. I'm no longer a slave to the abuse, and I'm learning to live in freedom a little at a time.

It wasn't my fault.

They are responsible for what they did to me.

They perpetrated the abuse because of their needs, desires, or addiction. I no longer need to attempt to control others and their responses to me.

I'm in charge of my decisions and my actions; I'm not responsible for others' choices.

The healthier my boundaries, the better able I am to love others.

Cec

Too many of us live with a fix-it mentality. If you're a woman, you're supposed to make sure everyone is happy. If you're a man like Gary and me, you have to solve each problem and make the family (or business or neighborhood or church) run smoothly.

Let's try a hypothetical situation. Your good friend comes to you and says, "I don't love my wife. I just don't know what to do." Chances are that you will immediately advise him about what to do. Right?

Maybe not. Suppose he added, "What should I do?" If you haven't jumped into the situation to guide him before, you surely are doing it now. *"He asked me for help."*

Many years ago a friend said to me, "You know, Cec, you don't have to die on every empty cross you see." I didn't get it then, but I do now. He was telling me that God didn't expect me to take away everybody's pain and problems.

As Gary quoted me before: My role isn't to solve your problems. My role is to love you and encourage you while *you* solve your problems.

Most of us who were abused struggle with taking too much responsibility (or rebelling and taking no responsibility).

Here's the reason I see this as such a big issue. As children, we were unable to take care of ourselves. We were overwhelmed and overpowered. As adults, taking on too much responsibility is an unconscious way to undo the pain of our past: I couldn't do *anything* for myself as a child; I *can* do something for everyone now.

> The need to feel responsible as an adult
> comes from my powerlessness as a child.

12

WHY ARE MY EMOTIONS SO CONFUSING?

CEC

I met with a friend who seemed to have worked though his issues, but he said something that made me realize that he wasn't as far along as I thought. "I wish I could let myself feel the pain."

That was a courageous statement. It's also one we need to address if we seek to be fully healed. My friend wanted to let go of the restraints and to experience what his words and his body said, but his emotional awareness seemed cut off.

I want to be clear about what I mean. My face is expressive, and people often say they know how I feel just by looking at me. For years I assumed my face was neutral, so I used to laugh when they said those things because I didn't understand.

"You're like a pane of glass," a co-worker once said to me. "I can see right through you." It happened at a time when I wasn't enthusiastic about something he said and assumed I was giving a totally neutral response.

Sometimes (most of the time) I didn't know what emotions I felt. I could get angry and not be aware of the inner rage; be overwhelmed with excitement and not realize I walked on a euphoric cloud. *I was cut off from awareness of what I felt.*

After I started to heal, the emotions loomed into my conscious brain, and I wondered if I truly wanted to feel those negative emotions. I became aware of the anger inside me, and I was shocked.

I focus on that emotion because I had never thought of myself as an angry person. I didn't know that words like *rage, wrath, seething,* and *fuming* described part of my emotional makeup.

As memories emerged, so did those feelings, and for me they were unacceptable. I didn't like them, and I didn't want to face their presence in my psyche. Yet they were part of me. For the first time, I admitted to myself that I felt rage—not all the time, of course—but I was capable of such strong responses.

When I was twenty-one years old and in the navy, I had decided I was a pacifist because I didn't think I could ever, under any conditions, take the life of another person.

About two years after I began my healing journey, Shirley and I watched the movie *Extremities*, which featured the late Farrah Fawcett as a woman named Marjorie. Marjorie had nearly been raped. Later when the perpetrator breaks into her apartment, she traps him inside a large fireplace, and tortures him emotionally and physically.

As the story unfolded, I felt intense anger toward the would-be rapist. I thought, *I could kill that man for what he did to her.*

That forceful passion shocked me. I hated him enough to think of *murder.* I wouldn't really kill him or anyone, yet my powerful response told me something about Cec Murphey: With the right stimulus, I was capable of the most heinous crimes. I held my wife's hand as we watched the film. At that intense point in the drama, she pulled her hand away. Later she said, "Your fingers pressed so tightly; you were hurting me. That's why I pulled away."

I wasn't aware of the pressure on her hand, but I was aware of my anger. That film thrust me into a rage. Or perhaps a better way to say it is that I vicariously experienced the hatred and anguish of Marjorie, and that second-hand experience unlocked my long-denied feelings.

Had I been that angry before? I'm sure I had. But the difference was on that occasion I *consciously experienced* the hatred. I *knew* those sensations as if they were bodily wounds.

That incident was both exhilarating and frightening. "I feel my emotions!" I yelled the next day as I ran through an isolated, wooded area. "I feel my emotions!"

But there was another emotion I felt: fear—dreadful, paralyzing horror. While I relished becoming aware of my intense fury, I was afraid of what I might do if I got in touch with that deep loathing and hatred toward anyone. Would I do something terrible to them?

When I explained to my friend David about the movie and my reaction, he said, "You haven't killed or physically hurt anyone so far. Why would you start doing it now?"

Perhaps that sounds simplistic, but it was exactly what I needed to hear. I feared that because I had opened the sealed box of emotions, I would behave in a frenzied, crazed, and uncontrolled manner.

No, I thought, *I'll probably behave much as I have before, but this time I'll be aware of the moods and reactions as I haven't been before.* I needed to admit, accept, and embrace every part of myself, especially the unacceptable parts. I sensed that if I wanted wholeness, being in touch with how I felt was a requirement. Unlike my friend whom I mentioned above, I had begun to experience the reality of my emotions. I didn't like many of them, but they told me who I was.

From then on, every day for at least a year, one of the things I prayed was, "God, help me feel my emotions." To be whole, I needed to experience anger, irritation, even rage. I was willing to take the risk that I might do bodily harm to another person.

And at times I really felt anger.

One time Shirley and I were driving down the expressway. A car cut in front of me to get off at the exit. I yelled (which he couldn't hear) and laid my hand on my horn.

"You're mostly a nice person," Shirley said, "but when you get behind the wheel of your car, sometimes you become someone else—an angry someone whom I don't know."

I'm not sure how I responded, but inside I was absolutely delighted. I felt rage, and I expressed it. Until then I hadn't been aware that I felt any strong, negative emotions while I was driving. I was so out of touch with that part of myself, her words shocked me.

I held on to one important thing: finally, finally I was in touch with my emotions.

Most of the time, I'm past that kind of outburst, but I needed to be aware while I expressed such fury. I assume I'd been just as enraged many times previously, but the line between head and heart had been severed. Now it was reconnected.

✦   ✦   ✦

For a long time, even before my healing began, I numbed out when I felt strong emotions. Once my wife lay in the emergency room, not expected to live (she did survive), but as I stood next to her gurney and gazed at her face, I felt absolutely no emotion. I didn't know how to cry for myself.

I sensed that once my healing began, I would experience suffering— and I did. What I hadn't expected was to feel the high emotions—great joy in daily living. I've always been fairly good-natured (or so people have told me), but part of my change was that I *experienced* unparalleled inner peace and lightness of heart.

As I learned to accept the negative side of myself, I also experienced the positive. I'm now comfortable with both.

GARY

I was so shy as a kid that I hid behind my mom or dad when we were out in public. I wouldn't make eye contact. I didn't know it, but I was feeling deep shame and wishing I could become invisible.

There was an insidious reason for those feelings. I remember being in a department store. My mom knelt down beside me and whispered in my ear, "Gary, take a good look. It's not safe here in the outside world. Anything can happen. There are bad people out here. Stay close to me. I'll take care of you." It still makes me shudder to think about it.

Looking back, I can now say I felt terribly insecure, worthless, and lonely. I was sad and sensed no one cared about me. Fear and dread were constant companions.

As I grew older, I began to feel and express some anger. It's interesting to look at pictures of me from childhood. Until I was about eight, I looked terrified, and I was almost always alone in the picture. After that, if friends were in the photograph, I was smiling, and you could tell it was real and genuine. If I was alone, I looked sullen and angry. But all too often, I was angry and short-tempered, especially when I was at home.

The anger continued to be there as I grew older, but true rage emerged after my flashbacks began.

At first, all I felt was shock and denial. I didn't want it to be true. Then came the anger—absolute fury at times. I'd bury my face in a pillow, scream into it, and pulverize it with my fists. I vomited my wrath onto the pages of my journal, not caring who might ever see or read my words.

When no one was home, I paced through the house, yelling at my perpetrators, "How could you? How could anyone do that to a child? How dare you? Who are you? *What* are you? Do you have any idea what you've done and what I've got to live with now because of *you?*"

My counselor encouraged me to continue to let out my deep-seated ire. He suggested that I begin talking out loud, putting my thoughts and feelings into words whenever I could. When I did that, it slowed my mind down enough to feel my way through my pain. For months, every time I got into the car to go somewhere, I yelled out loud about whatever was going on in my mind and heart.

At times, the fury and grief were so intense that I wondered if I would ever recover. The feelings seemed all-encompassing. The hole felt so deep, dark, and ugly that I began to wonder if there would ever be an end to it. I felt like a caged animal, frantically pacing with no way out.

Letting out the anger was a slow process. I tended to monitor and judge myself. My counselor kept addressing the issue of guilt. He used the word *congruent* a lot. He said things such as, "Is the emotion congruent to what happened? Does the depth of feeling fit the depth of what happened?" Those questions released me to criticize myself less and accept what I felt as being normal, and enabled me to be more aware of how I felt.

I now know I had to go back and feel what I couldn't allow myself to admit when I was a child. It would've killed me. It was just too intense. I shut down to survive. Now that I've gone back and felt what I couldn't then, I can move on. I'm no longer stuck. That means I can live and enjoy the abundant life that Jesus promises his followers. (See John 10:10.) I can also understand my emotional swings and my outrage. They are real, and they help me know who I am. I need to feel what's inside me. If I don't allow myself to accept my emotions, I will hide them deep inside, but they'll leak out later, most likely in unhealthy ways.

CEC

Like Gary, I assumed that once I began to feel and to accept my emotions, I had won my battle. Of course, I was wrong. I've come a long way in being able to feel, but I'm still on the journey.

One day my wife and I were on our way to church. I was driving and overflowing with powerful emotional verbiage.

She said nothing and showed no facial response.

"Don't you care about my pain?" I asked. "I'm vomiting all these feelings, and you're indifferent."

"Really?" Shock covered Shirley's face, and she said, "I thought you were merely giving me information."

Then I was shocked. I felt as if my emotional garbage had filled the car. I couldn't understand why she didn't get it. Then it hit me: What I felt came out as bland and understated. Until that moment, I didn't realize I ever came across that way.

"Until I learn to get the emotional valve regulated," I said, "I'll let you know when I'm opening my soul to you. If it's just to tell you things, I'll say, 'This is information.'" I also promised that if I wanted to lay bare my soul, I'd make certain she understood that, as well.

It has worked for me. Occasionally I still have to explain the intention of my words. And sometimes it is only information. But I'm getting better at making my intentions clear.

I mentioned this issue of emotional awareness in a seminar I conducted in late 2011. Afterward, I had personal conversations with participants. Jennifer and her husband came in first. She had been molested and was frustrated over his lack of response.

"When you tell him how you're feeling, what happens?"

"We usually end up arguing," she said.

"I don't know when she's upset or deeply troubled," he said, "because it doesn't come across in her voice or on her face."

We talked for some time, and their responses helped me to realize that we survivors may not be aware of how people "hear" our words when we talk about our abuse. Isn't it possible that we may think we're throwing our total selves into what we're saying but it comes out bland and perhaps even in a monotone?

If we're feeling our true emotions and not getting a response from a person we love and trust, we can ask:

"Did you understand what I was saying?"

"From what I've said, how do you think I feel?"

"Did you hear this as merely giving news, or did you know my words were emotion laden?"

God gave me emotions;
the more I heal,
the more aware I become of what I feel.

— 13 —

WHY THESE CONTRADICTIONS?

CEC

I remember the first time I heard the word *paradox* defined. It may not have been the dictionary explanation, but it helped me understand the meaning of the word and provided a strong lesson about life.

I was a first-year college student, and the class discussion centered on human free will and divine sovereignty. I understood the word *sovereignty*—and insisted that, although I didn't understand everything, if God is totally in control, that allows no room for human will. Otherwise, God isn't sovereign.

Another student took an opposing view, and soon eight or nine of us voiced opinions.

After perhaps ten minutes, the professor intervened. "This is what we call a paradox." After I asked him to explain, he said something like, "A paradox is when two statements appear contradictory, yet both are true." He spoke about how we live with the issue of free will and God's full control.

"You mean we have to live with contradictions?" one of the students asked.

He smiled before he said, "That's a good way to explain it." That's when the word *paradox* became part of my vocabulary.

Whether we call it a paradox or a contradiction, it's part of life and plays a significant role in the lives of those of us who are healing from childhood sexual abuse.

Paradox is a portion of our legacy. It's as if we push away at the same time we embrace. I mention this because for some of us, it's troublesome to feel two contradictory emotions.

For example, when we think of our predators, we may feel anger, even hatred, at what they did to us. That's natural.

Our abusers touched our deeper inner need that yearned for acceptance and affection. The contradiction is that it felt good to receive the human touch that we desperately needed. That's also natural.

They damaged our souls and caused us to feel endless pain and remorse. That's natural.

In the abuse, we felt something positive, perhaps exciting, and certainly stimulating. It lasted only a few minutes, but the experience was real. That's also natural.

If it happened so long ago that we have no emotional connection, we probably feel only disgust or perhaps no emotional response. Either is natural.

As I wrote the paragraph above, I thought of these words: Contempt is the weapon of the weak and a defense against our own despised feelings. So when people express disdain, I remind myself that they also have issues and their reactions may be their weapon of defense.

❖   ❖   ❖

Many of us need to admit to ourselves that when our abuse happened we weren't mature enough to see the experience as molestation. Our abusers seduced us, and temporarily we felt pleasure. Or acceptance. Or for a few minutes believed that someone loved us. At the same time, many of us sensed that something was wrong about what was going on, but we didn't say anything, or perhaps we were afraid we wouldn't be believed.

I focus on this paradox because I finished reading a book a few days ago that consisted primarily of first-person accounts of males who had been abused before the age of thirteen. It struck me that in almost every situation, the boys talked about contradictory emotions, even though none of them said it that way.

They referred to feeling loved or cared for, but at the same time they sensed it wasn't right, and they couldn't understand the reason for their confusion.

For many of us, the abuse brought out those contradictory feelings. I can't recall my emotions from the time Mr. Lee molested me; however, one of my relatives heard me warn my sister (whom Mr. Lee later abused), "Don't go into his room."

That warning indicates to me that I sensed something was wrong, even though I went back. It reveals not only my immaturity but also the contradictory nature of the abuse.

If I had talked about the abuse when I was a child, would I have been believed? Possibly. But I suspect the immature working of my mind concluded that I had been bad.

There's the paradox: I'm sure I liked what Mr. Lee did to me, but at the same time I sensed it was something bad.

◆   ◆   ◆

Do those opposing emotions stay with us? I suspect they do in some form. If we're aware of such conflict, we enable ourselves to accept our conflicting feelings.

As I point out in another chapter, many of us are heterosexual yet struggle with same-sex attraction. I see that as a fact of the incongruity that began when we were young. It's like an old allure that hangs on. We don't want to go back to it or do it again, but we remember.

I started to smoke at age fifteen, about a year after my immediate peers had taken up the habit. I quit at age twenty-one and never smoked again. But for five years after I quit, whenever I smelled cigarette smoke, I remembered how much I enjoyed it (translate: how addicted I had been). But I didn't go back to the habit. Even so, I lived with the contradiction that I hated cigarettes but at the same time I wanted to smoke again.

One expert told me that survivors worry about sexual feelings of any sort. Yet if they admit any feelings of attraction toward other men, they're filled with anxiety and confusion. If they feel attracted to women and stare at their bodies, many Christian men wonder if they are giving in to lust.

Paradoxes.

GARY

As early as I can remember, anything sexual was taboo. I viewed it as dirty and shameful. I don't remember anyone talking to me about that subject, so I formed my own opinion as a result of the abuse.

After I became an adolescent, I discovered that even though I was strongly attracted to several girls, I was also terrified of expressing that attraction. Part of it may have been normal adolescence, but I believe most of it stemmed from the fact that one of my perpetrators was female.

I was shy and tentative. Usually someone had to talk to the girl for me, which only compounded my view of myself as weak and worthless. When I got to high school, my life improved, and I dated quite a bit. But I was still tentative when expressing physical affection. Although I knew I was supposed to be the initiator, I was far more comfortable if the girl made the first move. Yet if she did, I was ashamed because my image was that men did that. (I hesitated writing this paragraph because shame still pulls at me.)

Sexual things were taboo, yet like any normal teen, my hormones raged. I didn't know what to do, and no one had ever talked to me about what I felt. I needed help, but the only people who had real input in my life were my peers.

Although I was fairly popular, I was terrified of offending the girls. When the relationship got difficult, or reached the point where I needed to lead to the next move, I backed off. I never allowed myself to get close enough to give or receive love of any magnitude.

In college a mentor described sex as something beautiful, designed by God. He likened sex to a river. A wonderful, life-giving force as long as it flows within the boundaries set for it, but it can be a life-taking terror that causes all kinds of damage if it overflows its boundaries.

My sexual experiences were warped and grossly outside the boundaries. No wonder I was full of contradictions.

Cec

As we move into healing, we punish or condemn ourselves for admitting our needs and our desires—and both are often present at the same time. One emotion temporarily or permanently overwhelms the other, but they're both part of us.

We needed affection, attention, love. What we received from our perpetrators wasn't love—but we didn't grasp the difference. They gave us attention, and what we assumed was affection. Their actions were deceptive and manipulative.

Consequently, many of us condemned ourselves for being needy.

One factor has helped Gary immensely. Like me, he reminded himself that what he needed but didn't receive in childhood from his family, he still yearned for and often sought elsewhere.

"I still want to condemn myself for being a lonely kid," he wrote, "one who felt emotionally abandoned and unwanted."

Gary's words resonate with me and with many other men. There's the contradiction of the healthy, human need for affection. We had to settle for temporary substitutes—even though we were too innocent to understand the difference. Many of us as adults carry the guilt for not being mature enough or wise enough to reason as an adult while we were still children.

Even if we admit we were children, we struggle with being compassionate toward the immature, innocent children we once were.

I remind myself that my self-contempt was also my defense against my own despised feelings.

"I've stopped judging and condemning myself for being who I was," one man said. I'm delighted he could say that.

Maybe one day I can too. I'm getting closer.
Closer. Almost.
But not quite healed.

> Life's paradoxes can be confusing,
> but the more honest I'm willing to be,
> the less often contradictions trouble me.

I NEED SOMEBODY.

CEC

"We need other people." That's become one of the commonly used expressions in mutual-help groups and the subject of many sermons. Another way I hear it said in the church is, "We were made for community."

And those statements are true. Even though some people yell that they need nobody, they're lying—to anyone who listens, and certainly to themselves.

I see two aspects to this inborn essential. First, we need to belong to some social group, even if we stand far off to the side.

Second, we have an innate desire to feel that we matter in some way. That's why we can talk about life having meaning. Not many of us will be highly successful or famous. But we yearn to be significant in some way so that our lives have purpose.

When I was a pastor, I faced families in which someone had committed suicide. In each instance, regardless of how they said it, in some manner all of the people who committed suicide declared that life was empty, useless, or meaningless. "I had nothing to live for," one woman's note said.

When meaning and purpose are gone, so is the will to live. Every human being wants to matter in some way and to belong. This shows up in the first pages of the Bible. In Eden, God created a man and put him in the garden to take care of it. "Then the LORD God said, 'It is not good for the man to be alone. I will make a helper who is just right for him'" (Genesis 2:18). And God gave him Eve.

Our need to be part of a group is as basic as our eating and breathing.

The most self-isolated usually realize they're alone, and it can be frightening and lead them to despair.

The tendency among those of us who are survivors is to feel that no one is like us; no one understands; worse, we feel no one cares. Too many of us don't tell, so how can others care? How can they know our pain?

I write about this because I'm convinced belonging is essential. Because of that, rejection and exclusion are the most powerful punishments we can inflict on another person. The Amish custom of shunning works because in that closed society, those who receive only silence feel isolated. They are alone, despite hundreds of people being around them. The "sentence" is to show them that they cannot get away with violating the laws of their community.

A PBS-TV documentary showed pictures of brain scans of people who felt rejected and isolated. They had the same configuration as those who experienced physical pain.

What surprised me even more was that it didn't matter if the rejection came from family or loved ones or from strangers. The effect is the same whenever we face overt exclusion. Some sensitive people, and that fits many survivors, feel shunned when other people merely turn away from them. What seems as unimportant segregation can bring about emotional reactions. When others obviously turn away from us or avoid us, it signals to us that something is wrong.

For most of us survivors, we interpret *wrong* as, "Something is wrong with me." To be shunned can threaten our social, spiritual, and psychological well-being.

Belonging to a group is an essential of being a human being, whether it's at church or with gang members. It's not only a preference or a desire. Studies indicate that if we're excluded, it lowers our self-esteem and we feel useless. "I'm nothing," I've heard. Those words say, "I don't matter, and my life has no significance."

If we're verbally pushed away by one group of people, we can still connect with others. But with total exclusion, such as religious shunning within a closed society, we're severed from human relationships. The imposed silence makes us feel helpless. We can fight back, but no one responds. Such isolation says to us the words perpetrators have sometimes yelled at us, "You are nothing. You are nobody."

We need to be somebody.

We *are* somebody, and mutual-help groups show the importance of this when the members stand up and say, "My name is Randy, and I'm a survivor." That simple statement affirms something powerful and primitive in each one of us. We have names; we're alive; and we have survived. By our presence, we silently affirm that we need the other survivors—and they need us.

For instance, the first time I attended a Celebrate Recovery meeting, I felt overwhelmed by their openness and their acceptance of me as one of them. "I feel I've found my tribe," I told my friend who brought me.

We've mentioned Celebrate Recovery several times in this book. It's not the only mutual-help movement. But they have groups around the country. Besides the mutuality of healing, they offer other human contact and acceptance.

✦   ✦   ✦

We're survivors and we yearn to be fully healed. We can't do it alone. We must have other people to love, rebuke, encourage, and inspire us. We need to talk with those who understand our pain and can assure us that we do matter.

Although the words of Jeremiah were written for the Jews after their return from Babylon, the essence of God's words through the prophet ring true today: "'For I know the plans I have for you,' says the LORD. 'They are plans for good and not for disaster, to give you a future and a hope. In those days when you pray, I will listen'" (Jeremiah 29:11–12).

I may feel lonely, but I am never alone;
God is with me.

— 15 —

WHY DO I HAVE TO TALK ABOUT IT?

Cec

Too many men can't speak about their abuse, and I never want to force them to do that. However, I urge them to talk about it—to bring the evil deeds of darkness into the light and to expose them. I firmly believe they need to do that for themselves. It's a vital part of their healing.

"We keep telling others about our abuse," one of my friends said, "because admitting the truth aloud helps us reach the other side of our pain and we experience healing." I think he was right.

We need to make our voices heard. Because I know how difficult it was for me to tell my story, I understand the hesitancy and fear of others.

My assistant, Twila Belk, recently updated my Web site. She asked for testimonies from several men she knew who had been helped by my speaking up.

Eric responded:

> Cec's ministry for sexually abused individuals has been the catalyst for my being open about what had happened to me. The healing that has taken place in my heart is priceless. Thank you, Cec, for your courage and for the platform you have created to help victims of sexual abuse speak up and heal.

Dann Youle wrote:

> Cec's abuse ministry has opened my own heart. Hearing him talk so openly and his willingness to write and teach on the

topic of sexual abuse have made me unafraid to tell my story. Cec is such a blessing, willing to admit he's still on the journey as well, but willing to walk with whomever needs him to walk with them. Whether for a short season or over an undefined period of time, and whether in person, at conferences, or through his writing, Cec speaks healing and hope straight to the heart.

❖   ❖   ❖

I assume all of us once-abused men have the innate need to tell our stories, even if we're afraid to speak up. And it's not only to tell our stories, but we also need hearers who will listen and believe us. Our abuse took place in secret, and our perpetrators isolated us.

As long as we keep silent, we protect the perpetrators and deny the harm done to us. Eric and Dann, quoted above, have realized that speaking out does more than give an account of their abuse. It is a powerful element in an ongoing, unorganized crusade to bring light into the dark, secret places.

Our silence guards our "guilty secret," and it can make us feel as if we were the only ones. Maybe friends or church members will ridicule us and call us a sissy or make harsh comments about us and refer to us as being gay.

Some men keep silent because their perpetrators convinced them that *they* caused the molestation to happen. "You wanted it," they accuse. "You kept hanging on to me all the time, so I finally gave you what you wanted."

If we believe those lies, we'll stay silent, and those perpetrators will continue to abuse children. VOICE Today says that the average pedophile abuses more than two hundred children in his lifetime. Our silence can empower these men to attack more innocent children.

And even if our attacker weren't a pedophile, if we were molested, we need to speak up *for ourselves*. If we don't talk about our abuse, we live in some kind of personalized torment. We'll never heal.

We can't be free as long as the abuse resides inside our head. We're raped each time we remember.

Some would go so far as to say that if we were sexually molested by someone close to us—a family member, friend, or a church member—the dishonesty of holding back the truth of that exploitation becomes a model for all our relationships. We expect dishonesty from everyone. We're suspicious of motives, words, and actions. Holding back may protect us from being abused again, but it also isolates us.

If we grew up in an environment where we didn't feel safe when we tried to be open and honest, we lied—probably by silence. We pretended that we hadn't been hurt by others. We were forced to relate to people who weren't honest about themselves. "Reality doesn't matter," may have been the subtle message we absorbed. "It doesn't matter because we don't matter."

When we speak up, we truly receive power. Strength. Encouragement. Permission to grow. We can choose whatever term we prefer because it means we have voices and won't be pushed back into denial or silence.

✦   ✦   ✦

Here's an important lesson I learned: Denial *through silence* is one of the most damaging forms of abuse. Our silence not only denies what happened, but it rejects the truth of what happened to us.

To open up, to talk to someone who will listen, is part of our human need to communicate with others. We do it for ourselves and not just to be understood.

The need to speak became clear to me a few years ago when I watched the film *Cast Away*. Chuck, played by Tom Hanks, washes up on a desert island, and he is the only survivor of a plane crash. He has been cut off from the entire world and has no one to whom he can speak.

Finally he finds a Wilson volleyball and paints a face on it. Chuck talks to the ball and takes it with him around the island. But most important, the volleyball becomes his companion and enables him to feel as if he's not alone. Chuck's friend, whom he appropriately names Wilson, keeps him sane during his years on the deserted island.

That film made me realize how natural, normal, and even necessary it is to share the deepest thoughts from our hearts. We need to speak up—for our sakes.

I think of the words written four hundred years ago by John Donne: "No man is an Island, entire of itself; every man is a piece of the Continent, a part of the main. . . ." He expressed poetically the reality that God made us creatures who need each other and rely on others to survive.

◆   ◆   ◆

At least a decade ago, I sat through an anti–Roman Catholic lecture in which the man railed against the confessional. Instead of agreeing with him, I came away with an appreciation of something that I hadn't thought of before. I realized the importance of speaking confessionally—from the depth of our being—and being heard by someone who represents God (and that individual doesn't have to be a priest). When that person understands, we have been affirmed, and the healing power is at work in us.

To put it biblically, "Confess your sins to each other and pray for each other so that you may be healed" (James 5:16a).

Our confession to others isn't limited to sins and mistakes. We need healing from God, but it seems to me that most of us also have to first experience acceptance from human beings.

We need affirmation and encouragement outside of ourselves. Until we share our inner pain, the agony stays inside. But once we speak about it and a human being makes us know we've been heard, the shame, guilt, and pain lose their power to enslave us.

Here's another way to look at it: Unless we speak our words to someone else, we become a slave to our worst thoughts. We allow them to torment us and to steal our peace.

I'll give an example. I did something during my high school days for which I was deeply ashamed. Jon Ludtke was my boss and the closest thing to a father figure I've ever known. On two occasions, I stole money from him—not huge amounts, but the amount isn't the issue.

I stole from someone who trusted me. And he never found out. But I knew, and I was tortured by that—especially stealing from Jon.

After I became a believer, I wrote to him, told him what I had done, and sent him a check for more than I had stolen. Because I was ashamed and guilty, I didn't want to face him. Whenever I visited my hometown, I avoided him.

When I went back for my fortieth high school reunion, Jon learned from one of my former classmates that I planned to attend. He told that former classmate that he wanted me to call him.

I didn't want to call, but the message was clear: Jon wanted to hear from me. I called him the next day, and he begged me to come to see him. I did.

As soon as I sat down, he asked, "Why haven't you come to see me? I know you've been in town several times through the years."

I couldn't even look at him as I said, "Because I stole from you. And no one was ever nicer to me or more loving than you." For another minute or two, I poured out my heart.

"That was kid stuff," Jon said. He dismissed it as a small thing. And perhaps to him it was; to me, it was a huge barrier to my relationship with my father figure.

Tears skidded down my cheeks. Until then, I hadn't known how much he cared or how easily he forgave me.

The point of this story is that the theft of a few dollars had chained me, filled me with guilt for forty years. But by speaking the words of confession (finally) and having my father figure call it kid stuff, I was set free.

None of us is an island, and even those who say, "I don't need anybody" are sad, isolated people. I'm glad I need people. And the more I've needed them and their acceptance, the more aware I am of God, who showers grace and love on me through other people.

◆ ◆ ◆

We may want to talk about our abuse, but fear or shame holds us back. We're acutely aware that we face negative consequences if we speak to the wrong person. Some individuals are uncomfortable with others' pain. Others are embarrassed by the subject of sexual abuse. I've met a few men who seem to despise anything that hints of personal weakness, giving off cues with their words and body language that say, "So? What's the big deal? Grow up!"

The good news is that we can choose those to whom we talk. We can decide whom to trust.

GARY

Deciding whom to trust is an important issue.

I was at a Christian writers' conference in Seattle. I was in a small group of six, one of whom was an editor. We were sharing what we hoped to write, and as soon as we finished, she gave us feedback. When it came to me, I simply said, "I'm a survivor of sexual abuse. I'm interested in writing something that will help others heal and begin to stand against this great evil."

When I said, "I'm a survivor of sexual abuse," the man sitting next to me leaned back and moved his chair a few inches away from mine. I don't think he was even aware of what he had done, but I immediately felt dirty and shameful. Afterward, one of the women came over and simply said, "Me too. I'm a survivor. Write it. It needs to be written."

That day I learned how volatile a subject sexual abuse is. I've repeatedly observed the negative reactions when I reveal to small groups what happened to me. Not everyone is going to affirm me. Not everyone wants to hear what I have to share.

I still need to speak.

I also need to be discerning. There are unsafe people—those with whom I shouldn't share. At times I have a sort of sixth sense about these things. I'll be talking with someone, and it's as if I hear the Holy Spirit whisper, "Don't go into your abuse story with him." I pay attention to that inner voice.

Feeling someone isn't safe to hear me self-reveal is significant because it convinces me that there are times to speak and to talk about my abuse and there are times when it's wiser not to say anything. There are forums or situations where it's appropriate for me to speak out. I don't go looking for chances to share about my abuse, but I try to remain open to opportunities as God brings them across my path. Even then, I pray, "Lord, do you want me to share?"

I don't simply share the agony of my past to anyone who'll listen. It has to be connected to the conversation or topic. Perhaps the other person is sharing about trauma in her background. Maybe someone asks about my childhood.

When I sense I have the green light from God, I usually share simply and directly and start with something like this: "My background was rough. I'm a survivor of sexual abuse. Healing has been a challenge."

CEC

Before we speak openly, here are some serious questions to consider.

First, what's my purpose in telling? If I'm doing it to feel better, or to gain support, or because it's someone I trust, those are good reasons.

Second, what do I expect to receive? I need to be prepared for disappointment or skepticism.

Third, do I speak up because I want help from the person who listens to me? If I don't, I start by saying, "I don't want you to do anything to help me. I need you to hear what I have to say. Just listen."

If the other person starts offering advice, we can respond simply, "Perhaps later I'll be ready for advice. Right now I need someone to listen who won't try to fix me."

Helping others, especially our friends, has become such a norm in the church (and perhaps in all phases of life), we tend to feel we've failed if we can't do something positive or speak exactly the right words that will make them say, "Thanks. That's wonderful advice."

We may need to learn to say firmly, "This is my problem, and I need to work it out. I just want to tell someone I trust. If you can listen to me and still love me, you'll have done a great deal to facilitate my healing."

Years ago I wrote an aphorism to define a good friend: A good friend knows all about me, still loves me, and has no plan for my self-improvement. I want friends who will love me in my imperfections and encourage me to grow even if they don't understand or agree with my choices.

✦   ✦   ✦

The first two people I told about my abuse were my friend David and my wife, Shirley. I *knew* without any doubt that they would hear me and love me anyway. I wasn't emotionally able to talk to anyone else about the subject for several weeks. I needed the support and encouragement of Shirley and David before I could open up any more.

I took my open confession in small steps. When I was ready, I told a small group of five other men with whom I met regularly. They were supportive and encouraged me. After that, I told a few select individuals.

About three years later, I was invited to speak to an organization called Lay Renewal. I did a keynote address at a church, and near the end of that message, I said I had been sexually abused and was learning to deal with my issue.

To my surprise, two people talked to me privately about my message, and they were the only ones who mentioned my abuse. One woman wrapped her arms around me. "I wish I could take away your pain."

I'm not sure what I expected, and I was disappointed that others didn't respond. At the same time, however, I felt empowered. I had revealed my secret to an audience of virtual strangers. The words were out there, and my level of shame diminished.

Since 2010, I've been going public as much as I can with this message. I now conduct seminars for survivors and friends of survivors of sexual abuse. I plan to speak to students at seminaries and Bible colleges—they are the ones who need to minister to those who hurt like I did.

> When I speak aloud about my abuse,
> I am healing my shame
> and empowering myself.

16

I DON'T WANT TO EXPOSE FAMILY SECRETS.

CEC

"Have you told anyone?" I asked the twenty-year-old man.

He shook his head. "Only you." He went on to say, "They wouldn't understand." He referred to his family.

"How do you know?"

He shrugged. "It wouldn't do any good. They won't believe me."

Our conversation went on for a few minutes before he admitted he was afraid to tell his family. I pleaded with him to speak up—but only when he was ready. "We have a term called 'the conspiracy of silence,' which means that no one in the family talks about it. No one admits the horrible, shameful acts. And we continue to suffer."

"It was no big deal for you, but to me—"

"It took me five years to tell my siblings," I said, "and more than a decade before I was able to write about my abuse."

"Really?" He stared at me incredulously. "You seem able to talk freely—"

"The longer we wait to tell anyone," I said, "the easier it is to pretend it didn't happen. Or to convince ourselves that it's not important."

My response surprised him because I talk openly and easily about the issue of male sexual abuse. I keep talking about it to help others—and to help me—get to the other side, which is freedom. Deliverance. Total victory. I'm still on the road to healing. "Even so," I told him, "shattering the conspiracy of silence was probably the strongest, most positive step I ever took."

I handled my abuse with amnesia (a form of denial) and was fifty-one years old before the first memories trickled back to my consciousness. As the painful memories emerged, my wife held my hand and my friend David gave me his shoulder. They encouraged me and infused me with confidence to speak about my molestation.

I often say that every time I spoke about my abuse, it emboldened me to speak more freely—and that's only a slight exaggeration. I'm glad I talked about it, but there was another huge step I didn't want to take. *I didn't tell my family of origin or my own children.* I made dozens of excuses for myself, such as:

> It no longer matters.
> They don't care.
> What difference does it make?
> I talk about it to others; why should I have to bring in my
>   siblings or my kids?
> It will only stir up anger and hurt.
> They probably won't believe me.

I grew up in a dysfunctional family. We didn't talk about secret things. My family didn't even use words like *pregnant.* My mother would say, "She's *that way.*" Her emphasis on those two words made it clear to me what she meant. It also reminds me of the way life was in those days. A thought came to me one day. Perhaps speaking to my siblings would bring healing *to all of us.* Perhaps all of us could face our painful childhood—even though our issues were not the same. Most of all, I admitted to myself that if I opened up, it would speed me on my recovery. By the time I was able to face my abuse, both my abusers were dead.

One sister had been molested by the old man who lived with us. I doubted that she had ever talked about the incident. Even though he targeted both of us (and possibly my two younger brothers), I have no recollection that we ever discussed what happened.

I decided that shattering the silence could bring healing to my then still-surviving five siblings and me. Even if it made no difference to them, it would mean that I could clear out the darkness of my childhood.

Around that time I lived in Louisville, Kentucky, and belonged to a group of men who met on alternating Saturday mornings. We wanted wholeness. Many of us had been sexually assaulted; others spoke of physical abuse. Some simply wanted to be able to talk openly with other men.

After I had been part of the group for a couple of years, someone brought up the matter of keeping silent. "We'll never be fully healed if we keep it a secret." Those may not have been his exact words, but that's the message I heard.

Until then I didn't realize that silence was also troublesome to many other men who had been molested in childhood. My focus had been on myself. I was aware only that I couldn't bring myself to talk about the topic. I gave myself many of the same reasons men often give for their indifference or disbelief of others, but that didn't stop the nagging voice.

I kept trying to figure out how to talk to my five surviving siblings, and I realized I didn't know how. On Valentine's Day that year, one of my sisters called me, and we chatted for perhaps ten minutes. She was the one who was abused by the elderly pedophile.

"Do you remember Mr. Lee, the old man who rented a room from us?" She admitted she did.

"He abused me," I said. I started pouring out my retrieved memories. We were poor, and Dad had been sick and out of work for months. "I don't think any of us ever felt we had enough to eat," I said. "Mr. Lee used to entice me to come to his room by offering me raspberry jam on saltine crackers."

"I had forgotten about the crackers." She went on to say she clearly remembered the abuse.

To my surprise, she was amazingly open. She helped me piece together more of what happened. Even more amazing, she didn't tell me I was crazy, judge me, or suggest I shut up and tell no one. I felt validated.

My two other sisters also helped me regain memories of that trauma and of the female relative who abused me. Later, when I visited my hometown, I tried to talk to my two younger brothers, both of whom I sensed had been molested. Neither wanted to talk about anything in childhood, but from their answers I inferred that my feelings were correct and they had been molested.

One sister said she didn't know about the sexual abuse, but there were indications. She apologized for not having paid attention. "Besides," she said, "in those days we didn't know what to do about things like that."

She was right, and this isn't to blame her for not knowing. But like many others, she remained unaware.

Denial. Ignorance. If I don't know about a bad thing, it didn't happen. Strange, but that attitude still prevails today, although sexual abuse isn't as hidden as it used to be.

GARY

A mentor once told me, "We're as sick as our secrets."

Sexual abuse wasn't the only secret in my family. Deception was an everyday affair. One of the main goals in life was to appear better, smarter, and more talented than we really were. We put on a show. We were fakes—not intentionally, but frauds nonetheless because we weren't truly who we tried to be.

Fear caused me to pull deep within myself. I was terrified of people. I hardly ever said anything. I began hiding. Keeping secrets became a way of life.

I created my own little world to live in. In this imaginary world, I was the hero, the rock star, the savior. And most of the time, my heroism led to a tragic end.

It didn't help that I wasn't allowed to play with other kids my age. All outside influences were tightly controlled. I got used to my rich inner world where I was in control.

The message I was living was clear. *When in pain, trust no one. I'm fundamentally alone.* My secret life was keeping me from real life.

I repressed the sexual abuse for forty years. Then the flashbacks started. That secret made me sick. When the silence was shattered, the healing process was able to start.

At times I still wrongly kept some things secret without realizing what I was doing. I withheld myself out of fear. That's the past, and I'm ready to make some secrets known. I'm tired of self-hypocrisy. I'm ready to live more fully in the real world.

I've also learned that sin, especially sexual sin, seeks to stay underground and thrives in darkness. My sexual abuse stayed hidden until I was forty-five, when the flashbacks began to flood through me. I thought I was going crazy. Terrified, I told my wife what I was experiencing. After hearing me out, she simply said, "I'm not surprised. I've always wondered."

I was already seeing a counselor for anxiety that had plagued me throughout my adult life. My wife went with me to the next appointment, and I described to him what I was seeing and feeling. I asked, "Am I crazy?"

"No," he replied.

"Did that really happen to me?"

"It's perfectly consistent with everything you've shared with me about your background, the people involved, and the struggles you've had in life."

From that point on, the counselor began working with me to bring into the light what had happened in the darkness. I slowly recognized the insidious nature of the conspiracy of silence. It kept me quiet and held me in bondage. The silence caused me to perform and work endlessly for affection and approval that would never be enough for me.

Several months after accepting the truth about my abuse, and with great trepidation, one Sunday morning I stood behind the pulpit and shared my story with the congregation I was pastoring. I didn't give them details, only the big picture. I wept and trembled throughout. I could hardly look at anyone. At one point, I could no longer speak.

One man got up, tears in his eyes, and came and stood beside me. I closed my eyes and continued to weep.

Soon I felt hands being placed on my shoulders and my back. Someone prayed aloud for me. Several others also prayed. Others wept. Finally, I looked up and realized that about thirty people surrounded me, either touching me or touching someone who was touching me. I felt such a powerful sense of relief.

That afternoon, however, I was struck by a powerful wave of shame. Now they knew my deepest secret. *How will they treat me? What will they think of me now? Do I disgust them? Do they want me to leave because I'm emotionally defective or ruined goods?* Fear and panic set in, and I expected the worst possible outcome.

To my relief, the church members accepted me and treated me as if nothing had happened.

In the next session, my counselor applauded my courage by saying, "You laid your heart out there. Some will meet you in that vulnerable place. You, not your mask, will get their love now."

A few weeks later, I took a trip to my home state of Texas. I was terrified, but resolute. I met first with the couple I often refer to as my adoptive parents. They made me feel that I was part of their family when I was in high school. I told them what had happened to me.

They had known me since I was six years old, so they knew my family pretty well. To my surprise they said, "We knew that something horrible had happened back there. We just didn't know what."

I began to weep when they said the things that every hurt, abused kid longs to hear: "We love you, Gary. We're proud of you. We're in this with you. We'll help in any way we can."

The next day, they drove for three hours with me to the place one of my perpetrators was living. They went with me and stood right outside the door during my seven-minute conversation with my abuser.

My counselor had worked with me on what to say and how to proceed, but I was still terrified. I was trembling as I walked inside and said, "I want to talk with you about something. I've had flashbacks recently, and in these flashbacks you're sexually abusing me. Could this be true?" I asked.

My abuser sat there, expressionless. "No," was the reply.

"Really? It sure seems and feels real. Did you sexually abuse me?"

"No," was the reply again, still eerily emotionless. My abuser was looking at the wall, making no eye contact with me.

"I know it's true," I said, "and I've forgiven you." I got up to leave.

As I got to the doorway, my abuser began to get agitated. By the time I walked out, she was shouting at me and yelling that I was mistaken and accusing her of things she hadn't done.

I kept walking.

My adoptive parents described the whole interchange as spooky. We expected denial and no remorse, and that's what we received.

I told other family members as well. Reactions ranged from supportive to shock to almost violent anger. The violent anger confused me, and it took me months to work through my own feelings about their responses. But I also grew closer to those who loved me and supported me.

It took several months to recover from the intense emotions of that trip. Although traumatic in many ways, the trip brought healing, as well. My abuse was no longer a secret, and everyone in the family knew the truth.

I'm glad I faced my perpetrator and told my family members. I couldn't live under that conspiracy of silence any longer.

Since then I've been fairly open about my abusive past. I don't broadcast it, and I choose carefully when, where, and with whom I tell my story. Each time I share, I still fight the fear of possible rejection.

I never know how the other person is going to respond. And almost every time I tell my story, I become introduced to more members of this not-so-exclusive club of sexual-abuse survivors. Dozens of people have responded with simple statements: "Me too. Thank you."

Bringing out the truth is one way I can fight and stand against the diabolical evil of sexual abuse. It takes a warrior's courage, and I'm committed to be that warrior.

Jesus' words encourage me. He said, "God's light came into the world, but people loved the darkness more than the light, for their actions were evil. *All who do evil hate the light* and refuse to get near it for fear their sins will be exposed" (John 3:19b–20, emphasis mine).

The conspiracy of silence revolves around fear. I refuse to carry the evil and the accusations of my abusers. It's their wrongdoing, not mine. I want to walk in the light, exposing the deeds of darkness whenever and wherever I can.

Cec

I received the following e-mail from my good friend Tom Scales with VOICE Today. He began with these words: "You are free to add the following to your blog or wherever. Use my name because that's part of continually breaking the silence and showing others it can be done." Here's his story:

> For me the silence was an impenetrable wall I constructed. It had many uses. As part of my abuse I did many things that, even at the time, were horrific, and I didn't want anyone to know the truth. I worked hard to isolate myself from intimate or close relationships. If anyone knew the truth about my childhood, certainly everyone would ostracize me.
>
> It took many years before I understood that my boundaries allowed behavior that was offensive to most people. Establishing proper, biblical personal boundaries has been a lifelong and life-changing process.
>
> The silence about being a survivor of childhood sexual abuse spilled over into other aspects of life. Because I didn't want people to find out my secret, I couldn't let them get close in other areas of my life. As a result, open and honest expressions of feelings and emotions were off limits. I kept hidden anything that would provide insight into what and who I really was. As a result, I didn't develop friendships with anyone.

The first responses I received after breaking my silence were so awful and humiliating, I clammed up again. Decades passed before I had the courage to shed the shame and guilt, to forgive myself, and to be able to allow God to use those horrible experiences for good in the lives of other survivors.

❖ ❖ ❖

By now I hope it's obvious that when we speak of shattering the silence, there are two significant elements involved. First, we need to speak up—to bring the evil out of shrouded darkness. As long as it stays inside, we remain tormented.

Speaking the words aloud to someone else tells us we have begun our healing journey. We need to take that vital step to continue going forward. Speaking up may not be the first step on the healing path, but it's too significant a step to ignore.

Second, to speak the words and to have others accept us validates our pain. Until we speak, we haven't taken ownership of our abuse or faced the depth of our pain. By speaking up, we're taking our stand and saying, "This happened to me, and I'm going to defeat the evil effect."

Both Gary and I feared we wouldn't be believed, but we were. We discovered allies in our quest for health and wholeness.

I'll never be fully healed if I hide the secrets of my past.
A big step—and a difficult one—
is to move out of darkness into light.

17

HOW DO I HANDLE FLASHBACKS AND RECURRING DREAMS?

CEC

We tend to repress memories when our suffering becomes unbearable. But those painful events don't stay repressed. Just to be clear, here's my distinction between *repression* and *suppression*. *Repression* is an unconscious act; it's a protective device. When something is too painful to accept about ourselves, an inner wisdom hides that fact from our consciousness.

Suppression is a definite act of the will. We know (or assume) things about ourselves that we don't want to share with others. We push them inside, but we're aware of their presence. Those facts often trouble us, and the more they torment, the more we tend to smother them.

Suppose I had once spent a year in jail for drug use and I'd be embarrassed for people to know that. I would push the fact as far away in my thinking as possible. I would probably be sensitively aroused whenever anyone brought up a topic that might "out" me.

Suppression doesn't have to be about bad or unacceptable things. It may simply refer to suppressing information from people whom we consider unsafe. We cover up or conceal facts because they're gossips or they could use the knowledge to work against us.

Suppression may keep us vigilant, but repression happens outside our conscious awareness. The problem with repression is that it tends to sneak into our lives as if to say, "I want you to know this."

What we repress sometimes resurfaces in flashbacks beyond our control, and we experience anew the horror of the past pain. We call that post-traumatic stress.

If we're committed to healing, the memories—and they're always partial and fragmented—return in some form. Two forms of agonizing memories hit many of us in the healing process.

The first is that we have flashbacks.

In those brief, in-an-instant experiences, we relive our molestation or events around the occurrences. They're painful and shocking. Despite their brevity, often they're so intense, it feels as if the abuse is happening again.

The other is recurring dreams. Gary experienced more of the former, and mine has been the latter.

Who wants to reexperience such terrible moments? Because they were painful incidents, it's natural that many of us want to deny them or medicate ourselves so that we don't hurt again.

I understand that, *but what if we valued flashbacks and dreams as gifts from God?* What if reexperiencing is a required step toward wholeness? What if they're signals for us to pay attention, to take notice, and to aid us in our healing?

A friend broke his leg a few years ago and went through terrible pain, but after a few weeks he was fine. Almost a year later, he went to his family doctor for another reason. He was limping (which he hadn't realized), and X-rays showed the break had healed but was causing damage by rubbing against another bone. A surgeon broke the bone again and set it straight. My friend was hurt twice, but the second painful time was to correct what hadn't healed properly after the first break.

That's not a perfect analogy, but apply that thought to dreams and flashbacks. If we see them as indications of our progress—as instruments of divine healing—we can accept them more readily. We can say to ourselves, "This memory came back to me because I'm ready to face now what I wasn't able to face as child."

Or it may be a statement to us of our maturity and encourage us to know we're ready to move forward.

GARY

I was young when my abuse happened, and it happened repeatedly. The perpetrators were close to me. I had no memory of the sexual abuse itself, but I grew up with a sense of deep terror and anger toward the perpetrators.

Years later, I began to have flashbacks. They started slowly and increased in duration and intensity. They came regularly, as if I had no will to stop them. I wondered and asked myself, "Am I going crazy?"

These flashbacks were intense, as if I were there, feeling the pain and turmoil all over again. It was unnerving, confusing, terrifying, and exhausting. The flashbacks continued for a period of two years.

I couldn't have handled it alone. If it hadn't been for a few committed, supportive people, I don't know what I would have done.

From those horrible flashbacks, I came to understand a powerful truth: isolation wasn't the answer. In fact, I think of isolation as one of my most powerful enemies. I had to share, to talk, and to stay connected with those who loved me to overcome the painful recollections of my past. Those important people in my life helped me to accept the flashbacks and not repress them—as I had in childhood.

My flashbacks were progressive in nature. I had my first one during a massage therapy session. The therapist was working on my left arm, and suddenly I saw and felt myself being dragged by my left arm toward the back bedroom of the house where I grew up. I couldn't tell who was dragging me, and when we got to the door of the bedroom, the flashback stopped.

After that experience, the flashbacks came with increasing frequency, as if someone had unlocked a door and left it ajar. For several weeks it was the same flashback, always ending when we reached the door of the bedroom.

At first, I felt emotionally detached from what I was seeing. It was like watching a movie with no real emotions about what I was seeing. I felt curious, and over time, increasingly apprehensive. I had a sense of foreboding about that bedroom door but was able to overcome my terror.

After several weeks, I wanted to know what had happened and prayed that God would reveal to me whatever he wanted me to experience. The next day, the flashbacks took a leap forward. The bedroom door opened, and for the first time as an adult, I was able to see some of what had happened to me inside that room.

I watched the same scene several times. After that, other events of the painful past flashed through my heart. As the pace of the flashbacks picked up in intensity, so did their duration and the amount that was revealed.

It became common for a whole scene to replay itself for several weeks, and that's when my emotions finally engaged. As a result, I felt as if the molestations were happening all over again.

After I had fully reexperienced my way through one event, a different incident would begin. At the time it was disturbing, but now I see it as a merciful and loving process. God was exposing me to what I was ready to face—for the first time. I could handle only so much, so it came over a period of time. As strange as it may seem, the progressive nature of the flashbacks assured me that the Lord was with me because he was directing the recall process. That became a source of great comfort.

After two years of those flashbacks, my health began to deteriorate. At random times my body flooded with adrenaline. Anxiety often took over. I felt like a deer being chased by a lion. My life seemed small and dark. Those flashback aftershocks continued for another few years.

Even though I constantly felt tempted to give up, I stayed with the flashbacks and talked to trusted people each time one occurred. I survived because I faced my fear and refused to deny what I knew was true.

Now the flashbacks are gone. They served their purpose, and I don't expect to have them again because I no longer need reminders of the past.

CEC

In contrast to Gary, I didn't have many flashbacks. The few flashbacks I had involved absolutely no emotion. I felt like an observer clinically watching something happen to another person. In fact, the most significant flashbacks were about the old man who molested me.

Mr. Lee invited me into his room. He had a small table that held a jar of raspberry preserves with a spoon, and next to it lay a package of saltines with a knife on top. I surveyed the scene from the doorway and watched as he took the little boy—me—and fed him. I was standing while the boy sat on a chair next to the old man.

After the boy had eaten the preserves, I watched as the old man pulled the boy toward himself and placed the child on his lap. He talked softly before he slowly began the abusive ritual. The entire time I knew I was that child, but I wasn't emotionally connected to him.

In my flashbacks, I didn't see most of what happened—I blotted out those painful episodes. Most remarkable to me was the lack of feeling—I experienced repression because I couldn't handle the emotional reality.

We've presented two ways flashbacks operate in the healing process. Our accounts point out that we're all different in our pain, and we go different routes in our healing journey.

✦ ✦ ✦

My repressed feelings surfaced in my recurring dreams. One dream became a regular part of my life. It seemed as if I had always dreamed it. I have no idea when it started or how often it came, but I know it started sometime in my twenties. The dream was always the same with minor variations.

Each time, I walked up the five steps to our white, wooden-frame house where we lived until I was fifteen. Recently a niece gave me a picture of that house (which has been torn down for at least twenty years), and it's exactly as I remember it.

The five steps led to a screen door. On either side was a mailbox. The only variation was that sometimes I noticed a letter in one mailbox or the other. On other occasions there was no mail. If there was a letter, I reached up, pulled it out. It had my name on it. As soon as I read my name, the dream ended.

If there was no letter in either box, I opened the screen door and pushed the door to go inside. The dream ended.

About two years after I began to heal, I had the recurring dream again, but that time it didn't stop while I was still outside. I pushed open the door and walked through every room of the house. I paused in front of two places I hid so I could be alone and no one would hurt me. Those spots were small, but as a kid, they were probably just big enough.

After I awakened, I felt confused because I could see only about three feet from the floor. Then I realized that's how I would have seen the house as a boy somewhere between the ages of five and seven.

✦ ✦ ✦

Both Gary and I can talk about our flashbacks and recurring dreams because we're now free of them. They were vital steps toward healing. It seems as if we had to reexperience our childhood trauma in order to be healed from it.

GARY

It's like we get stuck. Whatever we can't cope with remains inside us, internalized, waiting for the right time to manifest itself. When we're ready, the traumatic events come to the surface, inviting us to experience them again so that we're able to accept and move past them.

It's almost like there was a four-to-six-year-old Gary waiting to be rescued. Before he could be rescued, however, he had to be seen, acknowledged, and accepted. What he went through was horrific, and he deserved to be saved. Through the flashbacks, I went back and experienced it with "my little boy." Now he's an integrated part of myself, so I can move on to new areas of maturity.

My counselor referred to this experience as phenomenon integration.

It's as if I left part of myself back there. I couldn't be a whole person until I retrieved what I had left behind.

That's the function of recurring dreams and flashbacks. They are gifts that help us become whole. Because of the accompanying pain, they may not feel like gifts—at least not at the time. But afterward, both Cec and I were able to thank God for bringing them back to us.

CEC

I've mentioned that I felt nothing in either my flashbacks or dreams. That's a good way to look at the way I handled abuse as a kid.

My father beat me quite often. A large elm tree grew in our backyard, and Dad sent me to get what he called a switch from the tree. If it wasn't long enough, he made me get another, then he beat me for that as well. He liked them long and thin. I assume it was because they stung and bit into the skin. My sister Wanda and I often had marks on our legs from Dad's switches. So did my baby brother, Chuck.

Sometimes when Dad was really upset (today I'd call it out of control), he used whatever was at hand, such as his belt or a broom.

Because I refused to let Dad see me cry, I learned not to feel the beatings. Years later I went to a chiropractor who worked on me and kept pressing various places on my back. Each time he asked, "Does that hurt?"

None of the manipulations did.

"You have an extremely high tolerance for pain," he said.

The next day my brother Chuck and I talked by phone. I told him what the chiropractor had said. Chuck replied, "Don't you remember? We decided we wouldn't feel it when Dad beat us."

As soon as Chuck said those words, I vividly remembered the agreement he and I had made. Dad made us bend over, and the beating started. We'd look at each other and laugh and keep laughing while he struck us. Neither of us cried, and that made Dad even more violent and the beating usually intensified. But in ways neither of us could explain, we felt no pain.

The conversation with my brother marks the moment when I began to understand why I had no physical sensations and no connection with my emotions. I could finally understand the reason I became the observer during flashbacks of my sexual molestation.

GARY

The more lengthy and intense my flashbacks became, the more I began to feel them. I call one place in my flashbacks "the house of horrors."

An older man would invite me from the living room of the house to his room at the back. His voice filled me with fear. I was terrified, but I couldn't run. I knew it would be worse if I didn't do what he said. I walked through the living room, through the kitchen, where other people would be working or sitting, and I sensed they tried not to look at me as I went by. I was sure they knew what was happening.

I paused at the threshold going into his room. I stared at my feet, not wanting to go inside and silently pleading that someone would rescue me and I wouldn't have to go inside.

"Get in here, boy," he would command. I slowly walked into the room, still looking at the floor. In my flashbacks I heard his voice, and each time, fear struck my heart. It was going to happen again, and no one would help. I couldn't do anything to stop him.

He relied on my fear to keep me compliant and quiet. "See the top of that dresser, boy?" the old man would say. "That's where I keep my spiders and snakes." He would get up, walk to the dresser, and reach up out of my sight. "I've got a box right here, full of them. You do what I say, or I'll let them loose on you."

I believed these outrageous statements. I can still feel the terror. He would then sit down in his chair, call me to come to him, and the ritual assault began. I felt small, helpless, and dirty. I feel the same just writing this.

It's not strange that I grew up being afraid of the dark. Nighttime filled me with a sense of foreboding and danger. Bedtime was terrifying. *Who knows what might happen tonight,* I thought.

I steeled myself against the pain. After the first few assaults, I learned to detach so effectively that I felt nothing. Almost as if I went deep inside myself to protect my soul as my body was being ravaged. No wonder I grew up extremely shy. I was trying to be invisible.

✦   ✦   ✦

To say that I'm grateful now may sound inadequate, but I *am* grateful for the flashbacks and the aftershocks. I'm relieved to finally know what happened. I can make sense of my life and realize why I've behaved as I have. I understand what happened to me, why anxiety and dread frequently troubled me. For a long time, I wondered what was wrong with me. Until I connected those feelings with the abuse, I was confused about who I was and worried about what was wrong with me.

Like many of us in recovery, I endured the pain in childhood. I endured the pain a second time through flashbacks. Denial was survival in my childhood, but the time came when denial no longer served me well. It shackled me. I had to go back and remember what happened so that I could heal. I'm grateful. Now I can grow.

Cec

Our survival methods differed, and so did our healing. But two things are important to stress. First, we endured the molestation because we were helpless children. Second, we reexperienced the abuse through flashbacks as part of our healing journey.

At first, facing the abuse may seem as if we're being molested again. And it did. We *felt the pain* of those childhood assaults. We accepted our victimization, and the flashbacks were actually healing to us.

I look at it this way. We ran from our pain in whatever way we were able. We hated what happened to us, but reexperiencing is an important ingredient in the healing.

Repression became our form of medication. Many men, unable to repress or suppress, find their own way to relieve their symptoms.

I often think of the words of Kahlil Gibran: "And when you see a man drunken say in your heart, 'Mayhap he sought escape from something still more unbeautiful.'" That statement has given me compassion toward those who attempt to drown their sorrows through alcohol. It doesn't work, but the addiction shows they keep trying.

If we want healing—full healing—we can't mask our pain. As adults, we need to go back to those painful traumas. Once we go back and face the origin of our pain, we can leave it behind.

> I don't like to feel the pain again,
> but the only way out of the pain
> is to go through it again.

18

WHAT GOOD COMES FROM GRIEF?

GARY

Grief seems to have been part of my life for as long as I can remember. Some times were, of course, more intense than others. Grief stems from loss. And the losses that result from sexual abuse are numerous.

I have a picture that someone special drew for me at a pivotal time in my healing journey. It is a framed pencil sketch of a pillow and a box of Kleenex. The drawing effectively captured a large part of two years of my life. When I felt the grief coming, I grabbed a pillow and a box of tissues and sat on the couch. As the grief wave came, I hugged the pillow and let the tears flow.

The artist didn't draw a person in the sketch because the pillow and the Kleenex served their purpose. They are both now only a memory. The drawing depicts the healing that came to me through grieving.

✦ ✦ ✦

At first, I just didn't want to work through the grieving process. The recovery-healing stuff was interrupting my already way-too-busy life. I tried to shut it out. I tried telling myself that it was not that big a deal and that I just needed to suck it up. I tried harder. It was in the past, so why not leave it buried there?

My first response was denial. Denial didn't work and couldn't work for one simple reason. What happened was *real*. So if I wanted to live in reality, I had to deal with reality.

I couldn't avoid the process.

When that truth clicked, I entered a time of intense emotional pain. I now call it my hugging-the-pillow time. Decades of pent-up grief would suddenly assault me, pouring out of me like a cloudburst. Most times, I could feel it coming. I'd sit on the couch, hug a pillow, and begin to weep. My weeping often became sobbing, and sometimes even intense wailing. That period of intense grief went on for about two years. The grief came in waves.

On other occasions, the weeping hit me without warning. At home, at work, in the car, at the movie theater, at the gym, at church, in the pool, or in the doctor's office. It was especially bad early in the morning and in the middle of the night.

My grief often came with a high level of anxiety. At times, I intensified my anxiety level by trying to shut down my grief. I didn't want that overpowering pain to come back, even though it was necessary. I fared better when I quit resisting and let my agony overtake me.

During that period, I was seeing a counselor. Through our sessions, I learned to accept what I already knew was true, but I hadn't acted on what I knew by facing it.

I finally admitted that I couldn't go on holding the hurt inside. I couldn't have flashbacks and remain emotionally unaffected. I had to feel what I had repressed. The intensity of my grief gave dignity to that little kid who had endured so much abuse. My grief testified that what happened truly mattered. That I mattered. What happened was evil and shouldn't happen to anyone, especially a child.

Anger was a big part of my grief. For a time, I became angrier than I have ever been in my life. It leaked out in many ways. I was easily irritable. Little things set me off as if I were looking for ways to get upset.

That reaction was complicated by the fact that I viewed anger as forbidden for good Christians. In the church environment in which I grew up, true believers no longer felt anger, let alone rage.

My perpetrators had been angry, and they unleashed it on me through sexual violence. They screamed at me. At other times their anger was just under the surface, but I sensed it. It terrified me. As I grew up, anger in any form terrified me. I wanted nothing to do with that dreaded and feared emotion. It's no wonder I didn't express my fury.

But I was incensed and infuriated even though I couldn't express it in normal, healthy ways. I discovered I needed a plan, a way to really let loose and express the stored-up bile so that it wouldn't leak over onto my family and others who had nothing to do with the abuse.

I came up with several strategies.

I grabbed that pillow and punched the life out of it—in private (anger tended to scare my family so I wasn't comfortable letting them observe my behavior). Many times I got inside my car, drove down the street, and screamed. On other occasions I went to the swimming pool and splashed through a couple of miles, screaming into the water and whacking through every flip-turn.

I took small breaks during the day and speed-walked around the office or neighborhood, allowing myself to feel the intense emotions. I visualized my perpetrators and unleashed my rage in a verbal list of what *they* had done, the results of their cowardice, the devastation their sexual nuclear warheads had wrought, and how I felt about it all.

After several months, the distance between outburst episodes lengthened, and the rage became less intense. After more time passed, I had infrequent, short-lived anger spikes.

I had to remind myself that my anger was tied to the abuse and not to the current situation. Then I was also able to turn to one of the strategies I had developed and express it as quickly as I could.

◆   ◆   ◆

I also experienced varying levels of depression throughout, with intense bouts from time to time. Sometimes I sat and stared at the walls. My self-doubt was off the scales; my job confidence plummeted. I felt as if my chin scraped the ground everywhere I went. I felt worthless, incredibly sad, and hopeless. Trapped. I had serious doubts whether things would ever get any better.

I was finally allowing myself to really feel what I couldn't feel in childhood. If I *had* felt it back then, I wouldn't have survived. I felt the devastating power of feelings of worthlessness, hopelessness, shock, fear, anger, terror, and disbelief. I reexperienced the pain of being treated as an object, a target, as if I didn't matter or even exist. It felt as if my life were being slowly, deliberately mashed out of me, like a wrecked car in a crusher.

I was beginning to accept that there were lasting effects of the abuse that I would never get rid of. Certain things triggered my anxiety. At times I reacted more strongly than the average person would have. Fear might never be far away. My victim-thinking was deeply ingrained, and during stressful situations, it surfaced as automatically as breathing.

I said to my counselor one day, "It's like I'm handicapped."

He leaned forward and said, "You are. What happened to you was unthinkable and devastatingly evil. It has lasting effects that you will never fully be able to eradicate."

I was terribly depressed at that moment, but by the time I left his office after that session, something had happened. I felt hopeful for the first time in months. I got into my car and just sat there, marveling at the peace I felt. All of a sudden it was OK. What had happened, happened. I knew that day, on a much deeper level than before, that the abuse wasn't my fault. I happened to be innocently available. I was the victim.

And I survived.

I backed out of my parking place and pulled out onto the road. Soon I was pumping my fist, screaming, "I survived! I'm alive! I'm alive! I am alive!"

✦   ✦   ✦

When I hear the phrase, "good grief" I think of Charlie Brown from the *Peanuts* comic strip. He has just embarrassed himself in front of the little red-headed girl he likes. Or he has been belittled by Lucy again.

Or something else tragic has taken place. Charlie Brown hangs his head and simply says, "Good grief!"

I used to consider that the ultimate oxymoron. I think differently now. There is such a thing as good grief. Once I gave myself permission to grieve, what needed to come out, did. I have to continue giving myself that permission.

Good grief is essential to healing. I believe in this so strongly that I have a mini course on my blog called Good Grief.[1] We've all had devastating losses in life. It's how we interpret and respond to those losses that makes the difference.

Reexperiencing the sad trauma of the past means we revisit the old hurts. We have to plunge into the depths of our pain and despair. We not only have to face that it happened, but we also have to feel it. Too many want the healing without reexperiencing agony. It doesn't work like that.

As someone has said, "The only way out is to go in." That is, until we feel our hurt—and recognize it as our own—there is no healing.

Embracing the pain is a true expression. It means that I have to allow myself—perhaps force myself—to stare at the hurt and say, "This is my pain."

That's when the healing begins.

*   *   *

The grieving process goes on. I hugged the pillow again a few months back. Anything can trigger our sense of loss—a song, a movie scene, a smell, a photograph, or someone's innocent remark.

Grief resides in us, a result of the losses we have experienced. It is not our enemy. It can be a great friend in this healing process. I am still learning to let it out when it comes knocking from the inside.

Give yourself a great gift. Give yourself permission to grieve the many

---

1. www.garyroe.com

losses wrought by the abuse and by life in general. Cec and I give you permission. When it comes knocking, let it out. Embrace good grief that heals.

> Grief is not my enemy;
> it testifies that what happened
> really does matter.

19

I DON'T FEEL LIKE A REAL MAN.

CEC

Someone called it a fundamental obstacle for sexually abused men to reconcile molestation with their inner vision of what it means to be a man. Cultural perceptions and biblical examples about men and masculinity mean that many males aren't able to live up to those imposed standards.

A boy who was sexually molested likely feels challenged about his masculinity. He knows he has the same anatomy but may wonder (and worry) about muscles, strength, and penis size.

He struggles on two fronts. First and probably more significant is his self-perception of whether he is a real man. Second is the socially constructed ideal masculine self. For example, being a victim is something women face. He struggles to reconcile his attitude about manhood with his own sexual victimization.

❖   ❖   ❖

In January 2010, I began a twice-weekly blog for male survivors of sexual assault.[1] The blog's purpose is to offer encouragement and to be a healing forum to men. (We also have a few female readers.)

I want to make it clear that we don't ask readers to identify themselves. They may write anonymously, give us only a first name, or call themselves whatever they like.

---

1. www.menshatteringthesilence.blogspot.com

Occasionally, I'll post a topic by me or by one of our readers that elicits significant response. The topic of this chapter is one of two that has received the most comments on my blog. The other, lies we believe, is the subject of the next chapter.

Here's my entry that stirred up so much response, because it's a frequent question from men who were sexually molested in childhood. "What does it mean to be a man—a real man?"

We have cultural attitudes and expectations within our own social communities about masculinity. But no matter how it's said, most of us survivors face uncertainty about our manhood. We say to ourselves, but certainly not to anyone else, "If I were a real man, I would (or I wouldn't) . . ."

For example, I might remind myself that I was a victim of sexual abuse, so I can't be a real man, because true men are never victims. If I use the word *victim* when I think of myself, I may struggle or be aware of something I might say carelessly that will make others think I'm not a real male.

If I cry, my friends might laugh at me, imply that I'm a sissy, or taunt that I behave like a girl. Maybe I'm not athletic or don't enjoy watching football. Or perhaps I'm too thin or too fat. Too tall or too short. Almost anything can cause me to struggle with deeper issues.

It's sad because the question of being a true man is usually a silent, inner battle we can't share with others. We don't know how to trust other men so we can't talk freely—we fear it would open us to further criticism.

Years ago my friend Charlie said he played with paper dolls when he was a kid. He was an only child, and the dolls entertained him. One day he was with a friend, and they saw two girls playing with paper dolls. "Only girls play with dolls," his friend said and sneered.

"After that," Charlie said, "I played only in my room and made sure no one else would see them." He later said that he started dating girls at age sixteen, and even though he liked girls, later married, and was never involved in any homosexual relationships, he still wonders if he's really a man.

"How do I know if I'm a real man?" he asked.

◆　◆　◆

This anecdote came from a blog reader who chose not to be identified:

> Starting when I was five, and off and on for a couple of years afterward, my older cousin raped me and forced me to perform oral sex on him. I'm thankful that a decade ago the Lord showed me how to forgive him. Before that, however, I hated him and planned to burn down the house where everything happened.
>
> I'm now thirty-one years old, and I still deal with the effects of what happened. I rarely feel like a real man. I'm constantly plagued by inadequacy and not being masculine enough.
>
> I've struggled continually with same-sex attraction since the abuse happened. It seems that all I crave is to have a guy I consider a real man, tell me that I am man enough to be accepted. The only time I feel like a regular guy is when I'm working out at the gym. I spend almost all of my free time there.
>
> Although I've gotten bigger and stronger, when I look in the mirror, all I see is shameful weakness. At times, the shame is suffocating.
>
> I'm trying to convince myself to get your book.[2] I know it will be of tremendous help, but I can't—not yet.

---

2. He refers to *When a Man You Love Was Abused: A Woman's Guide to Helping Him Overcome Childhood Sexual Molestation* by Cecil Murphey (Grand Rapids: Kregel, 2010).

The pain has gotten more acute lately, and I've retreated into sinful behavior to buffer against the pain. The "fun part" is that I work at a church, and if they ever found out about me (my struggles, my sin), I'd be let go.

Your blog has provided great comfort. I watched a Beth Moore clip last week, and she asked, "Have you ever let God touch those deep, painful places in your life, or are you scabbing over them?" I asked God to touch the deep places in me, and that's when I found the link to your site. I think I will buy the book.

Through it all, the Lord has been so merciful to me and so gentle. I fight against myself every day to trust him.

Here's another person who chose to remain anonymous:

I am thirty-six, married with two kids, run a business, and have been a church high school staff volunteer for thirteen years. I was abused while on a family vacation, by the son of a family friend. I thought I had done something wrong. I was afraid if I said anything or told anyone, I would be in trouble. So I told no one for twenty-four years.

Three years ago a friend, a co–high school youth worker, shared his journey of molestation and confusion around same-sex attraction on a high school guys' retreat. For the first time, the lie, that I was the only one who felt that way, was broken. Further, my friend is thriving in life, and his words gave me a visual of what dealing with this could look like.

All I could do at that point was shove an anonymous note in his coat pocket that said "me too," because I was too overwhelmed, ashamed, and frightened at letting out my worst, dirtiest secret.

Two years ago on a youth trip, two of my guys confessed to me that they had been molested and that another friend of theirs had been, as well. My friend (same guy mentioned above who told of his abuse) and I formed a small group and started chasing after those hurting guys and diving into their pain. Their anguish combined with mine, which was completely walled off at the time, became overwhelming. But finally I started getting help, as well.

All of this is to say I deeply resonate with everything that you have said and feel. I have struggled and wrestled with the yearning for a "real man" to tell me that I am acceptable enough to be labeled a man. I, too, rarely feel like a real man. I know what it is like to stand on the edge of the cliff and be deathly afraid of what it might look like to start the healing process—the enormity and emotional upheaval of saying you were molested.

Right down to Beth Moore, our small group looked at one of her studies on Joseph, "Can't Quite Forget" where Joseph couldn't be whole until his past was put in proper place with his current life and God's future purpose for him.

Honestly, two years later, my life is so different—freer and better. I still have much to work through. The first part, right where you are, is like almost the worst, but like a remodel on a house, the tear-down process is super messy at first but then the new starts to take shape and it gets better rapidly.

This came from yet another anonymous reader:

I recently started a blog to write down my feelings in order to deal with my past. I also hope to help others in the same situation. I was abused (I don't remember for how long) and used drugs and alcohol to blot out the pain. I got sober nine months ago. Without the drugs and alcohol, it's tough to deal with the pain. I'm seeing a therapist and working on it, but it's a slow process.

I kept telling myself, "I'm a real man" or "I'm going to be a real man." One day it hit me: I am—I truly am a real man. I was basing my definition on what I read about in books or saw in movies. I wasn't like any of those guys. But I am a man, and I can define myself.

I have defined myself, because I've defined myself as a human being created in the image of God. I love the person I have become and am still becoming.

I am a real man, and I don't need anyone else's definition.

These comments are examples of how many, many male survivors still struggle with what it means to be truly masculine. We know it's an issue of more than physical anatomy and that it goes deeply into the psyche of those of us who were molested.

I recently saw a film made in 1980, called *The Elephant Man*, based on a true story in the late nineteenth century. John Merrick is extremely deformed and becomes known as the "elephant man." Near the end of the film, Merrick is part of a freak show in London. He escapes, but a group of boys harass him. They see him, chase him, and finally catch him.

Merrick screams, "I am not an elephant! I am not an animal! I am a human being! I—am—a—man!"

The story is different from that of any of us because Merrick's deformity is physically visible; ours is invisible, but the struggle is similar in many ways. People don't call us animals—in fact, they may not have any negative thoughts about us.

But just as our deformity is internal, so is our cry: "I—am—a—man!" And we are men, even if we don't feel like it.

✦   ✦   ✦

My answer to the question "What does it mean to be a real man?" is fairly simple: First of all, I am a male by gender. That's how God created me. Second, I get to define my description of masculinity. I don't have to be macho with a belly the size of a football hanging over the top of my pants. I don't have to know the name of every NFL or NBA player. I don't have to conform to the beer-guzzling stereotypes, because they don't get to decide who I am.

Most of all, I have to be who I am. If I am as true to myself (and to God) as I know how to be, I have defined myself as correctly as I know how.

I've previously mentioned the small group of six men to which I belonged. We met every Thursday night for four years and didn't miss a single week, not even Thanksgiving or Christmas.

At our first meeting, we asked each other one question: What do you want from the rest of us? I posed the question, so I answered first. "I want intimacy with other men above the waist."

They knew what I meant. And to my surprise, the other five said something similar. One of them said he had never talked deeply with another man—ever—and he felt he needed to connect with them.

I tell this because those four years (I moved out of state near the end of the fourth year) did something special to me. I was a male—a real male—a mensch—and I took risks and became the catalyst for the group. I spoke about feelings and pain, and each time I did, the others affirmed me (and I affirmed their words). Within weeks, we felt safe with each other—even though none of them were individuals with whom I'd do social things. But they were five men to whom I could open myself and by whom I felt supported.

Here's the most powerful lesson I learned during that four years with those other men: *That which seems the most intimate and private, when expressed well, becomes the most universal.* That is, when I took risks and let them peer inside my heart, to my surprise, they understood. They knew what I meant, and my speaking up gave them courage to open up. As they did, I understood their emotions as well.

That which seems the most
intimate and private, when expressed well,
becomes the most universal.

WHAT LIES HAVE I BELIEVED?

CEC

"I was abandoned by God," Mike Lewis said to me. When I asked him to explain, he said, "My pastor was God's representative to me and to the entire church. The pastor made that statement several times and informed the congregation that if we criticized our leader, we were fighting God."

Despite the craziness of that logic, many men have had the same emotional reaction. "It felt as if God himself had abused me," an altar boy said on a TV newscast.

Think of the implications if a boy believes his pastor or church leader is God's specially appointed representative on earth. From such congregations I've heard outlandish stories of inhumane treatment from "divine" emissaries. One man told me his pastor-father frequently tied his hands above his head and raped him to "chase the devil out of you."

He said he felt he was one of the worst sinners in the world, and his father convinced him that he deserved every bit of punishment he received. His self-loathing and fear became enormous.

A slightly less malevolent pastor said to his victims, "I want to rid you of the sin of lust. I'm going to help you overcome your evil lusts toward women."

What happens to those "purged" souls after they become adults? One of them said, "If I can't trust God, how can I trust anyone?"

On a call-in radio show, someone asked how I answered the question, "Where was God?"

"I didn't become a believer until I was an adult," I said, "so it wasn't anything over which I struggled."

He told us his painful story. "I was a Christian and was baptized when I was eight or nine. Right after that, the abuse started." His pastor began the molestation about that time. "I want to believe in a God who loves me." He went on to say that he read his Bible and attended church, so he knew *about* God's love, "but I've never felt it. Will I ever truly believe that God loves me?"

I didn't try to answer his question for two reasons. First, I didn't know the answer. Second, I don't see my role as providing solutions, but rather to care for hurting people and to wrap my arms around individuals when they hurt. I can't give them insight or faith, but I can encourage them and let them know I care.

I urged him to get help either from a professional or from someone he could trust. I told him that I felt powerless to solve his problem and I didn't try.

"I promise to pray for you every day for one full year," I told him. "I call this my prayer contract with you. Please stay in touch with me and keep me aware of your progress." I said that after a year, he could renew the contract if he wished.

I'm now in my second year of praying for him, and he has joined a Celebrate Recovery group. He is making progress, but like many others who struggle with the God question, he still has a long way to travel.

I have a daily list of more than thirty people for whom I pray every day. Many of them I've never met in person. I usually make covenants with them—I agree to pray daily for a period of time, up to a year. Long-distance prayer is the strongest thing I can offer. I believe God hears us and answers our prayers, and I also believe that the suffering souls can remind themselves that they're not alone because at least one person has their spiritual back.

Here's Gary's response to the God question. "I knew God was there, but he wouldn't protect me because I wasn't worth his time. Therefore, I deserved what I got."

✦ ✦ ✦

Some speak of trying to tell others and not being believed, then either getting punished for lying, being ignored, or told not to have such wild thoughts and to keep silent. Then they're abused again. They believe the lie that they're too bad for God.

One fifty-nine-year-old man told me at a conference, "I've been afraid to hug a man or let a man touch me in any way. I was afraid that because I was abused, I'd become an abuser. I don't ever want to hurt anyone the way I was hurt."

Here are some of the phrases I've heard men use—and all of them are lies we use in talking to ourselves. I've referred to some of them in another chapter, but I hear these so frequently they need emphasis.

"He was nice to me and bought me things, so it wasn't abuse." It was still abuse. He seduced you and made you feel special, but it was still abuse.

"I was molested, but that was such a long time ago. I'm grown now, and I'm over it." Time isn't the issue; rather, it is facing the issues and being healed. Suppose you broke a leg and did nothing about it. You would probably learn to walk again—with a limp and pain—but you could walk. Think of abuse that way, except that it's worse.

"It only happened once. Maybe twice. It wasn't a big deal." The number of times it happened isn't as crucial as *your* response to the abuse. You remember it happening, and that tells you that you haven't resolved the issues. Denial may seem like the macho reaction; it's really avoidance of pain.

"Even if it was abuse, it didn't affect me very much." That's a defensive statement and usually comes from a man who chooses not to face his anguish. It's as if he says, "If I don't admit to having pain, it's not there." But the pain is real.

"I'm highly imaginative and probably I made up those stories and it didn't really happen." Many of us who were abused tried to grab hold of that excuse. We don't want the molestation to be true, and if we can convince ourselves it was only imagination or we were caught up in the false-memory syndrome, we don't have to deal with the issue. Many of us have tried to convince ourselves that it was imagination, but we had too many symptoms to believe that lie.

"It's too late to do anything about it now. My abuser died ten years ago so it's over." You are alive, so it's not too late. The perp may be dead, but you still suffer from the effects of the abuse. You still need to resolve your unfinished business. You need to learn to find healing *for yourself*.

"My babysitter didn't abuse me. We had sex when I was twelve, so if anyone was used, it was her. I just got lucky." That's a typical macho response. You didn't get lucky, and it was abuse. You were a child, and she was older. She *used you* for her needs and desires. She was older and knew it was wrong to have sex with a minor.

"It felt good, so it couldn't have been abuse." Of course it felt good. Touch and sexual stimulation are God's gifts to us to enjoy within heterosexual relationships with a spouse. To say it felt good is true, but it's still abuse.

"He was just trying to help me discover if I was really gay." Oh? And who appointed him to do that? And how did it help you? You were exploited. You believed his lie.

"Boys can't be victims." That's one of the worst lies. You were a defenseless child and unable to stand up for yourself. You were not an adult when it happened. If you believe this lie, the most obvious and logical statement is that the assault was your fault.

"Women don't molest boys." They shouldn't, so we think they don't. But women can and do molest boys. On one Web site, I read that 38 percent of abusers are female. Both Gary and I were abused by female perpetrators, so from our own experience, we know the statement is a lie.

◆   ◆   ◆

I want to refer to special words of enticement. Pedophiles and abusers have an ability to say exactly the right thing to boys who are susceptible to abuse.

For years, I cringed when someone called me special. My immediate thought was to wonder what the person wanted from me. That's because one of the biggest lies I heard and believed came from my perpetrator.

"You're a special kid." Mr. Lee hugged me and said those words several times. He rented a room from us and invited me inside several times a week. *I needed to hear that I was special or worthwhile.* Or at least that someone appreciated me. I wasn't old enough or mature enough to reason that he was insincere or lying. I do know that he pulled me to himself emotionally because of the tender words he used.

Elsewhere I've told the story of Mr. Lee and that my father beat him up and threw him and his belongings out of our house (after my sister told of her abuse). A few months later I saw him when I walked down a street about a mile from our house. He sat on the porch in a rocker next to two other elderly men.

I called his name and waved to him. Instead of acknowledging me, he got up and went inside the house. I didn't understand why he didn't want to see me.

His rejection that day made me feel something was wrong *with me.* His action reinforced the lie I had accepted in our family that I was worthless. (No one in my family ever used such words, but the lack of familial warmth enabled me to believe that lie.)

Until the day Mr. Lee turned away from me, I still thought he loved me and I was truly special. I was too immature to understand what had happened, and his walking away was just one more piece of evidence to show how bad I was.

Because I felt worthless and shameful, the foundation existed for me to accept other lies uncritically.

In 1982, I wrote a book called *Devotions for Grandparents.* That was several years before I got in touch with my abuse. I have only the vaguest memories of Dad's mother and my maternal grandmother. I mentioned Mr. Lee in the book and said he was the closest thing to a grandparent I knew. In the fall of 2011, I revised that book, and I was horrified that I had written such a thing. But that's what I had done.

Worse, I believed it then. I mistook his bribery for kindness and his sexual abuse for love.

That experience reminds me that we often see things differently over time. Before an awareness of my abuse, I could remember only his "kindness" and that he listened to me talk when no one else would. Later, I remembered only the enticement of the jam and crackers that led to molestation.

GARY

I swallowed some powerful lies and didn't even question whether they were true.

"They're the adults. They know what they're doing." I must do what they say. This is the way life is. I've no choice but to submit and find a way to please them so they will take care of me.

"It's my fault." The perpetrators told me they did it because I wanted it. I deserved it. I should be grateful for it. I was a lucky kid.

"I'll never truly be loved, because I'm unlovable." They told me I was worthless, that I didn't deserve anything better, and I was good for nothing.

"I'll never be a real man." My female abuser called me "little man." She exercised total dominance over me whenever she could. Both my perpetrators laughed at me when I was naked.

"I must meet my own needs." The abuse drove me to try to get the love I needed some other way. I chose performance and people pleasing. I became codependent at an early age.

"I'm OK only if you're OK." If they were upset, they took it out on me. I began to live along the edges of life, performing in the hopes that no one would be upset.

"If I don't please others, I'll be punished." This put me on a performance treadmill where it's almost impossible to step off. It just keeps going faster.

You'll notice I expressed the above lies beginning with "I." They were lies, but I chose to believe them. As Cec alluded to before, once we believe the first lie, a door opens and all sorts of companion lies come flooding inside our minds. At the time, we don't see them as lies, and they begin to take root. Further abuse waters them, and the roots of those lies begin to reach deep into our hearts and souls.

I've recognized those lies for a number of years. I just didn't know where they came from until about five years ago when my flashbacks began. I've been trying to uproot them for a long, long time. Now that I know their origin, it gives me new perspective.

I get a mental picture when I think of the lies I believed. In my picture, I'm somewhere between three and six years old (the age when the sexual abuse took place). I live inside a dungeon. I wake up each day when the electric lights flicker on, revealing a cold, gray cell with carefully positioned video monitors on all sides. The monitors come to life, revealing the faces of my perpetrators, who begin speaking the lies I listed above.

Those images are on a loop and repeat themselves throughout the day, while I go about my life inside my enclosed space. I hear them inside my head, believe them, and make decisions based on those hideous untruths.

I shared these mental pictures with a friend. He thought for a moment and said, "I get it. But it's even deeper than that. More than video screens, it's like the lies have become part of some kind of microchip inside our brains, loaded in through what happened to us. The microchip sends its messages out to our brain continually, and we believe them and live accordingly."

Sometimes I hurt so much I think it would be easy to give up because reprogramming my beliefs is so hard. Those are my worst moments, but the rest of the time I'm ready to battle against that insidious, ever-firing microchip.

I've tried many things—some less successful than others. Below I've listed the sequential steps I take on those really bad days.

1. I remind myself, "They are lies. They are untruths implanted by terrible, evil abuse."
2. I acknowledge the powerful, pervasive influence of those lies in my life before I ask God to show me how the lies influenced or controlled me.

3. I confess to God that I believed those lies. If I had not, I couldn't choose to reject them and make changes.
4. I ask myself, "What's the truth?" I examine each one of the lies I believed and replace it with a corresponding truth.
5. I ask God to help me to *permanently* replace the lies with the truth about me.

I wrote those truths on three-by-five-inch cards and put them next to my bed. For months, I've read them every morning and every night. I remind myself, "I'm feeding myself the truth each day." That doesn't stop the implanted microchip of lies from firing. But it gives my mind competing messages. I can make conscious choices to accept the truth.

Here are the truths I recorded:

"They were the adults. They abused me and made me responsible for their pain. I was innocent."

"It's their fault. I was their victim."

"God loves me and I have eternal value, completely apart from anything that I've done or that's been done to me. God loves me, therefore I'm lovable."

"God made me a man. God only makes real men, and I'm a real man."

"God knows my needs and will meet them. I can trust him to meet those needs."

"I'm OK even if others aren't. I'll try to love others in my life without making myself responsible for their feelings."

"God has a plan and is working in my life in every situation. He protects me in ways I'm not aware."

"I choose to trust God and rely on his love for me."

CEC

Most of us didn't have one single event that shattered our childhood. With some, it was a prolonged abuse by a single perpetrator. Others speak of multiple incidents or several victimizers. Or it may have been only one time. Regardless of the number of times or perpetrators, something damaged our lives. We judged ourselves negatively because someone lied to us.

"I felt as if I had been stamped with the word *worthless* on my heart," someone wrote me. He held on to it until he was thirty-nine years old and then began to heal.

Most of us—probably all of us—were lied to or weren't believed when we tried to speak. That made us appear as liars, and sometimes we doubted ourselves. We were exploited, and sometimes perpetrators seduced us with soothing words of love and tenderness. Because we didn't feel loved, their manipulations worked.

✦   ✦   ✦

I met Kevin when I spoke at an Exodus International conference. He said, "The worst lie is when a perpetrator no longer wants us around. Mine yelled at me, 'You're only good for one thing.'"

For several years, Kevin was into the gay lifestyle because he thought that was the only place people would accept him. "In my gay circle, I met a number of others who thought their only value was as a sexual object."

Like Kevin, we were young and didn't know how to distinguish between the true and the false. We believed the falsehoods because those who spoke them were bigger and older and we were small and young. They were also people we trusted.

> I can turn from the lies I believed;
> I can embrace the truth
> because the truth sets me free.

WHY DID I BELIEVE THE LIES?

CEC

On my blog, *www.menshatteringthesilence.blogspot.com*, I presented a series about lies we believed. A number of readers responded with some of their lies. I have permission to share these.

"Lies I believed" by Dann Youle

I believed that somewhere, there really was a "perfect" family. Like on *Ozzie and Harriet* and *Leave It to Beaver.*

The Andy Griffith Show perpetuated this lie as well. Even though there were no alcoholics in my family of origin, and even though abuse didn't happen overtly in my family, I knew we didn't have the perfect family.

I was always the good boy, but even that wasn't enough. The *big* lie I believed was that I would *never* be a man. Being abused sexually and discarded by my grandpa, struggling with same-sex attraction, not receiving the love and affirmation from my father the way I needed to, I realize that at forty-five, I *still* don't always feel like I'm a man.

I know I am a man—a real man—and I'm learning to define myself the way that God sees me. The American ideal of a man I'm not, and I'm finally learning that that's OK.

For the longest time, I couldn't move forward in life because I felt like I didn't have what it takes to have real "masculine initiative" and do the things I know I'm called to do. I'm still learning and have a *long* way to go, but at least I've started back to school, and I know I can accomplish all God has for me.

It's a great feeling: I'm truly the *man* God has called me to be and I am "living into that" more and more.

"No one will ever love you" by Heather Marsden

Heather Marsden responded to the blog (and we have women readers) with these courageous words:

> The first time my father came into my bedroom, I was seven. "You are so stupid, dumb, and ugly, no one will ever want to marry you unless you put out," he said. "I'm going to teach you how to put out."
>
> Those words stuck with me most of my life. My first marriage was based on the fact that the guy asked me, and I figured no one else would. It was a mistake.
>
> Even today my self-esteem is not what it should be. My father's words hurt, and they stuck.
>
> My mother and sister convinced me that the abuse was my fault. I should have said no to him. I should have pushed his hands away.
>
> Later, my mom told me it was my fault my father died because of the embarrassment I caused them by being taken out of that house by the courts.
>
> Those two lies still hurt.
>
> But the biggest lie, the unspoken lie, was that I was not worthy of love. That no one could love me, not even God. I also thought all fathers were horrid, including God. It took time to trust in God the Father and turn my life over to the only safe Father there is.

"He said I was a sinner" by "Matt"

When I ask permission to reprint from my blog, I ask readers if they want me to use their name, a pseudonym, or simply "anonymous." The following story, which I've condensed and edited slightly, came from "Matt."

> The deacon, who was also my Sunday school teacher, started visiting me to help me understand the Bible. My folks liked him because he was friendly, and so did I.
>
> At first. But that changed.
>
> He molested me and kept doing it every week or so for about two years.
>
> You know what he told me? He said I was a terrible sinner and I was heading straight to hell, but he was there to help me get rid of evil thoughts and to be pure. It sounds crazy now, but I did what he told me, and that was supposed to make me into a good kid.
>
> Just four weeks ago a sudden realization hit me. "He was the sinner!" I told my wife.
>
> "Of course he was." She seemed surprised that I hadn't figured it out.
>
> I thought I was the one who had failed God and been evil. For more than twenty years, I hated myself because I believed his terrible lies.
>
> Those lies almost ruined my life.

"I believed the lies and I became a liar" by "Rodney"

Call me Rodney, which is my middle name. I'm a thirty-nine-year-old male survivor of childhood sexual, physical, and spiritual abuse. Ralph, my dad's best friend, molested me almost weekly for more than a year. I was eight years old, and at first I admit I liked it. He treated me nicer than anyone I've ever known.

But one day—and I can't remember the circumstances—I told my parents. My dad called me a liar, and my mother refused to listen to such "dirty, filthy talk. And if you don't stop that kind of thing, you'll always be bad and no one will like you."

Ralph said, "Don't be so hard on the kid. It's all right. I'm not sure what's wrong with him, but I'm not angry."

I never tried to talk about it again to the family. But it started me on the pathway to lying. I became a compulsive liar, and I made up stories about things that didn't matter. In all of that, I lied to myself: "It didn't happen," I said.

I went to church—a bad church I now realize—where the pastor said we had to pray for thirty minutes every day and read our Bibles for thirty minutes or we would fail God. Each week we had to write the amount of time we spent in prayer and Bible study.

Because I couldn't stay focused or fell asleep, I lied and wrote down what I knew he wanted. One time he had me stand up, and he told everyone that I was a good Christian. That was the last time I went to church until two years ago.

That church experience made me believe (and act out) another lie: I had to act a certain way for anyone to like me, and if I didn't conform, everyone would hate me. I guess I got that lie from my mother.

For the next twenty years, I learned to be what others wanted. Sometimes I failed, but mostly I was the nice guy that everybody liked. They liked me—but they didn't like the real me. If they had known who I was, I was sure they'd despise me. Of course, that was another lie.

I moved to a new city and told elaborate lies about my background and life. I had been in the army during Desert Storm, but I didn't see any action. But if you listened to me, you'd think I had been a one-man army.

I did go to college and, although I don't know how, I graduated and then found a good job in a bank. That's when I met Lori, who became my wife.

For nine years. Then everything fell apart.

I had lied to her so much, she said, "I can't stand this life with you. I don't even know who you are!" She took our son and left me.

I wanted to die. We had a few sleeping pills but not enough to "do the job," so I went to four different doctors and collected ninety-three Ambien tablets. I was sure that was enough. I swallowed all of them. And then—I don't know why—I realized I didn't want to die. I called 911, told them what I had done, and had passed out by the time they got there. They pumped my stomach, and I lived, but I have some liver damage.

A chaplain at the hospital talked to me, and for the first time since I was nine, I told him the total truth and held back nothing. He prayed for me, visited me, and called me after I left the hospital.

That was two years ago. When I become depressed, as I sometimes do, I start going back to the old lies that I wasn't abused and that I'm just a bad guy.

Most days I'm able to believe that God loves me and that I'm worth loving. But sometimes the old lies creep back in, and I have to call my chaplain friend and others and they pray for me.

I'm better, and it happens less often.

Lori has come back into my life, knows the truth now, and says she never stopped loving me. Three weeks ago, she said she'd remarry me.

"Lies on top of lies" by Arnold Caines

Television is one of the biggest purveyors of the world's lies. I remember being deceived as a child by that "classic" show, *Happy Days*.

Happy Days distorted relationships between men and women, especially as it related to dating. The focus of dating was to find some chick and to end up necking with her. The show's hero, Fonzie, personified that nearly every week. When I look back on the show, I'm astounded at the scale of the lie that was foisted on adolescents back then. Years after the show ended, I found myself battling concepts I learned from Fonzie who, in reality, was nothing but a womanizer. Amazing what a lie packaged up as a prime-time hit TV show can do.

✦ ✦ ✦

Regardless of whether the sexual molestation was a one-time-only event or it went on repeatedly, others deceived us. That was terrible, but even worse, because we were innocent and unsophisticated, we didn't know how to push away the false things we heard.

Because we believed the lies we heard, we felt useless, unworthy, and unloved.

We probably felt many of those qualities before the abuse, but the perpetrators exploited our neediness. Even as adults who are in recovery, many of us still struggle with trust and feeling loved.

GARY

"You're nothing, boy," one of my perpetrators said. "You'll never amount to anything."

I was immature and unable to evaluate those statements. Those were strong words that came from a trusted adult (or one who should have been trustworthy), so like many children, I believed them.

I translated those words into my life: I'm no good. I'm nothing and less than nothing. I'll never really succeed (no matter what it looks like). I'm a failure.

Those words still ring inside my head at times. "You're nothing, boy." They're far less effective than they were forty years ago, but I still hear them. And not just hear but embrace them as truth.

Perhaps that's why I became an overachieving student and athlete. I had great success in a number of areas. But I never felt like a success. The performance was never perfect, and there was always the next accomplishment out there waiting. And of course, because I knew I'd never be anything, perfection always eluded me. It would have anyway, but I didn't reason that way. I couldn't be perfect—not even close—because I was a worthless failure.

I never believed I'd succeed at anything. The tormenting part is that something twisted inside my brain, and I felt the only way I would be worthwhile was if I succeeded *at everything*.

I couldn't be outstanding at everything, so that proved again the words of my perpetrator.

I no longer believe that lie. I am *not* a failure. I could haul out a list of my achievements, but that's not the kind of proof that means anything. I finally, finally believe that there's only one success I need: to trust God. If I succeed in doing that, I am not a failure, even if I'm not perfect.

I've always learned that failing at something can be a powerful learning experience. As a child, I had to learn the word *no* before I understood the meaning of *yes*.

The rule by which I now live sounds like this: "Search me, O God, and know my heart; test me and know my anxious thoughts. Point out anything in me that offends you, and lead me along the path of everlasting life" (Psalm 139:23–24).

> The lies are many, and I believed them.
> The truth is simple,
> but I'm often slow to accept
> wonderful, loving messages about myself.

— 22 —

HOW DO I COMBAT THE LIES?

"I'm in control of my life" by "Mal"

Because of sexual abuse in early childhood, I grew up infected with a number of lies. The most basic one was *I'm alone*. Following closely behind were *I'm unlovable* and *I'm a failure*. I bought *I'm a failure* because I believed *I'm in control*.

The people who should have protected me were my abusers. That left things up to me. If it was going to stop, I had to act. I set out to control my situation and the people around me.

I truly believed it was up to me to keep bad stuff from happening. But I couldn't do it. I tried to make people behave the way I thought they should act. I told them what to do, and sometimes demanded their conformity. The lack of results left me with a sense of despair and failure.

The truth took me years to admit: only God is in control of life.

I've learned there are a few things over which I have power but not many. I can learn to make healthy decisions. I can choose my form of behavior (and often follow through and do what I propose).

I also admit that I'm not in control of circumstances, people, or my own instinctual, automatic reactions. I'm not that powerful, but I am significant and my life has meaning. The more I'm able to rely on the omnipotent God, the more I realize that he is the one who can enable me to live a life in which I joyfully surrender control.

"It was my fault" by Cec

Childhood sexual abuse implanted the lie *I'm alone* deeply into my heart. That lie brought other companions with it: *I'm unlovable. I'm a failure. I'm in control.* All of that led me to say, "It was my fault. I caused the abuse."

My perpetrators were adults. They were supposed to know what they were doing, and no sensible adult would hurt a child. So something must be wrong with me. Maybe I deserved this.

I did a quick survey of my life and focused on all the mistakes I'd made, so that convinced me that I deserved blame.

It's taken me years to change that picture and cast the blame where it belongs—on the perpetrators. I deserve no guilt. Not only was I a child, but I was also victimized.

"It was his fault. He did it to me." Perhaps that's obvious, but because I took on the shame and guilt for the abuse, it took me nearly two years in recovery before I could say those two sentences and mean them.

In my book *Committed But Flawed,* I told my story of not feeling loved. Below I've revised what I wrote eight years ago, but it's still essentially what I wrote then.[1]

I came to a significant crisis in my faith. My theology taught me that God loved me—me and everyone else. I didn't doubt the biblical teaching. Emotionally, however, I didn't *feel* loved. The Bible tells us that God "loved the world so much" (John 3:16) and sent Jesus to die for sinners. That included me. Even so, sometimes I felt as if I were picked up and accepted as part of a package deal. God had gotten stuck with me because of a sweeping compassion for everyone.

Getting the message of divine love from the top of the head to the bottom of the heart is such an ordeal for many of us. We think of our failures or hear the words our tormentors used. Or we focus on our shame.

1. Cecil Murphey, *Committed But Flawed: Seeking New Ways to Grow Spiritually* (Chattanooga, TN: Living Ink Books, 2004), 8–15.

Despite our inability to believe from the depth of our beings that God loves us, we *are loved*.

I grasped that intellectually, but I didn't know how to make it an emotional truth. Until I felt loved, my theology was orthodox, but my emotions were not.

One day I figured out a method that worked for me. In my devotional reading I came across Romans 9:13, where Paul quoted God as saying, "I loved Jacob but I rejected Esau."

That verse struck me as odd, even though I'd read it many times. The impact of those words stayed with me, and I pondered them frequently over the next few days. What did Jacob ever do to deserve love? Of all the people in the Bible, he was one of the biggest scoundrels and least deserving, yet God loved him. He did nothing to earn that love and should have received severe punishment for the underhanded and dishonorable things he did. Instead, he received God's love.

At first I wanted to be like Jacob as the receiver of grace. Then I decided I wanted *to be* Jacob—that is, I wanted to feel loved even though I felt unworthy and undeserving.

Pondering the story of Jacob caused me to think about Jesus' parable of the prodigal son. The father loved the younger son even though he demanded his inheritance, left home, and wasted all his money. When the son returned, the father embraced him, called for a feast, and gave him the best of everything. The boy wasn't hugged and blessed because he deserved those things. The father simply loved him and couldn't hold back his excitement. That's why there was joy over his return. (See Luke 15:11–31.)

I wanted to be embraced like the prodigal—who was loved despite the wrong decisions he had made. Instead, I felt like the older brother who stayed home, did everything required of him, watched his brother waste a fortune, and felt angry when the rebel received the hugs and a big celebration.

For most of my Christian experience, I had done what Christian leaders advised me to do—I constantly tried to do more of the religious things. I wouldn't have admitted to anyone during those years, and only much later could I admit to myself, that my frenetic activities were unconscious attempts to gain God's love. Or maybe they were attempts to prove to God that I deserved the blessings I had already received.

As I pondered the story of the prodigal and the life of Jacob, I faced one sad reality: *I couldn't earn God's love.* The best I could do was to accept that God loved me. I didn't know how to do that, but I kept thinking of the deeply loved but utterly undeserving Jacob. To my amazement, one morning I heard myself praying in deep anguish, "I am Jacob. I am Jacob."

The more I thought of those words and focused on what I was saying, I knew that was exactly how I needed to pray.

"I am Jacob, whom you love." Several times I spoke those words aloud.

I prayed exactly those words every day for months. As I prayed, I allowed myself to envision what those words meant. I could picture a son being embraced by a father. In my mind, no matter how much the wastrel protested, the loving parent kept saying, "I love you, and that's what counts."

One day I was nearly through with a six-mile run, and instead of saying, "I am Jacob, whom you love," I heard myself say, "I am Jacob. I really am."

I had focused on *being* Jacob for so long that I had *become* like Jacob. That is, I knew I was loved. The powerful assurance was there in a way I had never experienced before. In that sense, I was indeed Jacob.

My method may not work for everyone, but it worked for me. There was nothing mystical about what I did. I do believe that by repeating the words every day for weeks, the meaning finally got through to me.

The words I spoke were true, but I didn't believe them. My intention was to take that objective truth (Jesus loves everybody) and make it a subjective, emotional reality (Jesus loves me).

Each day as I prayed, I reminded myself that God's love bypasses achievements—or lack of them. I don't know if I understand even now about God's rejection of Esau. I knew what the feeling was like of being Esau; I wanted to feel like Jacob.

Some may have trouble with my approach. They can't easily say, "I am Jacob." I could have said, "I want to be loved like an undeserving Jacob," which is what my words meant. But to explain to God (who needs no explanations) and to unravel all the words for greater clarity would have made my prayer cumbersome. The simple concept worked for me. "I am Jacob" sounded direct; it enabled me to focus.

Each day as I prayed, I envisioned more clearly what it would be like to be fully embraced by God's loving arms. The more unworthy I felt, the more I could appreciate that love.

In my case, this went on for months before the realization struck me that I had become like Jacob. That is, I felt deeply loved and fully accepted without any qualifications and despite my shortcomings. Those simple words changed my life and escorted me along the path of closer intimacy with God.

I'm glad feelings are not facts. I now believe—with utter, undeniable certainty—that *I'm lovable.* I've turned away from the lie and accepted a powerful truth.

I don't deserve your love. I can't earn it.
Thank you, God, that I can accept it.

23

WHY AM I SO HARD ON MYSELF?

CEC

Kind.

Tender.

Compassionate.

Understanding.

Giving.

People have used those words to me and about me for years. And they sound nice, perhaps even flattering, and they're generally true. I do feel that way about most people.

When I was a pastor, many times parishioners would spend nearly an hour pouring out their pain, and I tried to say little. (Often I didn't know what to say.) When they left, they frequently said how much better they felt. Perhaps it was because they had opened up and let out their pain. Maybe it was because I listened nonjudgmentally. Or possibly it was a combination.

Regardless, I was a man of compassion, and I have no trouble acknowledging that quality.

But.

The *but* was that the person who deserved the most compassion instead received criticism and castigation. I speak of myself. For a long time I didn't know how to be kind to Cec Murphey. In fact, I don't think I'm aware of how self-critical I was.

Shortly after I started down the healing path, I made one significant change. When I did something wrong or behaved stupidly, I began to say, "This is not your usual way." It was a minor step forward, but it worked. That is, it worked when I remembered. I became less self-critical.

My friend David did more to help me in this area than anyone did. He refused to let me tear myself down. One time I said, "I really did something stupid."

He put his hand on my shoulder and stared into my eyes. "Don't talk that way about yourself. Don't you know it hurts me to listen to you talk that way?"

Hurt him? That shocked me.

"You're being critical about my friend Cec, and I don't like it when you do that."

I apologized to David (and to myself) for being so harsh. Even now, when I'm with David and occasionally blame myself in an unkind way, he stops me.

I've slowly learned to feel more kindly about myself.

GARY

Being hard on myself is as natural as breathing.

I have incredibly unrealistic expectations of myself. I'm not sure I could identify a realistic expectation without help. I'm merciless with myself if I make a mistake. *Mistake* for me is synonymous with *failure*. It's simply not allowed.

Yet I fail regularly. The awareness calls out the guilt, the fear, and the shame (usually all in a span of seconds). Depending on the failure, it takes me a great amount of time to recover. And by recover, I usually mean being able to do something as penance for my failure so that I can feel better.

In fact, I think I'm addicted to trying to feel better. It seems to motivate a lot of what I do.

Cec says to me quite regularly, "Be nice to Gary. I like him." I always smile when he says those words. It causes me to stop and think. I pride myself on being a nice guy, but I'm not particularly nice to myself.

God shows me infinite compassion. He welcomes me, no matter what. He's with me in everything, ready to help, protect, instruct, and lead. He wants me and is patient with me. I say I want to follow the right paths. Perhaps part of following the Lord is learning to be kind and compassionate toward myself.

I'm just getting started on this being-forgiving-of-myself thing. Being critical and hard on Gary seems obvious to me and therefore is my automatic default. Like an involuntary reflex. I can't stop it. Or at least I couldn't until recently, when I've made progress.

First, I need to recognize that I'm indeed hard on myself—relentlessly demanding and unforgiving.

Second, I need to discard that type of behavior. It's an immense amount of work, but I can learn to do that.

Third, I need to replace the negative behavior with a new pattern that honors God, such as being gracious, loving, compassionate, and forgiving—toward myself.

A friend said it this way: "We all have reflexes—automatic responses to certain triggers. I'm praying that, over time, God will alter my reflexes so that my automatic responses begin to change. Small, incremental changes each day are what I hope to make."

Those words helped me. I tend to want large changes, and I want them immediately. I want things to be easier and faster and my life to operate more smoothly. Good change is difficult, often painful, and takes time.

One of the primary changes I'm committed to make is to be more compassionate toward myself. The world won't disintegrate because of my mistakes. I'm allowed to be human. It's who I am. God knows that and is loving and compassionate toward me.

I feel as if I've just climbed on the be-nicer-to-yourself train. I have a long journey ahead. It's exciting, however, to think about how things might be different as I learn self-kindness and self-acceptance.

CEC

The lack of compassion toward myself has shown up in many ways. One day I talked to David about another writer who had attained a fair amount of success. I thought his writing was mediocre, perhaps even less than that. I not only told David how I felt but explained my reasoning. I watched David's blue eyes as he listened to me, and a slight twitch told me something was wrong.

"You're not critical of people in other areas. I've listened to you tell about people at your church, and it's never judgmental or unkind."

Although I no longer remember my exact words, I'm aware that I defended myself and talked about that writer's lack of ability or what I assumed was refusal to grow—something to justify my attitude. But David was correct.

"So why am I so critical of other writers?" I asked and assumed that it was because of my zeal for quality writing. "He's talented, and he could be better."

But even as I spoke like that, I knew it wasn't the full answer. In a twisted sort of way, I realized I was projecting on them feelings about myself. I was being critical of Cec. Although I tried to deny it, David had caught me.

For several days, whenever I'd start to think about those other writers, I stopped myself and said, "I accept them as they are, and I accept Cec as he is." After repeating those simple words many times over the next few days, I began to believe them.

In that simple act, I've focused more on self-compassion and can honestly say I'm more self-forgiving and self-understanding.

I can be—and will be—
compassionate toward myself.

24

WHY DO I NEED TO FORGIVE?

GARY

I used to think forgiveness was a simple one-time act of the will. Forgive. Let it go. Move on. When I found myself confronted with the same emotions again, I assumed I hadn't forgiven.

Forgiving my abusers has been a process. It certainly began, as all forgiveness does, with an act of the will. God led me to the point where I chose to forgive, trusting that over time the feelings would follow.

Then the person I wanted to forgive stopped the process. He or she said or did something that put me right back under that ugly, familiar cloud of anger, shame, and guilt. *How could I have forgiven,* I asked myself, *if I still have such strong and terrible feelings?* Instead of wondering if I had forgiven, I voiced my forgiveness again, determined to forgive once and for all.

I've repeated that process dozens of times. Each time, it seems to get a little easier. On most occasions, I feel a little freer. I'm learning that I have to *practice* forgiveness, and sometimes it feels as if I have to do it moment by moment. Whenever the trigger gets pulled or the cloud of shame descends, I'm learning to see it as an invitation to forgive. My negative reaction means I'm aware of my lack of releasing my grudge or pain against them. It also means I can learn to let go of the hurts they caused.

CEC

I like Gary's words above. And I've come to the same conclusion. Too often I prayed to forgive my abuser or anyone who had hurt me. I prayed and committed them to God. But the emotions didn't track with the will.

"If I've forgiven, why do I feel this anger? This hurt?" Those are the words that tortured me for a long time. I finally figured out, as Gary did, that feelings follow the act of the will.

Two things have helped me grapple with this. The first is the biblical command to love. One of the last things Jesus said to his disciples before his crucifixion was, "So now I am giving you a new commandment: Love each other. Just as I have loved you, you should love each other. Your love for one another will prove to the world that you are my disciples" (John 13:34–35).

Second, Jesus made it clear: love is a choice. They could decide to love. Love, as used by Jesus, is an attitude, not an emotion. The biblical command to love (Greek, *agapao*) means to want the highest and best for others. Like forgiving, love is an act of the will—a determination to serve or give.

One day I said this, "I forgive, but it takes time for my emotions to catch up with my decision."

Paul states the issue clearly as an action that we need to take: "Get rid of all bitterness, rage, anger, harsh words, and slander, as well as all types of evil behavior. Instead, be kind to each other, tenderhearted, forgiving one another, just as God through Christ has forgiven you" (Ephesians 4:31–32).

As I think of that verse, I remember the first time I met a couple who had an arranged marriage. Both came from India, and both sets of parents arranged the wedding. The couple knew each other slightly because they came from the same church. I met them after ten years of marriage. Moses, the husband, said, "I didn't know her, and I felt no love for her. But my parents and her parents had prayed and committed both of us to God. I believed that if I treated her with kindness, my feelings for her would grow."

Moses smiled before he added, "It took me about a year before the tender feelings came, but they did come. I obeyed God's will as shown to us through our parents. In time, we have come to love each other deeply."

That's how I see forgiveness. As survivors, we must want to forgive.

It may take time—perhaps even years—for the pain and especially the memories, to die. But eventually it happens.

✦ ✦ ✦

Forgiveness *is* a process. It's rarely a quick, easy-to-accomplish action. But why is it often so difficult? I can't answer for everyone, but here's something I've found helpful. My anger and pain focused on Mr. Lee and his actions. But I finally admitted something else: I had blamed myself for the abuse.

If I hadn't been needy . . . if I hadn't responded to his deceptive ways . . . We all have our own statements. But the point is that I no longer had to punish myself. I no longer blamed myself because I didn't do anything to stop him.

It's something therapists call misplaced anger. We feel worthless and useless, and that's easy enough to identify.

But why do we feel so terrible?

It's not only that we have some sense of being bad—although that's powerful. Isn't it just as true that we're angry at ourselves for failing to protect ourselves? Forget the logic, think of the immature, primitive feelings of a child:

> I let this happen.
> I didn't stop him.
> I liked what he did—at the time.
> I liked the attention and the affection.

Consequently, I hated myself for feeling that way; however, it's natural for us to transfer the anger onto the perpetrator—which that person deserves.

It's probably not only anger at myself. Forgiving my perpetrator involves forgiving myself *first*. Once I can forgive myself for being human, immature, a child, and show myself the compassion I deserve, I can move on and forgive the one who took advantage of me.

+   +   +

The more I stayed focused on what terrible things were done to me, the more I kept my wounds open so that they didn't heal. I don't attempt to ignore or deny the abuse, but I needed to put the emphasis on healing, on forgiving, and on growing beyond the experience.

In talking with others, I've become aware it's not who was abused the most often or whose molestation lasted longer. It revolved around the attitude of the survivor. Some sensed the pain much more deeply than others.

That's when I realized that the deeper the man felt the pain, the more he tended to focus on it and to remember. One former alcoholic told me, "I drank to forget. When I wasn't drinking, I was reliving the abuse."

Someone said it this way: the deeper the wound and the stronger the recollection, the more the past and present merge so that the past pain becomes present pain.

+   +   +

In thinking about this, I come to focus on three aspects of abuse. First, and the one we continue to focus on, is *our personal molestation*. It happened to me, and I suffer.

Second, the abuse involves *a wider social setting* out of which the abuse arose and the social world in which the survivors live. I wasn't abused in an isolated instance. There was time, setting, and opportunity for him to molest me. My parents remained ignorant of what Mr. Lee did because he chose the social setting of a room in our house in which to assault me. As serious and traumatic as it was, that puts abuse beyond only my pain and makes it part of the social milieu.

Third, this issue also involves *the abuse and the wrongdoer*. It's easy (and natural) to see my perpetrator as totally evil, and what he did feels that way at times. But wasn't Mr. Lee more than an addictive, awful act of sexual abuse? No matter how often it happened, that wasn't everything he did with his life. Was there nothing good in him and not a spark of decency? I've not heard this question addressed, but it's important to ponder if we are committed to forgiving. This was one aspect of the perpetrator's life, but it wasn't his total life.

I'm not trying to deny the wrongdoing, only to see his actions from a broader viewpoint.

✦   ✦   ✦

During my navy years, I worked in the legal department, and we reviewed court-martials. After the conviction of a sailor for any crime, and before the sentencing, the court allowed for what was called "extenuation and mitigation." It was the opportunity for the convicted person to show that he wasn't totally evil and had things in his favor.

Some of the stories that came out were pitiful and sad. They were guilty of the crimes for which they had been accused. That was no longer a question.

The single judge in minor cases, or a panel of officers for more serious offenses, listened. They often deliberated before announcing the sentence. Sometimes they decreased the sentence because of the terrible situations described. For example, a man went AWOL because his mother died and his commanding officer wouldn't give him leave to attend the funeral. In another case, a woman started divorce proceedings, and the man had no annual leave so that he could be present to speak up in his own behalf.

The accused didn't refute what they had done. They tried to show the court that even though they had violated military law, their crimes were only one part of their lives. Their behavior was an aberration and not the norm.

This isn't meant to ignore or to deny the heinous nature of the abusers' crimes against us, but it's to humanize the person—to realize that the perpetrator, guilty as he or she was—was not totally depraved and beyond the realm of any kindness or sympathy.

For me to say that is to confess that at one time I committed wrong against the two perpetrators of my childhood. For a time I could see them only in one color and without any compassion. I painted two individuals as totally beyond help and redemption.

For instance, I think of two different influential pastors in the Atlanta area, both accused of sexually assaulting young men. I know one of them well; the other I've met. For the sake of argument, let's say both are guilty as charged, and if so, they deserve punishment for their wrongdoing. No problem there for me.

The problem comes because I also realize that both of them have done an immense amount of good. They've given generously of themselves and their talents and taught others to do so. I don't excuse their evil deeds—I want to be clear about that. But as a serious Christian, I also have to say that they are more than their sinful actions.

GARY

I agree wholeheartedly with what Cec is saying. I still have trouble getting there. I tend to live in denial. I see things as I want them to be, rather than as they really are. So for me, I saw my perpetrators only as wicked criminals.

As time went by and I processed the pain, I considered that both my abusers probably endured molestation themselves at the hands of others. I wrestled with seeing them as human beings instead of evil incarnate. It had been easier to look only on their dark side.

Over time, my heart softened, bit by bit. One day, I took the step of thinking about other actions done by my abusers—good things for which I was thankful. In my case, they were family members, so I did have a number of good memories and could identify specific things. I admit that, at first, I thanked God for those things while gritting my teeth, almost against my will.

But as I practiced thanksgiving and appreciating their good qualities, it got easier, and so did the forgiving.

Just listening to Cec, though, reminds me that I have a way to go with this issue. At times, I still want to harbor feelings of anger and resentment, especially when I'm face-to-face with a struggle that stems from the abuse. I'm faced continually with the choice of whether I'm going to forgive, and forgive, and forgive again.

I don't think enough about, or appreciate enough, how much I myself have been forgiven. If I could get a grip on that, I think I could release others more fully. How can I not forgive others, whatever the offense, when I have been forgiven so much more than I can even conceive? As Paul wrote, "Be kind to each other, tenderhearted, forgiving one another, *just as God through Christ has forgiven you*" (Ephesians 4:32, emphasis mine).

I want to strive for that kind of continual forgiveness.

CEC

I want to stress the process of forgiveness for two reasons. First, those of us who have been in the church for a long time tend to feel we're defective in our faith if we can't push away all negative feelings. But we need to be as compassionate toward ourselves as we try to be toward others. Although our abusers need love and understanding, we need to take care of ourselves first.

Second, occasionally I hear from angry survivors who charge that we Christians keep insisting that we *have* to forgive. Once on my blog for survivors,[1] someone accused me of writing that. I didn't, and I won't. Instead I'll say it this way. You won't forgive until you're ready to let go of the pain and the agony. If you realize *your need* to release your hurts, that's the time to deal with it.

I would have resented (and even argued) if anyone had said, "Forgive them. They don't know what they did." Whether they knew or didn't know wasn't my concern then or now. I want to forgive them so I can be free and fill my heart and mind with healthy thoughts.

When I'm ready to forgive, I can embrace a saying I used to hear

---

1. www.menshatteringthesilence.blogspot.com

in my early days of following the Lord: "Hate the sin; love the sinner." Good statement. I think those six words say it well.

This also reminds me that God freely forgives, and I want others to forgive me, even though I may not consider my evil deeds to be as serious. I want God's forgiveness, and the next step—whether immediately or over a period of years—is "forgiving one another, just as God through Christ has forgiven [me]."

God not only forgives sin; God loves the sinners.
That's the example I want to follow.

— 25 —

WHY IS FORGIVING SO DIFFICULT?

CEC

Back in radio days, Red Skelton used to do skits with Junior, "the mean widdle kid." When he brought the show to television, he wore short pants and used gestures to give the impression of a kid.

The boy would consider doing something wrong and would say to himself, "If I dood it, I get a whippin'." His comic face showed his indecision before a full grin, and he yelled out, "I dood it."

His facial expressions made it laughable no matter how many times we watched the program. But the segment was more than comedy; it also reminded us that our actions have consequences. The mean kid knew he would be spanked if he misbehaved. He chose bad behavior and punishment.

We know that when we do wrong, we eventually pay for our deliberate disobedience. The purpose of this chapter is to focus on the consequences of our failure.

We were victimized; our childhoods were stolen. Our big step—and one that some men never reach—is to forgive the consequences, the results, of a perpetrator's actions.

We were wounded, and now we must forgive. I wrote *must* in the biblical sense that if we want our lives to honor Jesus Christ, it is a command. The fact that it may be difficult doesn't excuse us.

The following is one of the most powerful things my co-writer shared with me.

GARY

I had taken the step to forgive my abusers. I thought I had the forgiveness part of my healing down solid, and then a friend asked a deeper question: "You say that you have forgiven your abusers for what they *did*—the rapes, the acts of abuse. But have you forgiven them for the *results in your life*—for what their actions did to you?"

I stared in shock. I felt as if my soul were being ripped apart. Right there, in a chair on the deck behind my house, I began to cry. Soon I wept convulsively. The reaction grew more and more intense. It was as if I were throwing up emotions in waves. It went on for almost two hours.

My eyes were closed, and I saw myself walking toward my perpetrators, carrying a large, heavy bucket of filth. When I reached them, I set the bucket down in front of them. "These are all the horrid, devastating results in my life of what you did to me. These things have affected my relationships and the people I love. I won't carry this anymore. These things don't belong to me. I return them to you and leave them here. I forgive you." I saw myself leave the bucket and walk away from it.

When my sobs subsided, I knew God had broken through and enabled me to forgive at a new level.

It was devastating to think of the results of the abuse in my life. It was *the* most significant event of my childhood, and it affected everything I thought, said, or did. *Everything.* Forgiving my perpetrators *for the consequences* of the abuse as well as the acts of abuse themselves was like a sledgehammer that broke the chains of my bondage.

CEC

Gary told you his visual experience of forgiving. But for some individuals, it's not that easy. Neither Gary nor I want to make it sound as if forgiveness is a simple act of the will and then it's over.

It *is* an act of the will, but it takes preparation before we're ready to make that decision. Let's think about the consequences of what happened to us. We're all different and respond in various ways, so I'm going to list some of the results of sexual assault:

+ A lack of self-worth
+ Sexual promiscuity or the inability to enjoy a healthy heterosexual relationship
+ The inability to trust others—or trusting everyone and being victimized repeatedly
+ Depression or anxiety
+ Compulsive behavior and addictions
+ Illness or chronic disability

The list of consequences can seem endless. And they are consequences. But we can't stop with merely saying, "I'm this way because . . ." Jesus put it this way: "If you forgive those who sin against you, your heavenly Father will forgive you. But if you refuse to forgive others, your Father will not forgive your sins" (Matthew 6:14–15).

Those words of Jesus are far more than just a command to forgive, but they imply something else. They imply that we have been forgiven—that we have perceived God's unequaled love that's able to wipe away everything wrong we've ever done.

Jesus didn't say we forgive if those who hurt us ask or we forgive after confronting them. Another way to state the command is, "Forgive others; receive God's forgiveness." That is, if I understand God's abounding love and grasp that God forgives me even though I don't deserve it, the realization produces one powerful result: I forgive others. On every level and no matter how superficially or deeply I was hurt. My reception of grace says I understand God's favor as being undeserved and unearned.

The best way for us to respond to grace is to pass it on to others through forgiving them when they don't deserve it—just as we didn't deserve it.

+ + +

My method of forgiveness was different from Gary's, but with the same result. A female relative abused me until I was perhaps four or five. That was overt abuse. Until I pulled away from her at about age sixteen, she continued with a different form of abuse. She hugged me and threw her body into mine. She told me sexually explicit jokes, laughed, and acted as if she wasn't sure what they meant. It's sad, but I can still remember two of them after all these years.

My second perpetrator was an elderly man on social security who rented a room from us.

Years later I was ready to face my abuse, and I knew—without any question in my mind—that I would never be healed until I forgave both of them. It wasn't easy to release my pent-up anger.

For days I prayed about both of them. I *wanted* to forgive them, but I couldn't release the pain they had caused. I remembered my victimization too vividly.

After about a week of agonizing, I walked to a nearby park that has a small lake. I walked around that lake repeatedly, but this time my prayers were different. I visualized their faces—as well as I could remember, because both had been dead for many years.

I did something I'd never done before: I tried to see life from their perspective. They knew they were doing wrong—of that I'm sure. I also thought about how they must have felt after each attack, after each satisfaction. I can't know what's in anyone else's heart, but I assumed there must have been guilt, pain, and perhaps remorse. I can even believe that both of them cried out for help.

The woman claimed to be a believer, and I think she was, despite the bondage in which she found herself. I thought of her misery and how she must have agonized over her terrible, probably compulsive, behavior. That was what it took for me to change. I was able to say, "Yes, God, I let go of my pain. I truly forgive her."

I did the same thing with the old man and was able to forgive him.

GARY

You can do this! You can forgive. If Cec and I can learn, you can. There's nothing special about us. I encourage you to seek God and ask for the willingness and power to forgive. After all, the Lord is the forgiveness expert.

As I trust Jesus Christ to produce forgiveness in me, I'm able to relax a little more, knowing that real forgiveness is a truly supernatural thing. It takes God's intervention, activity, and power.

Forgiveness is difficult for me,
but it's simple for God.
He's the expert,
and he teaches me how to forgive.

26

HOW CAN I FIND COMPASSION FOR MY PERPETRATORS?

CEC

I'm not a perpetrator, but I could have been. As I've examined my life and heard the testimonies of many abused men, I understand that some violated others because it was learned behavior. They tended to do to others what was done to them. They followed a pattern they learned through their own sad victimization.

Instead of remaining the victim, they became the victimizer. I don't think it was an intentional, deliberate decision. It seems like a natural progression.

The injured child grows up and practices what he knows as a form of sexual or emotional satisfaction. He copies what he observed and what was done to him.

He wouldn't think in those terms, but by reversing roles he becomes the person with power. He reaches for what he wants, and he learned how to do it because he was once the prey.

Think again about ourselves as children. For a few minutes at a time, we unloved, needy boys received acceptance or physical intimacy. We had some awareness of what it felt like to be loved. It was false and transitory, but the experience was real. It may have been the only tender expressions we knew in childhood. At least for me, it's the only ones I remember.

I'm not trying to excuse exploiting children, but I am trying to understand those who do such heinous acts. It helps me to compare them with those who are addicted to drugs or alcohol. The honest ones speak of what it's like when they get high. They tell me they're free from worries, able to forget the misery of their lives, their lack of feeling loved, or the awareness of feeling worthless.

One of my three alcoholic brothers once said about being drunk, "It's the only time I don't feel any pain."

Almost from the beginning of my healing journey, I've been able to empathize with other survivors. It was more difficult for me to feel anything positive toward perpetrators. And it took me years to feel compassion. I categorized them with serial rapists (they often fit that label) or murderers. ("They murdered my soul," I declared.)

As I healed, however, I was able to revise my thinking about those predators. I began to see them as more than vile, heartless creatures. I don't excuse their behavior, because they did something wrong and terrible.

But they, too, live in pain.

I sometimes wonder if their pain isn't worse than the pain most of us survivors carry. If they were molested, they not only have to cope with those issues but they also struggle with the driving compulsion to do to other children what was done to them. It's not that they don't know what they're doing, but I see it as a drive so strong that they can't defeat it.

✦   ✦   ✦

As I've studied research on pedophiles, it's common for the perpetrators to rationalize their actions. Here's how I define *rationalize*: an attempt to provide a reasonable explanation or to justify wrong or unacceptable behavior with a reasonable explanation.

To rationalize isn't a thought-out action, but it's instinctive—an act to "save face" for unacceptable actions.

Our perpetrators sometimes insist that victimized children benefited from the experience. According to at least one expert, the predators explain it as a "mentor" relationship.

The research doesn't excuse them and might even make some of us angry. I also realize that it means the victimizers probably can't face the heinous crimes they committed, so they give themselves explanations to live with themselves. The only way they can live with their actions is to find some way to self-justify.

If they faced themselves—and it occasionally happens—they loathe and despise themselves and their actions. One former predator said, "It was like an addiction. After each time, I sat and cried, pleading with God to take away the desire."

✦   ✦   ✦

About four years into my recovery, Shirley and I moved to Louisville, Kentucky. After a few months, I became part of something called the Men's Gathering. As many as forty of us met two Saturday mornings a month at a local hospital annex. We drummed for almost an hour, which was popular in those days.

Afterward, any man could come into the middle of the circle and pick up what we called the talking stick, which gave him permission (and freedom) to speak about whatever was on his heart. Sometimes men shared their insights or talked about issues that pertained to men, but more rarely, a man might talk about his pain or his healing. Some were also members of Alcoholics Anonymous or Narcotics Anonymous. Some were men smarting after a painful divorce.

One Saturday stands out because two men spoke openly of their sexual addiction. It was the first time I had ever associated the two words *sex* and *addiction*.

For the first few minutes, I could hardly believe what they said. It wasn't that I doubted them, but I had no idea that a man could be a compulsive masturbator (or a true satyr—a term I knew from my reading).

One of them said that he had to have sexual relief eight or ten times *every* day of his life. Sometimes his penis was so sore he could hardly touch it, but he endured the pain anyway. "For years, I had to have frequent sexual relief, and I had no will to resist. The urge was stronger than my willpower. It wasn't a choice."

That's when I began to feel a slight sympathy for perpetrators. I say slight because I was still caught up in my scorn and disdain for those adults who took advantage of our innocence. The two men with the talking stick weren't perpetrators, but their actions made me realize that those who took advantage of children must have felt some of the same compulsion. How could they not have felt remorse?

That Saturday morning as I listened to those two men, I realized that they practiced (in excess) what they had learned as innocent children. Tears slid down my cheeks as I thought of the terrible bondage and addictive behavior that drove them. Their sexual obsession took precedence over everything else. No person and no promise or self-commitment was stronger than the overriding need for a sexual fix.

What miserable lives both of those had once led. They didn't molest children. They abused their own bodies and souls, but it could have been children.

One of them talked about being suicidal before he got help. "I hated my life, I hated myself, and I tried suicide twice." After he was hospitalized the second time, a psychiatrist came to his room and talked with him. "That's when I knew I couldn't survive without getting professional help."

That Saturday was a powerful revelation to me. Those two men followed the pattern of what had been done to them. Both had been molested, and they did to themselves what their perpetrators had done to them.

It made sense.

Eventually I was able to forgive *my* perpetrators because I saw them as victims just as I had been. The once-victims became victimizers by preying on the needy, the unloved, and the lonely. They repeated behavior they had learned.

Something else helped me to become aware. Right about that time, I watched a documentary special on PBS about the Watts Riots—a series of horrible, tragic riots in 1965 that lasted for six days in the Watts section of Los Angeles and left thirty-four people dead, twenty-five of them

African American. One thing struck me about the residents of Watts: almost all of them beat *each other* and looted the stores and homes of other African Americans. I wondered why they didn't go after the white people they blamed for their conditions. Using film from various TV newscasts, the documentary showed pictures of rioting in their own neighborhoods. I was struck by the reality that looters struck against their own neighbors.

I'm sure the answer is multilayered, but the two men in Louisville and the riots in Watts made me realize something. The human tendency is *not* to go directly against those who perpetrated the crime; the tendency is to act out and make others become the victims. We turn to those who are accessible.

Quite recently I saw this more clearly in reading the works of Mikoslav Volf. He doesn't write from the experience of sexual abuse but from having been a prisoner who was tortured in 1984 in what was then communist Yugoslavia. I particularly noticed two statements he made. What he had to say could just as easily be about molestation:

> Victims will often *become* perpetrators precisely *on account of* their memories. It is *because they remember* past victimization that they feel justified in committing present violence. . . .
>
> The more severe the wrongdoing, the more likely we are to react rather than respond, to act toward wrongdoers the way we *feel* like acting rather than the way we *should* act.[1]

In the case of abuse, I can see why. They were overpowered when they were innocent, young, and defenseless. Those who became pedophiles and perpetrators responded by repeating what was done to them—by seeking the disenfranchised, the lonely, and the weak—by victimizing others as they themselves had been victimized.

---

1. Miraslov Volf, *The End of Memory: Remembering Rightly in a Violent World* (Grand Rapids: Eerdmans, 2006), 8, 33.

✦ ✦ ✦

I learned a great deal from Volf. One of the other points he makes is that when evil triumphs, there are *two* victories. The first, for people like us, is when someone abused us in our innocence. The second victory is "when evil is returned."[2]

Volf points out that evil dies when it's not returned, but when the victim becomes the next victimizer, the old evil or abuse is infused with new life. On the same page, he states the purpose of his book is to explore the *"memory of wrongdoing suffered by a person who desires neither to hate nor to disregard but to love the wrongdoer."*[3]

That seems especially apropos because some men want to hold on to their hatred. "He deserves my hatred, and I'll never forgive how he ruined my life." I've heard those words many times.

The other response sounds benign, but it solves nothing: Just forget the past. Let it go away and move on. *If only we could.* That's my answer. We can't forget as long as the pain feels like a pound of iron in the pit of our stomachs. If we can't forget, we will do something—and perpetrators fall into perpetrating the evil.

Gary is just beginning to deal with and internalize this truth of understanding and feeling compassion toward those who sexually assaulted him.

GARY

I'm still at the difficult stage with this. It's not new, but it feels new. By that I mean that I haven't really dealt with this emotionally. I recognize with my head that my perpetrators were people who were desperately hurting. I know that their own pain drove them to do what they did.

Once I had a dream about this—at least, it was like a dream. I saw in my mind one of my perpetrators going about her daily life. As time

2. Ibid, 9.
3. Ibid, emphasis in original.

went on, she began to slowly swell, growing larger and larger. She hurt and the pain increased. When the pain became too intense, she sought me, found me, and suddenly vomited horrible black slime all over me. She just kept throwing up, and the slime kept coming until finally she had nothing else to vomit and she found relief. She took a deep breath and walked away, leaving me standing under an avalanche of black slime.

The slime represented the pain from the abuse that she herself endured. As time went on, her pain built up until she finally had to let it out. I was the convenient target. She vomited on me. Then she would feel better and return to normal life, until the pain got too great again.

My first thought was, that's evil. Just pure evil. The second thought was, she was hurting, really hurting. And she dealt with her pain by doing what her perpetrator did. The slime was passed on to another victim.

I'm still processing this. It hasn't fully reached my heart yet. I believe my compassion is growing, but I have a long way to go. What's helping me most at present is to think about how I'm vomiting my pain on others. I don't do it by sexually molesting them, but my behavior, the result of my victimization, sometimes comes out like black slime.

As I grasp the progression, I also feel the guilt coming for passing on my slime. And I'm developing compassion for my abusers.

CEC

Unlike Gary, I've been dealing with this for two decades. I've made progress; I feel deep compassion for my once-victimized perpetrators. They need compassion as well as judgment for their actions. By God's grace, I haven't sexually molested others, but what if I had responded to my hurts the way they did? What tormented souls they must have been.

I want my position to be clear: I don't defend their behavior. It's reprehensible. But, more and more, I'm able to accept their heinous actions as compulsion that was birthed in their personal pain.

Their personal pain.

I thought of those three words for a long time and realized how apt it is. Some therapists say that perpetrators are unconsciously trying to undo what was done to them by acting out on others. Instead of curing, it confirms their actions.

I've gone into a lengthy section because I think it's important for those of us who were victims to see our victimizers as human beings. They themselves were in pain. They hurt. They certainly weren't happy, well-adjusted individuals, but I can't believe their focused desire was to ruin the lives of children. Victimizing the innocent was their transitory "fix." They were like the enraged citizens of Watts.

I accept that and believe it, but it was a position to which I arrived after a long period of inner healing. I reminded myself, *They were acting out of their horrendous pain and not out of intentional evil.*

The nineteenth-century Swiss author Anne Louise Germaine de Staël-Holstein wrote, "To know all is to forgive all." I believe that.

After I was able to forgive those who hurt me, I was able to think about their anguish. Not immediately and not for a long time, but I gradually opened myself to them.

I could conceive of them as evil, monstrous, and devoid of decency. Or I could think of them as men and sometimes women who are so controlled by their pain, they're unable to care enough about the people they hurt to be able to change their reprehensible behavior.

Our perpetrators did wrong.
Our best revenge is to extend compassion.

27

WHY DO I NEED ACCOUNTABILITY?

GARY

I came home from the grocery store the other day with a container of cottage cheese. Later that night, I opened the lid and discovered that the transparent protective covering was already half off. I stared at it for a moment. When did that happen? I wonder how long it was sitting like this at the store. I wonder if someone pulled off the lid and replaced it. What kind of nasty microbial creatures bent on wreaking havoc in my body have already invaded?

I stirred the cottage cheese around a bit. It looked OK. I raised a spoonful to my nose and sniffed. Smelled OK. I took a tiny bit on my tongue. Tasted OK. I shrugged, spooned out the usual portion, and I ate it.

Far as I know, it was fine. I'm still here. But that event reminds me of something that happened when we were sexually abused in childhood. We were "opened up early." Our protective covering was pulled back. Our sexuality was exposed inappropriately and against our will. Once opened and the protective covering pulled back, we became easy prey for all kinds of harmful influences.

I have a theory that, because of the abuse, certain parts of our sensory nature are more active than they are in other people. Certain things impacted and affected us more acutely. Significant sights and smells trigger powerful feelings. Visual images such as movies, television, or video games may have a greater, more lasting impact on us. Our emotions overall might be more stirred and powerful than those of the average individual.

This isn't to deny those abuse survivors who have shut down emotionally. In stressful times, they numbed out, which meant that they often didn't feel pain, and it also meant that they didn't feel joy.

196 NOT QUITE HEALED

This doesn't mean that we feel those emotions for what they are. Cec often says, "My feelings are only my emotions; they are not reality."

Another way to put it might be, "Feelings are not facts." That doesn't deny the reality of the feelings, only that what we feel isn't the proper gauge of truth. We may feel something is bad or horrible because that's how it strikes us. We may decide someone's words are kind and loving when they may be manipulative and evil.

If we're not careful, our strong, sensitive reactors can lead to addictions that distract us or deaden those powerful, perhaps frightening, feelings. Because we're so sensitive to them, we want to push them away. Drugs and alcohol are common "painkillers." So is sexual addiction or pornography—anything that helps us distance ourselves from our pain fits that category.

Sexual molestation touches us at our core and skews things from that point on through the rest of our lives. It opened us to a sexual world that we didn't choose to enter and shouldn't have had to enter at that age or in that manner.

Think of what it must be like for children to try to run across a mine field with no training or expertise. All they know how to do is to run. Bombs explode, and some of those children are maimed for life. All of us are affected by abuse, even if we safely reach the other side.

After we experienced what we did, we were permanently changed. A door was unlocked and left ajar. Someone opened the lid and pulled back our protective covering.

What we choose to expose ourselves to is profoundly important. After the abuse, we're automatically set up for things like sexual confusion, pornography, dysfunctional relationships, distorted thinking, self-hatred, and repeated victimization. We're still racing across a minefield and often don't know it. We're aware of one significant thing: we don't want to get hurt again.

In our healing, we need to recognize certain things we can engage in but that are inherently dangerous for us. A movie or video might do it.

Being in a particular location. Conversations that we don't need to hear. Magazines or books. Web sites on the Internet.

Then we face recovery. Too many make it sound easy and natural. "Just say no to those things. Say yes to healing."

If only it were that easy.

Everyone who becomes aware of abuse isn't instantly healed—just like alcoholics. It takes deep courage and serious commitment. It also takes a strong support base. No one makes it alone.

I want to emphasize that: we need help, and we can't achieve healing without others. I also believe Jesus Christ and God's people can provide a strong, healthy support base.

But many of us don't get that healing help. Although we can list various reasons—and there are many—they come down to fear we can't do it or fear of going through the pain again.

Because we were opened up too early, we stayed open and we can't change that. But we can also open ourselves to inner peace, a sense of self-worth, and a knowledge that we're loved.

It's a process.

It hurts, and the pain may make us feel we'd rather medicate ourselves with our old forms of behavior. That happens. A lot.

But the door of healing is open.

We sabotage our own healing by not asking for help. We put off attending mutual-help groups such as Celebrate Recovery.[1]

We "forget" to call the counselor. Instead of getting help, it's easier to log on to that porn site again. We choose to isolate and try to gain relief from the pain through various kinds of addiction.

I want to mention two addictions that we don't seem to stress. Too many self-medicate through food. For some of us, the more we stuff our

---

1. In 1991, Saddleback Church in Lake Forest, California, launched Celebrate Recovery. It was designed as a program to help those struggling with hurts, habits, and hang-ups by showing them the loving power of Jesus Christ through a recovery process. www .celebraterecovery.com

198   NOT QUITE HEALED

bodies and feel full, the less anxiety or depression we encounter. We instinctively know we need something we don't have (love, most likely), so we start stuffing in food as our chosen love substitute. And in the church, overeating is an acceptable behavior to soothe the pain of abuse.

The other addiction is promiscuity. It can be running from one affair to another. Or it can be filling our lives with unhealthy relationships—being codependent or controlling others.

We can be highly functional and successful, putting off the healing work we need because we're too busy building careers or businesses. We point to our families and shake our heads. "I have to be there for my kids and for my wife." We're probably not aware of what we do to ourselves. We don't see that it's our hunger to be loved and accepted that's driving us along. It's like that song about "looking for love in all the wrong places."

Let's make this clear: until we address what happened to us and face our own issues that arose from the abuse, we will look to other people or to substances to help us feel better or more secure, make us happy, prop us up, and assure ourselves that we're handling life as it comes.

Except in those moments when we're alone.

Perhaps before sleep or when we awaken at 2:30 in the morning.

Without knowing it, we place other people in front of our healing and expect them to meet our needs so that we somehow do not have to deal with the junk that happened to us. We walk around as shadows, longing for substance but settling for substitutes.

CEC

I was once engaged to a woman whom I had known since high school. I loved her—or I thought I did—but something kept bothering me about her. I kept putting off the wedding. I castigated myself for doing that because the excuses were only excuses.

But one day I knew the answer. I wasn't a believer, and I hadn't yet dealt with my sexual molestation, so the only way I can talk about this is to refer to my inner wisdom. In an insightful moment I realized that, as sweet and lovely as she was, she was also needy. I would spend my life and energies taking care of her.

I broke off the engagement, and I handled it badly. I didn't know how to say to her, "You're too needy. I can't take care of you every day of our life together." Instead I said, "I don't love you enough to marry you."

I could have gone the other way and attached myself to a woman who wanted to spend her life caring for me. It would have been just as miserable a task for her as it would have been for me to be the caregiver for someone else.

Whether we're the needy ones (and often we are) or we attract those who perceive us as the providers for all their needs, we end up in unhealthy relationships. And it doesn't have to be sexual.

For a long time I've realized that some people are in the helping professions as an unconscious fix for their own neediness. Teachers, pastors, therapists, and medical personnel. That's not to condemn or judge, but only to say that some people become so intensively involved that their work *becomes* their life.

As a former pastor, I understand that. If my wife hadn't gently pulled me back a number of times, I might have made being a pastor my total life, or as one person called it, his raison d'être—a French expression that means "reason for existence." We've all met those kinds of people, haven't we?

GARY

As long as I repressed what happened to me, I wasn't engaged in healing. I functioned in my roles, so I assumed that meant I was healing from that nebulous something that troubled me.

My identity became whatever role I was engaged in at the moment. Student, college minister, husband, missionary, hotel service manager, interpreter, pastor, father. But these roles weren't who I was; they were what I did. Until I started dealing with my abuse, I didn't know the difference. Worse, I didn't know who I was. Had anyone asked, I would have pointed to my functions or roles.

I'm not sure I know now, but I'm getting closer. I still struggle with fear, denial, codependency, and a host of other issues. It's comforting to me that, even though my motives may not be perfect and my helping others may at times be driven not by love but to get my own needs met, God is still at work in my life and uses me anyway.

I can look back and see I've vacillated between being the needy one and trying to take care of others. For me, these two things go together and are intertwined. I can see that all the way back to elementary school, in my dating relationships in high school, in my marriage, and in my chosen professions. I want to heal. I want to really love others. I need help. I need my healing team.

✦ ✦ ✦

We constantly have choices. We can temporarily—and only temporarily—minimize our pain with unhealthy painkillers.

We urge ourselves and others: let's not put anything in front of our healing, because it's also a healthy way of loving ourselves.

Jesus said it this way: "'You must love the LORD your God with all your heart, all your soul, and all your mind.' This is the first and greatest commandment. A second is equally important: 'Love your neighbor as yourself'" (Matthew 22:37–39). Many people don't notice that Jesus stresses self-love before we offer ourselves to others, but that's the way it works.

Thus we need to focus on getting well because those are healthy steps toward loving ourselves, and therefore being able to love those around us.

Like us, you're not quite healed. So if you're not yet taking the significant steps, here are the most obvious ones:

- ✦ Call a counselor or therapist.
- ✦ Call a friend (or friends) whom you trust and share your story.
- ✦ Attend a recovery group.

✦   ✦   ✦

I spoke with a counselor friend and asked her about healthy coping mechanisms for those who have been sexually abused. Joangeli Kasper is also a survivor and seems to have coped well with her issues. I knew that what she said wouldn't be textbook language or a theory she had adopted.

Here is what she told me:

1. *We need a higher power.* If we stay at it and work hard, we'll get better, but those who have a higher power get there quicker because they have hope. So the first thing I do is steer the survivor toward God, the ultimate positive coping mechanism.

2. *We need a strong support network.* We've been alone, and we don't have eyes to see reality. We need the eyes of others to begin to see that where we've been is not real.

3. *We need to learn how to thought-stop.* We live in a society where we go with what we feel, but that's not based on truth. When we make a statement like "You make me mad," it wasn't the person but whatever thought was behind that feeling that made us angry. The thought comes first, then the feeling, then the behavior. I try to get people back to their thoughts. What were you thinking about yourself when that happened? Usually, it was something like "I wasn't important enough" or "I don't matter."

4. *We need to be physically active.* Exercise is a powerful, positive coping mechanism.

5. *We need to build a base of knowledge about recovery.* We can journal or read. We need to be informed.

"The greatest danger to recovery is isolation," she said. "We're becoming increasingly isolated as society becomes increasingly individualized.

We have trouble living in community. We need to link arms and go through this together. We need a support base of people who realize they are broken and who are willing to be open and honest about it. When you start this process, you're building from the ground up. You can do everything right, but if you are not in community and don't know God, it's going to be a long, hard road."

CEC

Slightly more than thirty years ago, David and I became good friends. We didn't use words like *accountability* or *being answerable to someone else*, but that was our intention. At the time, I felt accountability was like standing before a teacher and explaining my behavior and how I responded to my tasks. Our goal was different. Both of us wanted to be healthy and to mature by having someone else there—someone trusted—to guide us.

"You were everybody's best friend," David said to me or I said to him—we can't remember who said it. "But you never had a best friend." We determined to fill that need, and we've done that. As much as possible, every week we get together for an hour or two *only* to focus on who we are and on our growth. He challenges me; I nudge him. We've both grown tremendously through the years.

> Accountability is the first step
> toward livability.

28

I NEED HELP.

GARY

Admitting I need help is very difficult for me. But even more difficult is actually taking the next step and seeking help.

I don't know why I think I can work through everything by myself. I think it's a long-learned, ingrained pattern of isolation. My perpetrators cut me off from the outside world, so I continued to isolate myself. Even though I have many good relationships, I still detach myself.

Ultimately, it comes down to whether my healing is worth the effort. Are those I love worth the turmoil I'll have to endure? Will I decide to make my healing a priority and seek any and all help that would aid in that?

When my flashbacks began, I was already seeing a counselor for anxiety issues. I had seen three previous counselors for several months at a time, over a span of twenty years. I received help from all of them. They didn't delve into the matter of my molestation because I wasn't consciously aware of it. Even though the topic didn't come up, they helped me manage my anxiety and begin to deal—at least somewhat—with my guilt and shame.

The counselor I was seeing at the time of the flashbacks was exactly the right therapist for me. He understood me and provided a balance of affirmation and challenge. He instinctively seemed to know what I could handle and what I couldn't.

I felt safer, more secure, less anxious, more settled. I continued seeing my regular therapist. Then our circumstances changed and we made a move back to our home state of Texas. Because we were financially strapped, I didn't look for a therapist after the move. I thought I was doing well.

Two years later, things erupted in my marriage, and my buttons were getting pushed all at once. Every day seemed full of triggers. I connected with a therapist on the phone, who told me I needed to make my healing a priority.

The following week, I attended a Celebrate Recovery group at a local church. The leader heard my story and agreed to meet with me on a weekly basis. After about six weeks of attending, I joined a more in-depth men's "step study" (where men work through the steps of recovery). I don't know how I would have made it without that group. I found it refreshing, real, and practical.

One day I said to myself, "I no longer feel alone." My words surprised me. It was a new feeling.

"The best gift I can give myself and those around me is the healthiest me possible."

I share this because I'd needed help and finally admitted it. I had to seek other people—to lean on the wisdom and training of professionals. Whether we go to professionals or lay people isn't the issue. We need help. And if we face that reality, we can take the next step and seek that help.

I would never say anyone couldn't handle this alone; I will say I've never met a survivor who said, "I did it all alone." The healthy survivors pushed away their pride, their fear of self-revealing, and opened up to someone.

I believe that real, lasting healing occurs in the midst of good, supportive relationships.

Here are some questions that I found helpful to ask myself:

Why did I choose to go to therapists? I was falling apart, unable to function in healthy ways. I needed someone who knew how to help—someone objective enough to guide and encourage me so that I could take one tiny step forward at a time.

How did I find my therapists? In each case, the therapist was recommended by someone I knew and respected. Because of my skepticism and lack of trust, I learned about the therapists and what they were like before I would make a call.

Not every therapist is necessarily a good fit. A counselor once said to me, "Choosing a counselor is like buying a new pair of shoes. You may have to try on a few before you find one that fits."

One bad experience taught me the truth of that statement. He may have been a fine therapist, but he just wasn't the right person for me. Rather than get discouraged and decide I wouldn't try anyone else, I remembered the image of buying shoes. I simply needed to try another therapist.

How did therapy help? I tend to trust what authority figures tell me, which is somewhat amazing to me, given what happened to me as a child. I believed my therapists told me the truth. Each one helped me see a little more of the reality about myself and grasp the implications of what happened to me.

They pinpointed issues that I would never have seen on my own. The therapy cost me greatly in time and in finances, but it was worth it. I'm convinced I would still be stuck in my pain without those wise and caring people.

What did I get from a therapist that I couldn't get on my own? I realized that without professional help, I couldn't see myself or the world accurately (there's that denial thing again).

Cec sometimes says that it's like trying to see his backside. He needed someone to hold up a mirror for him to do that. That's a good example of what we receive from others. He didn't go to therapy, but he had supportive relationships with his friend David and a few other men.

I'd say it this way: If we could heal ourselves by ourselves, we'd probably all be healed by now. I needed skilled, empathetic assistance. There's no way I could have gone back into that pain alone.

I recently had an appendectomy. It wouldn't occur to me to operate on myself. As I lay in the ER, I hoped the surgeon on call was the best one around.

When it comes to serious issues such as sexual molestation, I remind myself: I didn't get into this mess on my own, so how can I expect to get out of it on my own?

CEC

As Gary pointed out, I didn't seek a therapist. The simplest reason involves trust, which is a common problem among us survivors. As illogical as it may seem to some, I felt I couldn't trust anyone I had to pay to listen.

It's a little more than that. I yearned to open up, but that person had to be, in my thinking, trustworthy. Those individuals became trustworthy because I told them little secrets and (so far as I know) they didn't pass them on or make them items of gossip.

When others spoke about going to therapists, I didn't understand how they could open up to strangers. Yet as inconsistent as it seems, I sometimes sent people to counselors. I just didn't trust them for myself.

Now that I've made that point, I'll also say what's more important than having or not having a therapist: we need a strong support system. I didn't do it on my own, and I don't know anyone who has.

My wife, Shirley, was there, and I didn't doubt her love and commitment to me. After I first opened up, she said, "I don't understand, but I love you and I'm with you." I hadn't expected her to understand.

I don't recall what words David used, but the same loving commitment was there. I could trust both of them. That's what gave me the ability to start talking. And the more I opened up, and the more receptive Shirley and David became, the more I was able to trust them. There were also a few people in distant cities with whom I spoke by phone.

If I had not had Shirley and David in my life, I don't think I could have gone through reliving the pain of my childhood.

GARY

Having that support system Cec talks about is critical. I've already pointed out the importance of therapists, but they're not enough.

As a counselor friend put it, "The therapist is the surgeon. You also need the rest of the team around the surgeon to heal."

That says it well—the rest of the team. As I thought about that, I asked myself, "Who is my support team?" The family that I lived with in high school has been a bulwark of acceptance and compassion since the days of my first flashbacks. I also have a few close friends with whom I share my healing journey on a regular basis. Cec, from the first day I met him five years ago, has been a tremendous, encouraging mentor and friend. Then there's my Celebrate Recovery team.

The people in my Celebrate Recovery group (CR) embody the word *commitment*. They're committed to God, to each other, and to healing—their own and each other's.

For the team to function, it takes work. I spend a good amount of time each week with CR materials, in CR meetings and small groups, and with my CR sponsor.

CR certainly isn't the only mutual-help group. There are others around the country. But it's the one I found the most accessible.

I can't possibly express how much that group of people has come to mean to me. My healing has taken huge leaps forward. I love them most because they won't let me hide from them or try to become invisible in their midst. They make me accountable, and I need them to do that.

I also need to help each of them be accountable. As I probe and listen to them and to their heartaches, I understand my own pain even more.

Healing is truly a team effort.

CEC

In her book, *Nobody Understands My Pain*, Linda Harriss writes about not getting help because of fear. With permission, I've quoted this section from her book.

> Because your ability to trust has been damaged by your abuse, you don't feel safe disclosing your secret to anyone. In

addition . . . you may also be afraid of being judged for your negative behaviors and poor choices rather than receiving the support you need.

If you've been carrying your secret for a long time, seeking help can seem more frightening than remaining quiet. Whenever you consider disclosing the abuse—whether to a friend, family member, or professional counselor—fear-provoking questions plague you:

> What if people don't believe me?
> What if they think it was my fault?
> What if they no longer want to be my friends?
> What if they don't maintain confidentiality?
> What if they start treating me differently?
> What if they think I've become an abuser?
> What if they see me as dirty, bad, and flawed? . . .

These fears can become paralyzing, causing you to stall in your process of healing.[1]

Gary still feels tinges of fear when he seeks support.

I still tremble inside each time I share my story. Perhaps there is an old reflex operating that still screams, "Be quiet! If you speak, you'll be punished. They'll come after you. No one will believe you. You'll be worse off than you are now."

My natural way used to be that I'd listen to that loud voice and refuse to evaluate my automatic reflex. I isolated myself from others. And by that I mean I was *with* people, but they saw only the surface, the facade. I kept trying to figure things out, and I rarely did.

---

1. *Nobody Understands My Pain: Dealing with the Effects of Physical, Emotional, and Sexual Abuse* by Linda Harriss RN, LPC (Friendswood, TX: Baxter Press), 129–30. Used by permission.

There's an old saying, "Do what you've always done, and you'll keep getting the same results." How well I know that. Fear is a maladaptive coping mechanism. It's powerful, but it doesn't work. It kept me stuck in my pain and dysfunctional patterns.

Lately I've come to see fear differently. When I submit to God's plan for me and pursue my own healing (reaching out to another person, going to CR, seeing a therapist, choosing to do something different, etc.) and I find myself becoming afraid (my natural reflex motivated by shame), I try to picture my perpetrators clutching at me. They are terrified. They are screaming their old lies at me, "You're worthless. You'll never make it. No one will ever love you. It's hopeless. You'll never get away. You belong to us. You got what you deserved. You're ugly, bad. You caused this."

The more I move toward reaching out and seeking help, the more frantic and terrified they become. I see myself choosing to turn away from them and toward Jesus, who is walking in front of me, inviting me to follow. His way is the healing way. I smile, put my back toward my perpetrators, and walk forward.

Seeking help is still unnerving and anxiety producing, but I've resolved the issue. *I will win.* As I do, I believe I'll be better able to resist the voices from the past and better able to accept what those around me (those with me on my journey toward healing and wholeness) are saying. Over time and through small, daily, incremental changes, I believe my reflexes will change. That's transformation.

Paul in the New Testament said it this way: "Don't copy the behavior and customs of this world, but let God transform you into a new person by changing the way you think. Then you will learn to know God's will for you, which is good and pleasing and perfect" (Romans 12:2). This is a command to give up the old ways of thinking that lead to old ways of feeling and acting. Think differently. Thinking differently will ultimately lead to acting differently and feeling differently.

I hunger for healing, and I thirst for transformation. I want change.

That will not happen quickly, but I have taken the long view. I want to keep the big picture in mind. I reach out and seek help. As I do that and am open to the changes God wants to make in my life, he will use me to help comfort and heal others. I'll have traveling companions on my road to healing and wholeness.

It's natural for me not to seek help. It's natural for me to isolate. I'm determined to eliminate every excuse. I want nothing in the way of my healing, and I need the strength of others to help me overcome.

I've heard excuses from men who won't seek help:

"Only weaklings need a counselor."
"My problems aren't that serious."
"I can do this by myself."
"I have God on my side, and that's all I need."

Excuses, not reasons. They're ways to diffuse the issue while enabling us to avoid getting help. More than excuses, they're actually lies spawned by our shame from what happened to us.

What they're really saying is:

"I'm ashamed and embarrassed."
"I'm terrified of being rejected. I can't risk it."
"I'm not worth it."
"I hate this, but it's what I know. Being alone is familiar, and I can't live with any more unknowns."

Whether you go the therapy route like Gary or have a strong support system the way I did, you need help.

Someone smirkingly said, "Therapy is only a crutch, and I want to walk on my own." My answer is simple. If you had serious heart problems, would you say the same thing? If you knew you were diabetic, would you refuse medication? Are physical illnesses any different?

GARY

For my situation right now, I know my healing team needs to consist of

+ a supportive, well-led group of fellow-strugglers/survivors;
+ a few good, nonjudgmental, supportive friends; and
+ a local church where I feel safe and can worship and serve with joy.

Admitting I need help is a sign of humility, not weakness. Reaching out for help is a sign of courage.

29

WHAT'S WRONG WITH MY COPING MECHANISMS?

CEC

Two therapists interviewed me for a state-funded group called something like "Men Who Were Sexually Assaulted in Childhood." They chose fifteen men, although I have no idea how many applied—perhaps only fifteen.

At my interview, I told the two men I had been dealing with my abuse for about three years. After we talked for almost an hour, one of them said, "You learned coping devices that helped you survive childhood. You don't need them anymore."

I asked him what specific devices he meant, but he shook his head. "We'll discuss that during the weekly meetings." The topic never came up—specifically—during the year the state funded our group, but I've become increasingly aware of my coping devices.

For me, denial was the strongest and most powerful. I often refer to it as amnesia. It's not something I figured out and tried. It was unconscious. It's important to mention that because that's the core of my personal coping devices.

Our coping devices are not consciously chosen. We were children who were too immature to grasp such things. Because we were fragile and innocent, we resorted to what worked for us.

We can't change what took place in our childhood, and our molestation will always be part of our history. *However, we can move away from self-destructive and self-defeating behavior.*

The previous sentence may come across as simple or easy; it is neither.

One of the problems is that we can't simply dig inside and pull in our memory as a whole piece. Even more than a quarter century since I started to heal, my memory has gaps. Some parts are vague and seem unconnected to anything else. A few smells or certain phrases such as "You're special," still bring back sad but partial memories. Most of us don't and can't remember all the facts, and if we move forward in our healing, the pain will usually be intense.

For the first couple of years after facing my abuse, I felt as if I were being victimized a second time because of the intensity of the pain. Yet I knew I had to face the past before healing would occur.

Gary

Denial was the most obvious coping mechanism for me. For four decades I didn't remember what happened to me. That's serious denial. And the denial took other forms as well. I pretended it wasn't happening. I would have described my family as a loving, caring family. I would have said back then that my mother loved me and was a good mom. I made excuses for everyone's behavior. And most pervasive of all, I developed the habit of seeing people and the world not as they were, but as I wanted them to be.

I lived in my private fantasyland. By calling it fantasyland, I don't mean a land of sexual lust or whimsy, although for some of us it may include that. Fantasyland is the world as I see it through the lens of my past abuse. I can now say clearly that my fantasyland was a distorted concept of life. It's a worldview full of lies, and because I accepted those lies, I could make the rules on the way I lived.

I assumed other people thought and felt the way I did and behaved the same way I did. That form of denial allowed me to not feel my emotions. It's as if my feelings were frozen, and I had no idea what they were or that I even had them.

Instead of living in the present and dealing with real issues, I avoided the past by fretting about the future.

My denial also created anxiety, because I had to work hard to keep the fantasyland going. I had to control situations and fix things to stay in denial and try to get things to work out the way they should. That anxiety was immensely time and energy consuming. It kept me worn out. It takes tremendous energy to live on a level that avoids facing reality. My denial kept me inside a fictional world, and I avoided the truth. Therefore, it prevented me from fully engaging in the present and drastically affected the quality of my relationships.

I mistakenly felt that denial protected me from additional pain. Eventually I learned that living in a world of fantasy only extended and hid my pain from myself. Pain that is not felt and released stays inside, festers, and gets worse. For me, it festered into guilt and shame. And then the cycle continued.

I've vacated fantasyland even though it beckons to me almost every day.

CEC

We cope in many different ways. One man "invented" a friend so he would have someone to whom he could talk.

Years ago, my late friend Steve Grubman told me his story. It was the first time I had heard about an invisible friend, but it made sense to me. Steve had been sexually molested many times while living in a number of foster homes. He told me, "I had an invisible friend, and I was the only one who could see him. It was our secret." He said that talking to his companion was the only time he was fully at peace. While the abuse went on, in his mind, Steve was able to talk to the unseen friend and push away the agony of the rape.

As an adult, Steve no longer needed his friend. He doesn't remember when the invisible companion left him, but he said he thought it was when he was in college. He said, "I didn't need him any longer, so he went away."

I could say the same thing about my amnesia. When I was ready (we often refer to this as *feeling safe*), my memories seeped out. I use the word *seeped* because most of them came slowly and gradually. In retrospect, I think my inner wisdom (for lack of a better term) allowed only enough of the past to emerge as I was ready to deal with.

✦ ✦ ✦

I've mentioned two types of coping: amnesia-denial and Steve's invisible friend. A subscriber to my blog wrote these words: "Another way I was still being victimized was by an overwhelming fear inside that was turning into what one doctor diagnosed as 'the third stage of agoraphobia.'"

He went on to say that he understood it as a generalized fear of anything and everything. For some people, it becomes so debilitating, they're unable to leave their house for fear of what will happen. "I wasn't too far from that level," he said.

That terrible fear was his method of dealing with his molestation.

✦ ✦ ✦

Occasionally I hear men justify the abuse and realize that's their form of coping. In the state-sponsored group I was part of, one man insisted early in the year, "If I hadn't been so handsome, he wouldn't have done that to me." Later that man told us that the perpetrator said that to him and he believed it.

An unhealthy coping mechanism shows itself by justifying the molestation. They quote the victimizer's words:

"You were always hanging around me."
"You kept after me."
"You deserved what you got."
"You liked it, didn't you? You can't fool me. You wanted it."
"I'm just helping you become a man."
"You should be glad to get what I give you."

Other survivors resort to minimizing the event:

> "It only happened four times."
> "I was so young, it didn't really affect me."
> "It really wasn't that bad."
> "It was no big deal. It happens all the time."
> "They didn't really mean it."

GARY

Most of the coping methods we struggle with are known as *maladaptive*. They may have helped us survive at the time (and we need to be thankful for them), but as we matured into adulthood, they became handicaps. They kept us from engaging in healthy, peaceful living.

If we allowed them to be part of our arsenal of coping, they became habits and formed part of our character. They became our automatic, reflex reactions to life.

I call those maladaptive coping mechanisms *character handicaps*. I can easily trace my dysfunctional behavior back to them. Those character handicaps were the driving force behind the thoughts and behaviors that kept me stuck for years.

Here are other examples of character handicaps with which we survivors struggle:

+ *Fear.* It's not the terror that overwhelms as much as it is the emotion that wants us to hide from what's happening.
+ *Negative thinking.* We seem unable to grasp things as positive or good; we're programmed to focus on the bad side of people and situations.
+ *Self-condemnation.* Not only do we see the negative side of things, but we're aware of our attitude. Instead of changing, we blame ourselves for the way we think of or perceive the world.
+ *Passivity.* This is the inability to act even when it's a simple

loving act. Or we can't speak up against those things with which we disagree.

+ *People pleasing.* We need the approval of others, especially the important individuals in our lives. We base our actions on whether others will like us.

+ *Lust.* Sometimes situations arouse us and foster unhealthy desires or appetites that often lead to sexual acts.

+ *Self-importance.* Because of our neediness or sense of powerlessness, we cover up and overcompensate by seeing ourselves as powerful, important, or better than others.

+ *Self-justification.* We defend ourselves by explaining or rationalizing our behavior. One of the common responses we give when confronted is, "Yes, but if he hadn't . . . "

+ *Lying.* We probably resent the word, but we lie by silence, by exaggeration, or by allowing other people to believe we're something we're not. For example, we may imply we have a more prestigious job than we do or that we have greater financial assets than our bank account shows.

+ *Obsession.* We focus on a person, an object, or a goal. That fixation controls our lives. It may be getting ahead in our careers, having the cleanest yard in the community, or being the parent of the brightest student in the local school. It's anything that stirs such a passion in us that we can't let go or we think about it constantly. Prejudice and ethnic cleansing are powerful examples of such fixations.

Some people get caught up in a political issue—probably any topic can work. Take abortion or a woman's right to choose. Whatever position you take, if that issue controls your thoughts, your anger, your commitment, then that's obsession.

Other examples of character handicaps might be gluttony, greed, laziness, criticalness, perfectionism, procrastination, resentment, envy, intolerance, and insensitivity.

This can be a discouraging list. We mean it only as a way to say: "Think about these things. If they describe you, do something to change them."

We need to remind ourselves that the root of these handicaps (those that stemmed from the sexual abuse) was not our fault. We were violated and hurt, and we were powerless to prevent or stop what happened.

And we survived.

We survived because we embraced methods to take us through the pain. They worked then; now they hinder. Now we're adults, and we don't have to follow the patterns of childhood.

Our handicaps, if unidentified and unaddressed, keep us stuck in the cycle of abuse. What happened to us will continue to set the tone for our lives and relationships.

Discovering and overcoming our character handicaps can be one way we come out of denial and forever vacate the premises in fantasyland. We can fight against the massive evil of sexual molestation.

Don't expect immediate change, but you can expect progress. Once we're cognizant of our maladaptive behavior, we're already taking action. For most of us, healing consists of small, daily, incremental changes.

With God's help—and it's available to us—we can change. We can overcome the maladaptive behavior that has controlled us.

CEC

Only after I started to write this book did I hear stories from men who suffered from dissociative identity disorder (DID) or the older term, multiple personality disorder (MPD). That is, they dissociate or distance themselves from the conscious circumstances.

I want to state candidly that I was quite skeptical of such a diagnosis until I heard stories from men who shared their experiences with me. I'm now a believer, but I also see this condition as beyond our level as writers and survivors to deal with. I'm going to relate stories because they're important to the survivors and to those of us who care about the abused.

When I lived in Louisville, Kentucky, a man in our group whose name was Ted spoke about his dissociative personality. I didn't understand, but I didn't forget either. It's now been twenty years, so this is the best I can do at telling his story.

"At times I feel like two different people. Most of the time I don't feel much of anything—not bad and not good." When he spoke, I thought of his being bipolar, or as we called it then, manic depressive. Yet it didn't seem to fit with the typical descriptions I had read or heard about.

He said something about losing awareness of who he was and "the other part of me takes over."

Andy, another man in the same group, said that he became four different people. He said he used each persona as a way to cope with the diverse situations in his life.

"When I attended church, I was truly in a state of worship and praise." He went on to say that at work, "I seemed to have switched into somebody else. I became loud, obnoxious, and laughed at every phase of religion."

At first I didn't understand. "We can all shift our thinking or behave according to the people we're around," I said.

Andy nodded but added, "You can make that decision, but that's different. My shift was out of my control." He said he even had nicknames for each of his personalities. "I knew who they were, but I wasn't able to stop them before I went through intensive therapy."

◆　◆　◆

Gary is of the opinion that, to some degree, all abuse victims detach from themselves to survive the trauma. Put that way, I raise my hand.

Gary adds, "I believe all of us survivors are on that continuum." His counselor frequently used the word *integrate*. "We're meant to be whole people, but our lives were distorted and skewed through abuse. It's as if part of ourselves got left behind."

The place we each find ourselves on the continuum depends on our general psychological and spiritual makeup, the severity of the abuse, and our response to the molestation.

Regardless, most of us survived by leaving behind a part of ourselves. For me, it was the abandonment of feelings. (I didn't stop feeling, but I lost the connection between feelings and the awareness of them.)

Gary said he shut down emotionally and went inside himself—that means he focused on intellectual responses rather than trying to cope with his feelings. That was a way to hide from the abuse; the less others saw inside him, the safer he felt. Or perhaps it's better to say *less exposed*.

All of us used some form of coping mechanism to survive. Instead of being hard on ourselves for using such strategies, we need to appreciate ourselves and our ability to find a way that took us through the terrible ordeals.

Not everyone survives; not everyone heals. Some survivors have been so beaten down, they give up. Hopelessness overwhelms them, and the ultimate response is suicide.

But there is hope because there is healing. That's why we've written this book. We used a variety of coping mechanisms to protect ourselves. Now we can say, "Thank you and good-bye" to our old, inefficient, unhealthy ways.

For example, elsewhere in this book I've mentioned being driven. Call it anxiety. I didn't know how to relax and enjoy the now because I hurried to get to tomorrow's victories.

I used to brag that I got more out of my day than most people did. By that, I referred to productivity, as if doing more meant being superior. I tried to cover my inadequacies with greater accomplishments.

I tended to overschedule myself and then work double shifts to get everything done. And I usually accomplished everything. But what about the cost? I kept so busy racing from one activity to another, I allowed myself little time for relaxation or personal reflection. A few months ago I decided I was going to slow down my engine.

I'm a strong believer in self-affirmation, so I incorporated it. Each morning I run or walk for about an hour, and that has become my prayer and meditation time. On three-by-five-inch file cards, I wrote several affirmations and repeated them every day for months:

> *Today I have time to do everything I need to do today.*
> *I relax and take time each day to enjoy my life.*
> *I am loved and lovable and have nothing to prove to myself.*

For me, the simple, daily reminders enabled me to slow down. Instead of working twelve- to fourteen-hour days, I'm now functioning at six to eight. I don't accomplish quite as much, but I enjoy my life more.

I'm learning that I don't have to protect myself, that I don't have to let the engine drive me. I can control the accelerator and the brake.

The tools that helped me survive as a child
are no longer the tools I need to enjoy my adult life.
Now I consciously choose my tools.

30

I AM WOUNDED, BODY AND SOUL.

CEC

Sexual abuse affects every part of our minds, our spirits, and even our bodies. Some don't think of the body as being affected, but it is. I know abused men who can't stand to have someone touch them. Others seem constantly to need to touch other people.

A number of therapists teach that we store our emotional pain in our physical bodies. They talk about stiff necks (mentioned in the Bible), and some people push their anger into their lower back.

I used to assume that frigidity was strictly a female issue, but I've spoken with men who have no desire for sexual activity with their spouses or only do so occasionally.

God made us so wonderfully that our bodies respond to all affected emotions and actions. Most of us know the links between nicotine and cancer; heavy-fat diets and obesity; high levels of activity for healthy weight loss.

One of the effects of the physical beatings from my dad was that my mind taught my body not to feel pain. I wasn't aware of that, but I do remember that my baby brother, Chuck, and I determined that we wouldn't let Dad see us cry. My mind taught my body not to feel the pain.

Years later I was hospitalized on two separate occasions for peptic (stomach) ulcers, and I never felt the slightest bit of pain. I vomited blood, but that was my only symptom. I commented to a nurse about how great it was that I didn't feel the pain.

"Oh, how sad," she said. "Pain is the way your body tells you it hurts." Twenty years passed before I understood why I felt no pain.

GARY

Abuse does indeed affect us physically. I can't stand to be tickled. I can't pinpoint it, but being tickled evokes feelings of fear and shame, so I assumed that was one phase of my abuse. I have also had times where I wake up in the middle of the night, shaking with fear. A couple of times I have woken up in terror, feeling as if I'm being pinned to the bed.

My adopted daughters have some similar physical reactions. One reacts strongly whenever her left arm is grabbed, or when she is hugged from behind. Another daughter freaks out when her shoulder is squeezed. All these are reactions from their past sexual abuse. The body remembers even when the mind forgets. When the trigger is pulled, muscle memory kicks in, and the message goes out that the molestation is happening again.

I believe that sexual abuse can produce physical illness as well. When I had my flashbacks, I was in some ways experiencing the abuse all over again. It impacted my health. I went for test after test. Doctors couldn't find anything. But I could barely move, shook all the time, and couldn't sleep. I've had weird physical illnesses or issues for as long as I can remember, except for the time when I was living with my safe family in high school and college. I don't remember having any health issues during that time.

Cec mentioned that his body reacted by feeling no pain. My body reacted by becoming highly sensitive. I've become extremely aware of what's happening inside my body.

Physically speaking, trauma and prolonged stress suppress our immune systems. We become easier targets for illness and disease. Guilt and shame are incredibly stressful and sap our energy—energy that could be spent living well.

Sometimes our harmful coping mechanisms contribute to ill health. For instance, in my work with hospice, I've seen many people who dealt with abusive backgrounds by becoming addicted to drugs or alcohol, winding up very ill way before their time. They often say things like, "I did this to myself" but don't often see the strong link their chosen life-style has to what happened to them as children. Most of them have not dealt with their past and are still in denial. Perhaps they didn't know they could heal.

Once we make the commitment to heal, our bodies will be affected, too. If you are afflicted with a serious disease, I'm not saying that healing from your past will cure you physically. But I do think that even in those cases, there will be a positive impact. We are whole people. As we heal, the whole of our person is affected. If we heal from the brokenness inside, it only seems natural that our bodies would respond to that, as well.

Cec mentioned earlier that some men have little to no desire for sexual activity. To be honest, I'm frightened of sexual activity. I enjoyed sex with my wife immensely, yet I didn't seem to be able to maintain a consistent level of intimacy. I tended to be hot or cold. There would be several days or a week when I'd pursue her sexually, and then I'd back off; and weeks or even months passed before I was in that mode again. I don't know how to describe it, but fear and shame were behind that hot-cold attitude. Perhaps fear of rejection. Maybe terror of messing up, of not pleasing. Perhaps a lack of confidence stemming from the deeply imbedded thought that I am something less than a real man.

I can try to change that all I want, but the fact is, until I make my healing a priority (this means removing my excuses about how I don't have time to go to Celebrate Recovery meetings, or lack the finances to go to therapy), I will keep doing what I've always done. It's what I know. It takes focus and work to consistently choose to think and behave differently.

We are whole people—spirits, souls, bodies. What affects part of us affects all of us.

Cec

Though sexual abuse is basically physical in nature, its most devastating effects are spiritual and psychological. It's like a concussion. A blow is delivered to the outside of the head, but the bruise develops in the brain. The injury is from the outside, but it affects us internally. Sexual abuse is a blow, a devastating one, from the outside, but it creates all kinds of bruises in our souls.

We have to focus on the psychological or spiritual pain. This is where most of us struggle. We can call it poor self-image, lack of self-esteem, or low self-worth, but all those terms come down to about the same thing.

Too often we simply don't feel good about ourselves. We feel alone, as if we don't belong anywhere, or feelings of worthlessness trouble us. That's bad enough, but we then compensate by self-medicating. The pain is so great that we just don't know what to do with it, so we try to block it out.

Beer became the medication of choice for my three brothers. Others move into hard drugs. I have a friend who now weighs nearly four hundred pounds. He faced a crisis a few months ago because of heart problems, diabetes, and the early stages of renal failure.

He was finally able to admit the reason for his obesity: "I was abused repeatedly by a cousin because he said I was so cute. I determined that no one would ever call me cute again." Adding pounds was the easiest way for him to become unattractive.

GARY

People self-medicate in all kinds of ways. In my work as a hospice chaplain, I've seen a number of patients dying due to alcohol or drug addiction in their past. In many of these cases, sexual abuse was at the root of their destructive habits. These forms of self-abuse are usually evident in other members of their family as well.

I have relatives who are counselors and work with "cutters" (people, usually in their teens, who cut themselves for relief from the psychospiritual pain they are constantly experiencing), and sexual abuse is often lurking in the background too.

I've heard that male abuse victims often head to the weight room. Makes sense. It's like saying, "I'm going to beef up. No one will dare do that to me again." Or maybe it's part of proving that we're masculine, more like real men.

I'm an avid gym goer myself. I was a competitive swimmer growing up and always liked it when we would do weight training. I'm kind of a small guy anyway, and there is something about weight training that helps me feel more at home in my body. Maybe I feel more protected. Maybe fear drives me there more than I realize. Exercise can be a form of self-medicating. It's a fairly healthy one, but it can be an escape from pain nonetheless.

CEC

Steve told me his stepfather sexually abused him until he was thirteen. "He'd sexually abuse and then verbally assault me by frequently yelling about how worthless I was." His stepfather was the only father he had known because his birth father died when Steve was eight months old. How powerful was that message to Steve? Naturally, it took root deep in his soul. Such messages want to define who we are.

Such messages send us onto a treadmill of performance, or into a tailspin of depression. Maybe both, by alternating between them. Most of us try to prove ourselves one way or another. We struggle to justify the space we take up on the planet.

"What do I have to prove to anyone?" some people ask, while others declare, "I have nothing to prove to anyone." I suspect that's a self-deceptive statement. If they have nothing to prove, why would they need to think or talk about it?

Abuse injures us and steals part of our soul. We feel worthless, inadequate, unsure of ourselves. Those are results of our injured spirits.

> Because of my abuse,
> I have a hurting soul and an injured body.
> But I am healing in both soul and body.

31

EMBRACE MY INNER CHILD?

CEC

I used to respond negatively to statements like these that are easily thrown around:

> Love your inner child.
> Until you connect with your inner child, you'll remain isolated.
> Take care of your little kid, and you'll take care of yourself today.
> Your six-year-old self has been making most of the decisions in your life.

For years I thought the get-in-touch-with-your-inner-child talks were something from New Age devotees. They seemed like some new psychobabble or gimmick to sell more books. It confused me to think of any part of my psyche being an independent entity.

I knew Carl Jung referred to the *divine child*. In the late 1980s, I read pop therapist John Bradshaw and watched him on public TV as he talked about the wounded inner child. At a lecture around 1993, someone referred to the *child within*. A therapist friend regularly refers to "my little kid."

I resisted those messages for years until I grasped what those many voices were saying.

My awareness and acceptance started with a series of simple dreams. Each one followed in time sequence over a period of about ten days. In the first one, I saw myself as a baby in a high chair, even though I don't think my parents ever used one. The infant was crying and reaching out for someone to hug him.

In another dream, I fed the child who was about a year old. I picked him up, hugged him, and held him. Just that.

In still another dream, the child was a little older, perhaps four or five. He was standing alone, wearing a brown coat, and had a tam in his right hand. (When I awakened, I remembered seeing that sepia photograph of when I was growing up.) In the dream, I sensed he was lonely. Sad. I put my arm around the boy, who stared ahead and didn't seem to feel my concern.

My dreams stopped when I (the boy) reached the age of thirteen. In that last one, I was walking down Third Street in my hometown. A light rain was falling, and I hurried down a block where there were no streetlights. Tears mingled with the raindrops. (That was a literal scene, and afterward I remembered many details of that evening.)

I pondered those dreams for several days, and then I started talking to myself at various stages. I said things such as:

> "You hurt and felt alone. You're no longer alone."
> "We survived—and now I can show you the tenderness and compassion you needed."
> "You had the courage to keep going. You're stronger than you thought."
> "You made it. I am who I am today because you didn't give up."

GARY

Like Cec, when I first heard people talking about "getting in touch with your inner child," "healing the inner child," or "finding the child within you," I thought it was rubbish. And I was a psychology major in college.

When I first heard about the inner child, I was living in a cerebral world, trying to control my own inner pain (of which I was unaware) through logic and a restrictive belief system. I was fairly emotional, but clueless about where my emotions were coming from or what to do with them. Due to my amnesia (I like Cec's term), I was out of touch with my past and, therefore, not connected with my real self.

My disdain and rejection of the inner-child concept was part of my denial. I was unaware that the concept threatened me because I didn't know how to cope with it. Later I realized that if I embraced the inner-child idea, I'd have to go back to those places of horror and abuse. I had no idea I was protecting myself by trying to keep the past deeply buried.

Years later when my flashbacks occurred, I became thoroughly introduced to the little four- to six-year-old me. In some flashbacks, I was outside myself, looking at that little boy and observing what happened to him. At other times, I was that child, seeing things through his eyes and experiencing his pain. Over a period of about a year and through many flashbacks, a picture of young Gary came together.

Through those flashbacks, I could see little Gary pulling further and further inside himself. The life went out of his eyes; he ceased to feel. His life was shattered and meaningless. One day, he went into his room, walked to the farthest corner, and sat down with his back to the wall. He looked up at me and said, "I'm going away now. No one loves me." He began to cry convulsively.

Then I felt as if another me emerged—a kid who had resolved to trust no one. He would live without emotions. That kid was like an automaton. He would figure out what people wanted and wear an appropriate mask to please them. Then it was as if that new kid looked back, said good-bye to the one crying in the corner, and left the room to do life as Gary.

As strange or weird as this reads, that's the only way I can make sense of it. Part of me got left behind. It took me awhile to realize that if that were the case, I had to go back and retrieve that part of myself. I had to go back and pull little Gary out of the corner, hug him, and affirm him.

If I wanted to be whole, I had to return and find him. Once I saw that, I was on a rescue mission, determined to find and honor that little kid who had endured so much.

CEC

Although my path was different from Gary's, we both arrived at an acceptance of that inner child.

Here's where I am now. My understanding is that the inner child refers to that emotional part in each of us that is still alive. "It's where our feelings dwell," one friend said. The hurts and wounds our inner child received destroyed our innocence and messed up our childhood. The harm done to the inner child continues to contaminate our adult lives.

By contaminate, I mean abused and messed up our lives. We reacted with feelings of loneliness, abandonment, and self-hatred. Because someone we trusted abused us, trust becomes a painful, difficult issue for us. We each have to return to that childhood and embrace that hurting, wounded child.

For a long time such teaching seemed strange to me. Here's the way I explain it to myself. Many of us who were molested didn't tell anyone. We might have been afraid. Or we assumed our parents didn't care. They wouldn't believe us. Or it may have been incestuous abuse, and we had no one to tell. If we did tell, we might be blamed for causing the abuse.

We survived—with pains and wounds intact, but we did survive. We adapted to our hostile environment. Most of us who truly survived became extremely good at adapting.

Adapting is a good word—and a true one. We learned to protect our wounded souls and to survive in a chaotic, unfriendly environment. One friend said it this way, "We did what we had to do until we could escape our terrible milieu."

By the time I was twelve years old, I had decided to leave home as soon as I finished high school. I wasn't sure how to do it or where I'd go, but I made up my mind. I never told anyone, but within three months after graduating from high school, I was in the United States Navy. Enlisting in the military became my escape route.

As I learned, we can leave our environment. As I also learned, we still carry the hurts and the pains inside us—the wounded child is part of who we are. Like me, many suppressed it, others ignored it, and some acted irresponsibly.

We lived through and endured our childhood, but we carried negative messages inside our heads. We probably couldn't have articulated them, but they were there. Here are two ways I might have said it: "I'm alone—and I have to take care of myself. No one else will do it." The other is, "Nobody really loves me. And why should they?"

GARY

Even after I was confronted by my flashbacks, I was reticent to accept the inner-child concept. I experienced those flashbacks and thought: *That was crazy. Ridiculous. A little me trapped back there?*

After I was able to accept those flashbacks as being part of myself—something I needed to face—it became easier to accept the concept.

I now look back and see that, like Cec, I was so focused on getting out of that environment, I didn't care what I left behind. Of course, I didn't know I was leaving anything behind. I told myself that if I could just get out of this situation or circumstance, things would have to change. I remembered a Jackson Browne song I used to sing often that said no matter how fast we run, we can never seem to get away from ourselves.

In my case, many of my maladaptive coping mechanisms (my continued dysfunctional behavior) stem from denying and running from my past. One of my friends put it this way, "You can get the child out of abuse, but getting the abuse out of the child is a different ball game."

Now I see that part of getting the abuse out of the child means going back and reconnecting with that child. Is he worth it? Does he deserve to be loved and comforted? Does he deserve to be rescued? The answer to all those questions is yes.

I've sometimes said that it might be helpful or easier to think about the inner child as a separate person. Others may find it more helpful to see the little boy as part of themselves, which is really true.

Regardless of how we explain it to ourselves, we're working toward wholeness. We cannot be whole without going back and dealing with what happened to us during those formative and abusive years.

Our purpose is to heal, to become fully self-integrated. We need to thoroughly connect with our past and what happened in order to finally leave the trauma in the past and live as free men.

CEC

As I grappled with that idea of the inner child, one of the things that helped me was to ask myself how I felt about young Cec. I felt sorry for him and wished he had had a safe place to hide. He had no one to defend him or guide him. No one to help him make decisions about which clothes to buy (he was able to pay for them himself) or classes to take in high school.

At about age eleven, he seriously contemplated suicide. One of the things I remember saying was, "No one will miss me." I thought of my six siblings. Three of them were already married with children. "Mom will cry for a day or so, and then she'll forget."

I never felt anger toward my younger self, only pity and compassion. I think that's what opened me up. I saw reaching out to my younger self as a way to touch the unhealed wounds and to embrace that unloved part of myself.

Logically, it still doesn't make sense to me, but emotionally, it worked. For weeks, I had mental images of the little boy; I hugged him tightly, and I talked to him. I told him I loved him. So much of who I am today is because he was a brave little boy, even though he had no one on his side.

One friend told me that for more than three years he wrote daily letters to his inner child. He expressed his sadness. Sometimes he wrote about his anger, his doubts, and trying to be someone the inner child could trust.

"I asked my wounded child to forgive my adult self," he said. At the time that still sounded bizarre to me, but I listened.

He knew I was skeptical, so he said, "You're so hard on yourself, Cec."

I acknowledged that. "I'll bet you were hard on your little child and the teenager inside you."

As he spoke those words, something clicked. That's when I realized that I've always been extremely demanding of myself. In an earlier chapter I've written about feeling lazy and how it propelled me to work, work, work. I thought of the demands I laid on my younger self and carried into adulthood.

Whether it made logical sense or not, I no longer cared. I talked to myself. I spoke to little Cecil, the teenaged self, and the young adult Cec. I'm amazed at how easy it became to talk to those parts of myself.

I've heard people speak of parenting their inner child. I find that word *parenting* difficult to use because parenting was one thing I didn't receive. I've rephrased it to say to those parts of myself, "I want to care for you and love you with the unconditional love you didn't receive." That works for me.

GARY

After almost a year and a half of flashbacks, one day in the midst of EMDR therapy (rapid eye movement therapy involving visualization, designed for victims of trauma), I had a mental image of the little Gary completely at peace, happy, content, and laughing. He looked at the adult me and got a mischievous look on his face. Then he suddenly jumped inside me.

It surprised me, and it felt weird, but I knew what was going on. I had gone back and spent months reconnecting with that little kid. Now a new step in integration had taken place. He had been rescued or "assimilated" into me, as my therapist said.

I'm not done with the inner child. I now believe that when I get triggered, it's the little boy in me who's responding, mostly in fear.

The EMDR therapist worked with me to help me develop a mental image of a safe place that I could go to in my mind when I was triggered and fearful. For me, it was a beautiful meadow. Jesus was there, and it was always peaceful and secure. It was a place where no evil was allowed entrance. When my therapist asked me what little Gary was doing, he was always sitting on Jesus' lap, with a huge smile on his face.

Perhaps this sounds like we're running from reality, but we're actually running toward it and into healing. What happened back then was evil and skewed our lives horribly. Part of us got stuck; we're not whole without integrating that part of ourselves. Those little kids left behind deserve to be retrieved. We need to do anything we can to rescue them.

We can't do that unless we go back into the pain again, not as victims this time, but as victors. We return as warriors on a rescue mission. As we rescue and assimilate our inner child, we become more whole. The more whole we become, the more we can help others do the same.

> My childhood was stolen from me,
> but I can rescue my inner child
> and become whole.

— *32* —

HOW DO I CHANGE WHAT I SAY TO MYSELF?

CEC

I talk to myself all the time. So does everyone else. As simple as that statement sounds, I didn't realize I did that. One friend refers to the constant chatter inside our heads.

The truth is, we constantly think to ourselves, which is probably a little more accurate. That unconscious voice never silences itself. If we're awake, so is the voice.

My late friend Kiki Macabe and I talked about the voices inside our heads. She asked, "What do you keep saying to yourself?"

"I don't know."

"Sure you do," she said and laughed at me. "We're oblivious to the messages, but they're there."

Kiki was absolutely right. Later when I thought more about our conversation, I realized that I had to know *what* I was saying before I could do anything about the messages I gave myself.

Years earlier I had learned the sort of question *not* to ask myself: any question that begins with the word *why*. The human brain will always give us reasons, but even if we know the causes, nothing changes. I recently heard a man say, "Information isn't transformation."

But when I ask myself what those messages are saying, I listen, and I learn about myself. My interior voice speaks the truth to me—as I know it. No matter what I say with my mouth.

Once I understood, I was able to take the next step. I was able to think about the internal, frequently repeated messages. I said certain things to myself so often that I wasn't aware of the messages or their implications.

Here's an example. Once I said to my friend Eddie, "That was a stupid thing for me to say."

Eddie said to me, "Please don't say that. You're not stupid."

"I know, but it was a stupid—"

"Try this. Say to yourself, 'That is not my common form of behavior.' You're saying out loud the messages you keep feeding yourself. Change your message-giver."

I shrugged and said I'd do that. To my amazement, I had to say the new words several times over the next two weeks. About that same time, I began to read about transactional analysis (TA), which was a big thing a generation ago.

The advocates of TA referred to the incessant chatter as the tapes inside our head. I didn't get into TA, but I took one thing from them: I could change the tapes.

I think of the CD that's now playing on my computer as background music. It plays for two minutes short of an hour (I read that on the case), and then it repeats itself. It will go on and on until I stop it. After I've heard the same CD five times in a day, I usually change that CD for something new.

I'm still learning to change the tapes. Whenever I catch myself saying negative things to myself, I stop and give them a positive perspective.

I go by this idea: If I say it to myself, I believe it. If I believe it, I'll behave accordingly.

"I never do anything right" becomes "I often do things correctly."

"I really messed up again" becomes "I failed this time, but I often succeed."

"People are negative" becomes "I have chosen to be positive."

I don't have to keep listening
to the same words inside my head.
I have the power to change them.

I FACE WHAT I COULDN'T ACCEPT.

CEC

In our reflective moments, we can probably list most of life's markers. They're not the same as milestones. For me the difference is that milestones imply achievement and success. We've completed something and moved on to the next event.

By contrast, markers identify those times when we wrestled with issues that profoundly altered our lives. They refer to what I think of as significant events that mark us and shape us into who we are. For us, the molestation is one of the high markers in our lives.

For example, I lived just shy of six years in Kenya, and it was a powerful marker in my life. During those years, I read widely. We had no electricity. Yet I borrowed books from many sources and expanded my knowledge. But more than that, I lived in a foreign culture that taught me invaluable principles that mark me even today.

Suppose we call them the wrestling times—periods where something happened so that life didn't go on as usual. We changed. We grew. And we left pieces of ourselves behind. Sometimes intentionally; most often unconsciously. These markers can be about the events themselves, such as the death of a parent, or a "zero" birthday when we enter into a new decade of life. The deaths of our abusers can also become markers.

Regardless of how the markers come, they represent drastic changes in our lives. For us, dealing with the pain of our childhood assault may be the biggest marker we have to face, even if we're forty or sixty years old.

This also fits into what many refer to as the midlife crisis or male climacteric—a rarely used term that comes from the Greek, *klimacter*, which refers to the rung on a ladder. Some refer to the time as male menopause. Others dispute there is a condition that in any way resembles female menopause. They prefer to speak about a gradual masculine decline.

The usual term is *midlife crisis*. Carl Jung invented the term more than two generations ago, and by the 1980s and '90s, it became fashionable to use the term.

When I first read about Carl Jung's concept of the midlife crisis, it became a powerful source of healing. Regardless of the term we use, many of us hit a point where we change directions in our outlook. With some it may be because of illness or what we call physical decline. Something *does* happen and we have to go back and pick up the discarded or ignored parts of our past.

I explain the midlife crisis this way. We men spend the first half of our lives seeking the tribal goals (success, education, family, love). At midlife those are no longer the issues. It's as if we say:

> I'll probably never rise any higher in this business.
> We raised our kids and we're empty nesters.
> Our marriage is stable.
> I can stop working hard and enjoy this phase of my life.
> Is this what I've spent years working for? Isn't there something more?

Jung assumed the normal life span was seventy years, so he projected about age thirty-five to be when men faced that change of direction. Today, I assume the midlife crisis, male climacteric, or whatever we choose to call it, probably takes place after we've hit forty and maybe as late as our fifties.

The age isn't as important as what happens to us. From my perspective, it's the time when we go back and pick up the lost parts of ourselves. It's like moving from the left side of the brain to the right. It's a shift in the way we view the rest of our life span.

I wanted to insert this chapter because a large number of men with whom I've spoken have begun their healing journey after the age of forty.

I write that while recognizing that some men, aware of their abuse, struggled from childhood. Some fight with the issues in their teens or early twenties.

But in this chapter, I'm referring to those men like Gary and me who lived in denial or pushed away any thoughts of being affected by abuse. Then something happened. Usually memories start to return or we say, "Uncle Joe molested me, and it's time to deal with it." That's when most of us begin the healing journey. I was fifty-one years old when my memories seeped back into my consciousness and I remembered my abuse. Gary was in his mid forties.

As I read testimonies of other men, many of them began dealing with their past abuse around the same age. Perhaps it's because once we hit midlife, we have less to protect. We're safer. We've dealt with the tribal goals.

To apply Jung's concept, we start picking up those pieces. We face what we didn't deal with earlier in life. At one point, I wondered why I waited so long. But almost as quickly as I asked, I knew.

I began when I did because it was exactly the right time for me to focus on that phase of my life. I have an inner wisdom (which I believe is often God's way to speak to me) that lets me know that I'm safe and that I'm ready.

If we start too soon, we give up in fear or decide it's not worth the pain. The grief is too much for us to handle if we begin prematurely.

I liken it to teaching children to read. A few children may be ready to read at age five, but that's not generally true. Educational theorists know that the average child is ready to read at about age six. It's not just the ability to grasp letters and words, but there are other skills that they have to master such as eye-hand coordination and the ability to move into conceptual thinking.

GARY

We have to be ready to engage in this journey.

At first, I thought I was a real weirdo. I grew up with no memory of certain events—nothing—until the flashbacks started in my mid forties. About that time I read *The Wounded Heart* by Dan Allender, and it was exactly what I needed then.

The most significant thing Allender did for me was to point out that it's common for men abused by family members in early childhood (as I was from ages four to six) to have no memory of the events until their forties, when flashbacks often occur.

"He's writing about me!" I shouted to myself. "That's exactly my story." Even though my counselor had assured me I wasn't crazy, occasionally I still wondered.

"You're not crazy." I can still hear his voice inside my head. "But you were raised in an extremely crazy environment."

I was also living in Washington State at the time, far away from Texas where I grew up and where the abuse took place (where one of my abusers still lived). I was already seeing a counselor for anxiety issues. The stage was set and the drama was ready to begin. The curtain went up, and revelations of my childhood sneaked out of the hidden areas of my heart and came on stage.

In midlife, I was discovering more of where I came from and understanding the reasons I thought and behaved the way I did.

As the flashbacks continued, it was evident I had an immense amount of "stuff" to work through. I had no idea what it was going to mean or who I was going to become.

My life was in crisis mode—a prolonged crisis that lasted several years. But I knew I had not asked for the abusive treatment and hadn't wanted it. The adults came to me when I was young, weak, and vulnerable.

Now I grasped what had really happened—not everything but enough that I knew the truth about my childhood. And I knew the molestation was real. Perhaps I could have continued to deny it, but I wanted inner peace so badly, I refused to return to living a life of ignorance or denial.

It was unsettling—and not just for me. My family was profoundly affected by what I was going through. My adopted daughters were also survivors, and my flashbacks triggered their repressed memories. They began having flashbacks as well. It was a difficult time. The best thing I could do for my family was to work on me and heal.

I prayed often and fervently during that time. I quoted the words of Paul: "For I can do everything through Christ, who gives me strength" (Philippians 4:13).

Some would label my experience a midlife crisis, and that's all right. It was probably that, but it was more. It was a midlife correction. And it fit within the usual definition of pondering where I'd been, evaluating where I wanted to go, and deciding if I was willing to make the changes.

I thank God for my midlife correction.

CEC

What if we thought of picking up the pieces as our midlife transformation? What if we said, "This is my chance to be different"? This frees us to change careers, or to retire and spend the rest of our lives serving humanity.

This is a time to "become who we were meant to be." Or as one friend said, "We can become who we once dreamed of being." But it's also a time of crisis, even though a good crisis.

And for many of us, it's the time when we become aware of our painful past. Even if we didn't forget, we lived with our shame as we tried to cope, and often felt as if we were frauds. We decide it's time to pull off our masks or to rid ourselves of our false self-images.

At last we have the motivation to move into freedom and out of our bondage. The opportunity comes when we're ready to pick up those pieces.

We have the motivation: the yearning to be a whole person. My theory is that we all have a basic, inner need that pushes us toward yearning to feel like a whole person. We want to get rid of the sham and the pretenses. We throw aside our masks and refuse to hide from our pain. We also have pain—but we're stronger now. And wiser. We can cope and overcome. The stabbing, persistent hurts remind us that we were abused and we need to do something to heal those gaping wounds. The inner torture tells us we'll never be happy until we do. We will not settle until we can say, "I'm healed."

It may start with a time of tears (as it did for me) or restlessness. It's a gnawing inside that insists we have to do something. Or we can resist— and many do that. Some may see it as easier (perhaps safer) to hold tight and close our eyes. Denial works—but it leads to greater pain, anxiety, and depression.

When we face the turmoil and confusion and say, "I can't go on like this," we're ready for transformation. The pain of staying the same has become greater than the pain of changing.

For those of us who have faced our abuse (and possibly our abusers), we can look back and see it as the most transforming period of our life. As I wrote those words, I thought of how the writer of Hebrews refers to divine chastisement or discipline: "No discipline is enjoyable while it is happening—it's painful! But afterward there will be a peaceful harvest of right living for those who are trained in this way. So take a new grip with your tired hands and strengthen your weak knees. Mark out a straight path for your feet so that those who are weak and lame will not fall but become strong" (Hebrews 12:11–13).

That's how I envision this time of picking up the pieces. Painful. Feelings of shame and inadequacy slapped at us. We were tempted to retreat into a state of powerlessness. But even in the confusion and turmoil, we had a quiet assurance that we would eventually experience freedom. Sometimes discouraged, we continued going forward. We weren't sure who we were or who we were becoming, but we kept on. For me, some days the pain became so intense that I wondered if I truly wanted healing.

I kept on.

Now, years later, I'm different. Happier. More at peace. I think of the words of Walt Kelly's comic character Pogo, who said, "We have met the enemy and he is us." I've met the "enemy," that is, the dreaded parts of myself. And that enemy has become a person I love. He was bruised and seriously wounded by someone else, but he's almost whole now.

GARY

At times the pain was so great that I felt completely surrounded by darkness.

I slogged through mud two feet deep, and no matter how hard I pushed forward, I could only encounter more ugliness. I had never been in such a desperate situation. The terrain was unfamiliar, and I wondered if I would ever find my way into the light.

I'm grateful for my support team (a counselor, my family, Cec, and a support group at church), which assured me I was on the right path and urged me to keep on slogging.

It was exhausting, but the more I trudged forward, the easier the slogging became. After a while, the mud seemed only a foot deep and not quite as bad as it had been; or perhaps I had grown stronger.

Although it seemed as if my life was in pieces, in reality, it was like working a complicated jigsaw puzzle. At first the sheer number of pieces overwhelmed me. But as I stayed at it, made connections, and fitted things together, the intended design of the puzzle began to emerge. I still have a few missing pieces, and maybe they're forever lost, but I have enough to know what I'm doing. As each piece snaps into its proper place, I realize that my life is taking on its true and intended shape. I still have a few pieces to pick up, but I know I'm nearing the end of the great puzzle.

To change the metaphor, once I understood where I really had been, I could decide where I wanted to go. I now had the necessary map to guide me so I could move forward. I didn't know if I was doing it correctly, and at times I wondered if I had misread my map. But I kept going and continued to focus on forward movement.

CEC

I don't want to give the impression that facing our pain is simply taking one step forward after another, because it doesn't work that way. We take a few steps, stumble, perhaps fall backward, but we get back up—sometimes slowly—and take a few more steps.

It's not an easy journey, but it's the right journey. It's the only road that leads to health and inner peace. We make mistakes and blunder, but we also learn to forgive and to feel more kindly toward our wounded selves.

"Sometimes in my emotional travels I felt as if I were standing still," Gary says. "Maybe I was. I needed to rest, revive myself, and marshal the strength for the next forward phase.

"I wondered how many steps there were yet ahead of me. I was thinking about healing as a destination, rather than being thankful for the journey. Once I accepted that I was on a lifelong trip, I was able to relax more and be kinder to myself along the way."

✦   ✦   ✦

Years ago a male survivor told me that he wrote in his journal exactly how he felt about his life, career, marriage, family, and everything he could bring to the surface. "I especially wanted to put in words every negativity in my life."

He did that so he could look back later and say to himself, "That's who I used to be. That's not who I am now."

Claudia Black wrote a book called *It's Never Too Late to Have a Happy Childhood*. In one sense that expresses us. We're reclaiming a stolen childhood. We're picking up the pieces of the past so we can be full and complete.

"Picking up all those pieces is hard work," Gary says. "I can view it as a chore, or I can express it as a joy. There are times it is so painful that I don't want to even touch another piece. But that passes, and I'm soon back to picking up pieces and connecting them to other parts of my life."

We keep picking up the pieces. As we do so, the true picture emerges. By focusing on those seemingly small pieces, we realize they are major parts of the pattern.

To those still staring at a confusion of shapes and colors, don't quit.

Keep working because your life picture will begin to make sense. You will heal and become more whole, more your true, lovable, wonderful self.

I can't change the past,
but I can pick up the painful pieces of my past
and become whole.

— 34 —

WHAT DO I WANT?

CEC

In early 2011, I invited Angie Williams and Tom Scales, who head VOICE Today, to have lunch with me. Tom suggested we eat at a Chinese restaurant, and I agreed.

The problem was, I didn't want to eat Chinese. Why didn't I say so when Tom suggested it? I don't know.

"I don't know what I want," I said to myself. Twenty years after I began my healing process, it wasn't that I always acquiesced to everyone. But I realized from that simple experience that I often didn't know what I wanted.

My role had been to find out what others wanted and do what I could for them. My years as a missionary and as a pastor certainly reinforced that idea. I suppose it's a form of people pleasing—but it's certainly not anything I had sensed about myself before.

I was aware that when it came to important issues, I was able to stand up for myself. But the question about what I wanted just for myself seemed different. And that simple difference was another leaf off the artichoke—another way to help me grasp a little more truth in my life.

For a couple of days, I struggled over the matter of the restaurant choice. "It's so silly," I told myself. "It's only one meal at one restaurant." And it was, but I grasped that the one meal represented more than a single choice.

"What do I want?" I asked myself. "What do I really want?" In quizzing myself, it wasn't just about whether to go Chinese. I sensed it tapped into a deeper issue.

"What do I want?" I didn't know. Then the light flashed inside my

— 246 —

head. Regardless of what I questioned—my career, buying clothes, or seeing a film—too often I didn't know what Cec Murphey desired. Too often I said yes to others when inside, something whispered no. It was easier to placate than to disagree.

I don't remember if I handled the restaurant issue by phone or e-mail, but I finally was able to say, "I'd prefer Mexican." Tom immediately suggested a good place in his area.

When we met, I was embarrassed and apologized for being indecisive, and they were both gracious. I also felt ashamed (I was good at relying on *that* emotion). It was also a liberating moment.

I had broken yet another chain of enslavement—small as it may have seemed. But it didn't feel minor. It felt like a magnificent achievement.

*   *   *

The way I slept with my pillow has helped me see my progress. For as long as I can remember, I've slept on my stomach with both arms hugging my pillow tightly. That's just the way it was, and I didn't think about it. I've also had a great need to feel loved for myself and not for what I do.

A couple of years ago I realized that when I slept, both my hands were still under the pillow, but they were more relaxed. And this was happening as I was becoming less needy for love and acceptance. I now truly believe I am loved, and earlier this year I realized that my arms are at my sides when I drift off to sleep, not hugging the pillow at all. This change wasn't a conscious effort on my part, and that made it even more significant to me.

I realized that the more I admitted to myself what I wanted, asked for it, and assumed I had the right to choose, the better I felt about myself. My sleeping position and the position of my pillow was just one way I could view my needs and my progress in having those needs met.

GARY

I can relate to what Cec writes above. Several years ago my counselor asked, "What do *you* want?"

I just sat there, stupefied. It's as if that was a completely foreign concept. Actually, it *was* a completely foreign concept. In some ways, it's still strange and uncomfortable.

I get up in the morning thinking about what I should do, what I have to do. And I begin to do it. That's been my pattern for as long as I can remember. Like Cec, the decision about what I'd do on any given day often came down to what I thought others wanted me to do or needed from me. As I've mentioned elsewhere in this book, people pleasing was my way to try to control my surroundings to minimize further abuse. Pleasing others became so ingrained, I didn't realize my choices were really *my* choices.

The saddest fact is that people pleasing is an impossible task. It has no end except failure. Because I made myself responsible for pleasing others, I held myself responsible when they weren't pleased. And often, they held me responsible too. It was a vicious, never-ending cycle. Exhausting.

I've realized that when I'm engaged in people pleasing, I've actually given them control over me. I end up living as a shadow instead of as myself.

What do I want? That's a big, big question I still have trouble answering. But at least I'm thinking about it and slowly, often tentatively, saying, "I want . . ." or "I'd like to . . ."

Another thing that I do is apologize and explain myself a lot. If I'm asked a question, I'll launch into a thorough explanation. It's as if I'm covering every possible aspect, making sure I hit all the possible pieces of information the other person might be searching for. Again, people pleasing—born out of my basic lack of safety.

In childhood, it didn't seem to matter what I wanted. It was what *they* wanted that counted. And they took what they wanted, whether I wanted to give it or not. The message was clear. What I wanted was immaterial.

I wouldn't have said it this way, but I've heard people say, "The world is out to get me." I understand that feeling. I wore myself out trying to figure out what everyone else wanted and giving them enough to keep them from coming for more. But they always came for more anyway. It was as if I didn't exist separately from other people.

When I first asked myself honestly and truly, "What do I want?" the question terrified me. Would they laugh at me if I told them? Would they ignore what I wanted? Would my wishes inconvenience them or (worse) stop them from getting what they wanted?

No one said it, but on some unconscious level, I believed the needs and desires of others were more important than my own. It was easier and certainly safer to deny my desires and stay on the people-pleasing treadmill.

As I've worked on this, I realize I haven't been loving toward myself or toward the people around me by trying to please others while being detached from my own desires. That form of behavior is hiding from life.

I'm not my true and total self when I do that. I want to bring all of myself into the interaction. I can truly love others only if I'm being me. How can I be me if I'm not in touch with what I want?

I sat down and thought, "What do I want?" Here is what I came up with:

> I want a close, trusting relationship with Jesus Christ.
> I want to be an excellent father. I want to be a good example to my daughters.
> I want close, trusting relationships with other people. I want Jesus to live through me. I want my life here to really count.
> I want friends, good friends. I want to be a good friend. I want to feel connected.
> I want to feel safe (which comes from knowing and believing I'm safe).
> I want to live with faith and courage. I want to be tenaciously faithful, honorable, a man of integrity.

I want to learn to rejoice and consider it pure joy when trials
and difficulties come.
I want to be a person who eats problems for breakfast.
I want to heal. I want to grow. I want to love being challenged
more than being comfortable.

In looking back over this list, there seem to be no specific, measurable goals—such as I want to publish five books over the next five years. The things I hunger for the most are relational and character-oriented. That makes them somewhat unpredictable, moving targets. What I really want seems to have to do with knowing who I really am and living with that knowledge.

As I learn to be more and more of who I am, what I want in the small things of daily life should become more evident. But I'm betting that works both ways. As I identify simply "What do I want?" in the midst of daily life, the more I will be living as myself.

What do I really want?
It's a question I'm learning to answer for myself.
As I face my desires, I continue to heal.

35

WHAT DO I GIVE TO OTHERS?

CEC

"Why do you hug so intensely?" the man asked.

I stared at him, not comprehending what he asked. "I don't know," I said.

I spoke the truth.

Yet the memory of that experience stayed with me. I was one of about fifty men who did a three-day retreat in the Sawtooth Mountains of Idaho. The conference was to help men build healthy intimacy with each other.

About a month later, I was in the shower, my mind free floating, and a thought struck me. I grabbed a towel and rushed into the bedroom and yelled to my wife. "My mother wasn't warm and affectionate! I was a warm person."

Shirley stared at me for a moment before she said calmly, "She was one of the coldest women I know."

"You never said anything—"

"You used to talk about how loving she was, and I didn't want to spoil anything," she said.

As I went back to the bathroom to dry off, I kept thinking about that. In graduate school, one of my professors asked me about my parents. "My mother was warm and emotional. My dad was cool and quiet." Strange that I remember that conversation. Perhaps it's because even though I believed what I said, some deeper, inner wisdom knew it wasn't true.

What is true is that I am a warm, caring person. That's not to brag but only to point out something I clearly know and have accepted about myself.

Over the past couple of years, I've thought about that from time to time. Because of my need to be cared about, to yearn for parental affection but not receive it, I sought acceptance and affirmation elsewhere. For example, school was a marvelous place for me because I realized that the teachers liked me and gave me the kind of encouragement I didn't receive from my parents.

Gary admits that he, too, gives what he wants to receive. He claims touch as one of his "love languages." He responds when others verbally affirm him.

How does he react? "I go around touching people. And I tend to tell people the good I see in them. I believe we all tend to love others in the ways we want to be loved."

Gary also admits that he didn't see that response of giving what he wanted to receive as his motivation. But he says, "That explains to me why I do it."

✦   ✦   ✦

I've been a full-time writer since 1984, and over the years I've ghost-written or collaborated on many autobiographies. About a decade ago, I realized that there are certain stories that grab me. I love writing about the underdogs—those who make it by overcoming the odds. I like working with what some call the "invulnerables." They're the people who survive, succeed, and live fulfilled lives despite poverty, hardship, rejection, and even abuse.

Ben Carson, for whom I wrote *Gifted Hands*, is probably the best example. He was virtually illiterate in fifth grade. His single mother told him to go to the library and check out two books every week and write book reports. He did exactly what she told him.

Over the next six years, he became a top student. Before he graduated from high school, Ben received a full scholarship to Yale University.

For the past quarter century, Ben Carson, at the Johns Hopkins Hospital, has been one of the world's leading pediatric neurosurgeons.

I've done books about other people like him, and I find deep satisfaction in telling their stories in print. They appeal to me because, in a sense, they're my story as well. Our situations were different, but they all had that common element of feeling like the underdog. I identify with them.

It's easy and natural for me to reach out to the hurting. During my school years, I befriended many lonely, ignored kids. I never asked myself the reason. I just did it.

As an adult, I've always worked in the helping professions. When I taught sixth grade in a Chicago suburb, we had six classrooms. I asked for the kids with the lowest grades and IQ scores, and the other teachers were delighted to let me take them to my classroom. Not one of them was then reading at grade level.

All that year I worked with those children and stressed the basics of reading and spelling. Every day, we did arithmetic story problems. We did only the minimum of art, science, and social studies. I pushed them to learn, and most of them were able to read at sixth-grade level by the end of the year.

I became a pastor—again I turned to a helping-where-people-hurt profession.

Now I understand that I was unconsciously responding to my own need.

Although I didn't perceive this fact for years, I sought love by giving love. I gave what I wanted to receive.

I left the professional pastorate in 1984, but my wife insists that I'm still a pastor to people who hurt.

GARY

I have also loved the underdog, whether in the movies, on the basketball court, in the classroom, or in general life situations.

I saw myself as small, an underdog, even though I performed at the top of almost everything I did. Deep down, I knew differently.

I wanted to serve people. I was pre-med in college. I set my sights on pediatrics until I sensed God changing that direction. I ended up at seminary and in student ministry. After seminary, I served as a missionary church-planter in Japan, then as a pastor for the next seventeen years. I also worked in the hospitality industry for two years. I now realize there was one consistent theme—serving people.

Even as a child, I wanted to help others. I was drawn to hurting individuals. Those with big needs seemed to find me.

Some might say that my need to be loved drives me in that, through my serving and helping others, I'm looking for the love that I didn't get in childhood. That's true. I believe God used my need to enable me to meet the needs of other people. And that's probably the way it works with most of us.

CEC

Here's one additional lesson I learned. *If I give to others what I wish to receive from them, I am blessed or edified* (or choose your own adjective) *by my actions.* Something mystical and powerful transpires over time.

"When I make a visit to a hospice patient or family," Gary says, "I usually walk away blessed and encouraged. As I genuinely affirm another person, listen to the words of his or her heart (even if unspoken), or hug a nursing-home resident who can't hug me back, I find myself smiling. Maybe it's part of letting God meet my biggest needs by using me to meet the needs of others."

Or as Jesus said in what became known as the Golden Rule: "Do to others whatever you would like them to do to you" (Matthew 7:12a).

I find it strange that I wasn't aware of what I was doing. As I look at it now, it seems obvious. For the past few years, I've tried to observe what I give to others. For example, while I don't do it perfectly (which I readily admit), I've learned to listen to people in their pain. That's certainly a reminder to me that, in childhood, I had no one to listen to me.

I also try to help other writers achieve success and realize how little help I received during most of my life.

> I give to others what I want to receive.
> That's part of my quest for wholeness.

36

HOW DO I COMPLETE THE CIRCLE?

CEC

A few years ago I became fascinated with what people called "The Hero's Journey." We who are survivors have our own version, yet it's not altogether different. Instead of calling it the hero's journey, I'm more comfortable with calling it "completing the circle."

The experts tell the story several ways, but it always involves returning to the place we started—now as experienced, wiser individuals. The more I understand myself and the effects of the abuse, the more I identify with the concept of completing the circle.

Although there are variations to the story and some make it into two-dozen steps, I want to give it in a simple form. The call to adventure starts the process. Often when the call is given, the future hero refuses to obey. He may be afraid, feel inadequate, not like the assignment, or have any of many excuses. I think of Gideon in the Old Testament. He was of the smallest clan and claimed to be the youngest in the family (see Judges 6:15). That's a typical reaction. Moses argued with God and poured out his inability, but God didn't listen (see Exodus 3:7–14).

The called one has no intention of becoming a hero, even if he has some idea about the end or purpose of the adventure. Again, Gideon knew God wanted him to defeat the Midianites. In his excuse, he was probably also afraid, even though the summons came with these words, "Mighty hero, the LORD is with you!" (Judges 6:12b).

The man certainly didn't see himself as a hero, but God did.

Gideon also countered by asking why God had stopped delivering his people. The angel (or messenger) of the Lord brushes aside these words. "I will be with you. And you will destroy the Midianites as if you were fighting against one man" (v. 16).

God had to show Gideon signs until the reluctant deliverer took on the challenge. Again, that's in the same vein as most of the hero stories—circumstances or divine action force him out of his old way of life, and he begins his journey.

In the Bible, the story of Jonah depicts that same struggle, although we don't get a happy conclusion to his story. God commands the prophet to go to Nineveh, and he refuses. He tries to run away and gets on a ship. A storm ensues, and the sailors throw him overboard.

Jonah finally and reluctantly does the task assigned to him, although even to the end of the book, he's still resentful.

Perhaps a better example is Moses. God tells him that he'll deliver the people of Israel, but after he kills a man, Moses, in fear, flees to the land of Midian. After a forty-year stay, Moses hears God through the burning bush. Moses doesn't want the task. "Send someone else to do it," he says. But God doesn't waver. This is Moses' destiny. The reluctant leader returns to Egypt so he can begin to travel the circle.

Even King Saul begins his life by hiding when they want to crown him king. He doesn't want the journey. But the hero's response doesn't matter. The call to adventure is the circle's starting point in the hero's life, whether he knows it or not.

Once the journey begins, it's never easy. The hero faces terrible battles and ordeals. Often the hero fails in those tests. Remember Moses' anger when he struck the rock twice, after God told him to speak to it? Jonah certainly failed. King Saul failed early and never recovered.

The ordeals are important because they are the means of transformation for the reluctant hero. By enduring (and sometimes failing), the hero continues on his voyage. But as he moves on, he changes, and when he completes the circle, he won't be like the naive young man who left in fear.

That's the important part to emphasize. He changes because of what he goes through, and the result is not just that he's stronger and defeats his enemies, but something more. The hero becomes more compassionate and tolerant of others who fail.

Finally, the hero completes the circle—he returns home. The true hero retains the wisdom he gained on his quest and integrates it into his life. This is where he says, "It has been worth the journey."

A learned philosopher lectured about the end of the hero's journey and said, "He now has the freedom to enjoy his life. He has learned to live in the present without anticipating the future and not regretting the past." He has become a role model without being aware of what he's done.

Those of us who have lived through our pain, survived, and grown from the experience are certainly heroes who are completing the circle. We may not want to think of ourselves as heroes, but we are.

Consider it this way. As children we were violated and lost our ability to trust. We were severely wounded, and some of us became suicidal. We may have hid like Saul or run away like Moses. My response was to run away—that's what amnesia amounts to—denying the trauma and running away by "forgetting."

Jonah is an angry man, and there's no evidence he lost his anger. And without losing the anger, he can't complete the circle. Like King Saul before him, he fails in his journey.

For us, the abuse survivors, as we heal, we relearn to trust and accept ourselves and our pain. We reach out to others and comfort them. (After all, that's what heroes do.)

The healing process is like making a full circle: the hero's journey brings him home. He remains aware of the past and doesn't flinch from facing who he was, but he's strong because of who he is to become.

We not-quite-healed survivors are the heroes in our own stories. The journey home enables us to break the emotional paralysis with which our perpetrators ensnared us. We speak out and break the conspiracy of silence. We become advocates for those who feel lost and still hurt.

GARY

What if this life is not meant to be smooth? What if this life is about coming to the end of our own abilities and our own maladaptive strategies for running from our pain, and turning to God?

The Bible is full of people stories. Some accepted God's call, albeit reluctantly, and lived out their destiny. Others couldn't seem to escape the snare of their pain and then failed.

The contrast between Peter and Judas comes to mind. In the twelve or so hours leading up to the crucifixion, both men betrayed Jesus. Judas became the inside informant, took cash, and handed Jesus over to the authorities.

By contrast, Peter, out of fear and to protect himself, denied three times that he knew Jesus.

After Judas realized the Romans had condemned Jesus to death, he couldn't live with the consequences of his actions. He committed suicide. Peter, although emotionally devastated by his own betrayal, accepted forgiveness.

No wonder Peter became the leader of the early church. The strong-willed, be-in-control, often-tell-Jesus-what-to-do fisherman became a humble and bold witness for Christ.

That's another hero story. Peter refused to give in to his past. He chose to embrace his God-given destiny. He completed the circle.

CEC

"That sounds nice," someone might say to me, and I understand that response. As a serious Christian, I'll try it another way. I was violated and wounded. Even though I didn't know it, even then the "call" was there.

I ran from my pain until I was fifty-one years old. That's when the transformation began to take place. (I was a Christian long before that, but for this, I refer to the healing transformation that occurs as we trudge forward and defeat the painful, horrendous abuse we suffered.)

How do I know I'm home? Simple. I've grown through the years. I've become more self-accepting and self-affirming. But that's not all. As I embrace myself, a strange thing happens: I'm able to embrace others who struggle with their trauma and turmoil. Jesus commanded us to love our neighbors in the same way we love ourselves. (The implication is that we first love ourselves.) As I grow in loving myself, it spills over into love for others.

But it's even more than that.

I am the hero in my life, and so are others who survive and enjoy their lives. We've been to the depths of emotional hell; we've experienced rejection and an amazing amount of agony. All of us have failed at some point, but we didn't give up because of our weak moments. Even when we felt depressed or discouraged, we kept on. We didn't just survive; we endured and overcame our pain, our self-pity, our anger, and we forgave those who sinned against us.

We live the truth of Romans 8:28–29. I hesitate to quote those verses because they are misused in so many ways. I often hear people try to comfort others in their pain and loss with verse 28: "And we know that God causes everything to work together for the good of those who love God and are called according to his purpose for them." And they stop.

As they bandy the verse around, it's similar to the words of Friedrich Nietzsche: "What doesn't kill us makes us stronger." I agree with those words, but it's more than that—more than knowing God works for our good. In fact, it's misleading to quote only those words, because they're only giving part of the meaning of the passage.

Without quoting verse 29, we miss the point of the journey and the hardships. The apostle Paul added, ". . . and he chose them to become like his Son."

Now we get it. The purpose and fulfillment of the circle is to "be conformed to the image of his Son."

That's why our suffering has purpose and meaning. God is leading us and teaching us to be more like Jesus Christ.

And what does the Bible say about *the prototype*, Jesus himself? "Even though Jesus was God's Son, he learned obedience from the things he suffered" (Hebrews 5:8).

Are we better than Jesus? Don't we learn the same way?

As we look back on our suffering and our pain (and I never want to minimize that), we can see that God had a purpose in it. Depending on our theological position, we can say God allowed those things, or we can state that God sent those horrible things into our lives.

Some will strongly object to that last phrase, even though it's my theological position. I can't believe our troubles caught God by surprise. To "allow" seems weak to me or that God had to adapt to circumstances outside his domain. I believe that, horrendous as our experiences have been, there is an ultimate purpose. God planned for us to start *and to complete the circle.*

How else can we comfort and encourage others? Can we talk about the pain that we haven't experienced? I have the "street creds" because I was victimized, survived, and have grown through my pain, so I can help others as they complete their own heroic circle.

✦   ✦   ✦

In my pastoral days before I dealt with my abuse, our church sponsored an Alcoholics Anonymous group. Occasionally I sat in on their meetings. They welcomed me even though alcohol has never had a strong appeal to me.

One man named Johnny said to me, and he didn't mean it unkindly, "You can't really understand us. You haven't been controlled by an addiction. You don't know the pain and the torment we've suffered and some of us still do."

I didn't argue with him, although I wasn't sure I agreed.

But now I do.

As I speak to others about my abuse, many of them don't grasp what we went through. How could they? They can't comprehend why some of us contemplated or attempted suicide. They can't grasp the torture of feeling useless. Worthless. Like spoiled goods. If they came from a loving family, how could they understand what it's like to feel unwanted and unloved? I don't condemn or judge them for not understanding.

What I do know is that my heart is much bigger and softer because of my painful childhood. I never, never, never want any child to go through what Gary and I and thousands, perhaps millions, of other men endured. But I also believe that, by completing the circle, we have been enabled by God to transform our pain into healing balm for others.

In the hero's journey, transformation is an absolutely essential part of making him the hero. Until he's been tested, failed, risen, and kept going, he's not the hero.

I want to point to two other verses that have been God's encouragement to me. They're also often quoted carelessly. But I quote them because of the power of their meaning. Paul wrote to the Corinthians, "God is our merciful Father and the source of all comfort. He comforts us in all our troubles so that we can comfort others. When they are troubled, we will be able to give them the same comfort God has given us" (2 Corinthians 1:3b–4).

The apostle went on to write, "For the more we suffer for Christ, the more God will shower us with his comfort through Christ. Even when we are weighted down with troubles, it is for your comfort and salvation! For when we ourselves are comforted, we will certainly comfort you" (vv. 5–6a).

Here's how I see this completed circle. We suffered, we found help (and are still receiving it), but that is not the end of our journey as heroes. It's not only a self-centered journey where we become transformed by our suffering. Most people can grasp that. But what do we do *after* our transformation?

If we fully complete the circle, we give to others what we have received. We complete the circle by helping other survivors complete their circles.

✦ ✦ ✦

I stress the passing on of responsibility because it's God's will for each of us heroes. But I also do it because of my observations.

For a decade I belonged to something called the "men's movement." I learned a great deal from them and received a great deal of help. But I also observed that many hurting, pain-filled men came to us. We ministered to them, and we shared their joy and excitement as they were transformed from victims and emotional outcasts into peaceful and joyous individuals.

Then they left us.

They had received healing, and that was their purpose in coming. It saddened me that they didn't stay with us and become the wounded healers—the true heroes. They didn't fully complete the circle. They got better, and I can always rejoice in their personal victory. I wish they had used their victories to help other hurting men.

They received immense encouragement, brotherly affection, and attention from us. We accepted them when they didn't know how to accept themselves.

Yet they left.

We victims want help, healing, and encouragement to become the victors. As victors, it is our responsibility and honor to stand against this great evil of sexual abuse. We need to begin to live like the compassionate warriors, the wounded healers, that God wants us to be.

✦   ✦   ✦

Where does our responsibility lie? Isn't there a principle in life that says if we give, we also receive? The more freely we open ourselves to others, the more grace, joy, and strength God gives us.

Luke 6:38 records these words of Jesus: "Give, and you will receive. Your gift will return to you in full—pressed down, shaken together to make room for more, running over, and poured into your lap. The amount you give will determine the amount you get back."

The principle isn't just about giving money, but it's about giving of ourselves to bring healing to others. When we unflinchingly open ourselves by telling our stories, by inspiring others, and by reminding them that they, too, can have victory, that's the proof that we've completed the circle.

> When I give of myself to those in pain,
> I fulfill my calling as God's hero.
> I complete the circle.

37

HOW WILL I BE DIFFERENT?

CEC

If we move forward, we change. Even if the changes are minimal, they're a beginning. We don't remain who we were or who we thought we were.

"If I become different, will I like who I am? Will I like the new me?" That's a question I used to ask myself. I wish I could have shouted, "Yes, I like the new me," but I didn't know.

One day I thought about how much I had talked to my wife about my day-to-day progress. As a full-time writer, I worked at home, and Shirley worked for a publishing house. A few minutes after five in the afternoon, she arrived at home and I would have a pot of tea for us. We sat and talked.

I want to make it clear that Shirley never complained about listening. But I assumed she must have grown weary of hearing reports each day. I felt I whined and sounded like a self-pitying weakling (and I've learned that other men have felt the same way).

For at least a year, I did have almost daily insights or fragments of memories returned, or I put together odd pieces of information.

"I want you to keep listening to me," I said. "If you don't, after I'm healed, we'll still be married, but you won't know me."

Shirley's eyes flickered with shock and then pain before she took my hand. "I want to hear everything you tell me."

Looking back, I'm sure I knew that. But I was on a perilous journey and feeling extremely unsure of myself. I wish I had been honest enough to say, "Please tell me that you'll continue on the journey with me."

Part of the reason for my insecurity, I assume, was because I knew other men whose wives or girlfriends had left them. One woman told her husband before she moved out, "I have enough problems; I can't add yours to mine." She added, "I married you because I thought you were strong and I needed someone to help me."

Her response sounds heartless—and I don't know the circumstances—but her response is one many of us quite naturally fear. What if the other person can't handle my emotional and spiritual baggage? Will my problems overwhelm the person I love?

That's part of the risk we take if we want to be whole and be true to ourselves.

In my case, divorce wasn't an issue, but I feared abandonment nonetheless—emotional abandonment. Why wouldn't I? The people I had most trusted in childhood had ignored me, pushed me away, and deserted me. Shirley wasn't one of my parents, but she was the person most important to me.

Shirley gave me the right answer—the answer I needed—the assurance that she was with me.

Those of us who ask the question recognize that it involves fear. A lot of fear. It goes back to our pain-smeared past. But the question also refers to our future.

If I was going to be whole (or healthier) I knew I had to focus on my anger. There was a lot of it, hidden deep inside me. Most of the time, as the good boy and the helper, I was able to repress it, but sometimes it slipped out.

How would I handle anger if I gave in to my emotions? We can ask the question in many ways. Anger was my major concern. For others it could be any number of things.

For at least two weeks I struggled with opening myself to the heated flames inside me. I was afraid that no one would love me. If they truly knew my heart, everyone would abandon me. That's why I needed Shirley's assurance of being there for me.

That sounds obvious to me now, but it was one of those powerful, breakthrough moments in my healing. I had been so fearful of facing my inner demons that I didn't confront them.

"I can face them now," I told myself. "I'm an adult. I'm not a kid who is powerless. I don't have to worry about what it would mean to be shunned by every person I love."

The next morning I began to pray, "God, help me feel my feelings. Help me face my neediness."

In retrospect, I can say that I had doubts, but I had begun to face other emotions and with similar results. The hidden emotions are deceitful frauds. They have power over us as long as we tremble and refuse to face them. But once we open the door and let them come out, they're never as awful as we assumed they would be.

◆   ◆   ◆

It's easier to show this when I face my anger. I had worried that if I faced my feelings, I'd become violent. My friend David helped me realize that I wouldn't do anything like that.

Did I have a temper? Of course.

Did I get angry? Certainly.

Did I go on a rampage? No. That didn't happen to me, yet I was afraid that I'd "go postal" and tear up or destroy anything in my path. It hasn't happened; it won't happen.

I have become different, and Shirley has stayed at my side through the years. So has my friend David. They have been my support.

But there's something even more important than staring down the threat of my unreleased emotions.

It's the result. For as long as I kept being pulled back into my childhood, I didn't feel good about myself. I felt inferior, ashamed, insecure— and I could easily include most of the other negative emotions other men face. But once I faced the demons of my past, I was free from the past.

I like being who I am. I honestly, truly enjoy my life.

I am becoming different.
And I like the new me.

38

WHEN I'M HEALED, WHO WILL I BE?

CEC

One of the questions that troubled me is this: "After I'm whole, who will I be?"

Many men dread asking that question because they're unable to project their imaginations that far into the future. "I can hardly make it each day," Jerry Gear said. "How can I look toward the future?"

"Because that's your goal," I answered. "That's why we strive to change."

I didn't think those were particularly wise words, and they came out before I pondered the question. But in retrospect, I think it was a good response.

Jerry frowned, and then he smiled. "I've been so slammed and pummeled, I hadn't thought about what will happen later. But it's the final end that's more important than what I go through now."

Before I could add anything, Jerry said, "It's like being a Christian, isn't it? No matter how bad things seem, we know we have a wonderful, glorious future ahead."

Afterward I thought about Jerry's words. I hadn't connected my battles for healing from abuse to my spiritual battles. But they flow together. We win by refusing to give in or settle for less than total healing. Or as the saying goes, we keep our eyes on the prize. The more vigilant we are about our spiritual growth, the more readily we heal from our emotional, painful abuse.

In the book of Hebrews, we are encouraged by these words: "Therefore, since we are surrounded by such a huge crowd of witnesses to the life of faith, let us strip off every weight that slows us down, especially the sin that so easily trips us up" (Hebrews 12:1a).

For me and for many men, the "sin that so easily trips us up" is often fear. That dread shows itself in many ways.

Some are afraid they won't like who they are at the end; some hide from facing themselves with no illusions. That's new territory for them.

Early in my healing, I felt fear and anxiety. I realized that, if I became whole, I'd have to focus on my anger—I carried a lot of that deep inside me—as well as other issues that I had avoided.

Some of us are too afraid to face those inner demons, so we don't confront them. They won't control us, but we'll never know that until we face them. The threat of the evil behind the door can prevent many of us from stepping forward and turning the handle.

I understand. At one point, I wondered if I would despise myself for my failures and weaknesses.

The passage in Hebrews goes on to say, "And let us run with endurance the race God has set before us. We do this by keeping our eyes on Jesus, the champion who initiates and perfects our faith" (12:1b–2a).

Run with endurance.

Don't quit.

Keep running. There is victory ahead.

That's the message for us to hammer into our minds. I've met too many men who started the healing journey and quit along the way.

✦　✦　✦

I had a good marriage, and Shirley had always been supportive. But about two months into my healing journey, this question began to trouble me: Would Shirley stay with me, or would our marriage become a casualty?

When I was a pastor, I saw the pattern frequently. One person in a relationship changed—which was fine. But if the person changed alone and without the full support of the spouse, deep, deep trouble entered their marriage.

When two people are married, they soon find a balance. For some, it may mean a lot of arguing or it may mean silence. But it's their pattern, and their relationship survives because they continue to go back to that balance. What I call balance may not be healthy, but it works. And on some level, both of them know and survive.

I was concerned about my relationship with Shirley. Not only had she been supportive, but our marriage was the only stable relationship in my life. I had gone through a lot of chaos before we met and also throughout our years together. I had been able to struggle through and survive everything because she was my anchor. I depended on her—at times more than I was aware.

For example, I'm an enthusiast with a lot of energy, a quick decision maker, and I constantly seek new mountains to climb. If I was totally on my own, I'd probably change churches every couple of years. By contrast, Shirley has always been stable, slow to make decisions, and able to tolerate unfavorable situations. She tends to sift out the noise and confusion and allow everything to grow calm. I'm usually in the midst of the chaos.

If I changed—and I knew I would—how would this affect our relationship? We didn't have a set of rules, but before we married, we firmly agreed on one principle: we would never fight.

She's gotten angry at me a few times, and I've certainly upset her, but before we married, we asked God to help us so that we could retreat from a situation before either of us responded with anger. God has helped us to stay with that commitment.

Although I don't recall that we ever set it up as a principle in our marriage, we had a tacit agreement on another factor. I'm a talker. I'm aware that I have to talk things out to know how I feel about anything. I used to say to people that I'm like a fountain that's always pouring out water.

Shirley is like an artesian well. Her reasoning takes place underground. She'll sometimes mention something that concerns her, but no matter how much I'd like to decide an issue in nine seconds, she doesn't work that way. She goes underground, and when she's ready, the water spurts out.

Could we—would we—retain that aspect of our marriage? It had taken me a few years to accept her silence or lack of decision making. She had learned to accept that I've often decided something before she finishes giving me details.

Would that change?

I sensed something in the early days of my healing: for it to be effective and lasting, Shirley had to become part of my healing. It wasn't a journey for me to take alone. For the first few weeks, I had no doubts about her holding my hand as I faced my personal demons.

After a few months, however, doubts crept in. In retrospect, I think it was my old issue of trust and my need for assurance.

One day I said, "When this is over—after I'm in some kind of healed stage—I'll be different. If you're not with me through this journey, we'll both be married, but you won't know who I am."

I stared into her blue eyes as I said those words. Immediately a flicker of pain came over her. I realized in that moment that I needed the assurance and felt I had to hear her say she would stand by me.

She leaned forward, took my hands, and said, "I'm with you, and I want to know everything that's going on."

True to her promise, Shirley has remained by my side, and she's grown along with me. That's not true in every marriage. When one spouse changes, the relationship is no longer the same. It means both have to take the journey together.

When I was a pastor, I saw this principle in action, but it wasn't until after I became heavily involved with other men in their healing process that I frequently saw the results when only one person was healed. These days when men start to heal, I urge them to solidify their personal relationships—to do whatever they can with their partner so they can both grow.

Part of this also comes from the realization that I was a victim, but my wife was also victimized. She met me years later and had to live with the consequences of my abuse. As I healed, I wanted Shirley to adapt to the changes that were taking place inside me.

Until quite recently, whenever I became overwhelmed with emotions, I shut down. I froze and felt nothing. On several occasions, when I most wanted to be with Shirley in *her pain*, I couldn't open up. I had no access to my emotions.

A few times I was able to say that to her—long before I was healed—even though I had no sense that I could change.

Another way it showed up was that I tended to stay busy. I like activity and I'm a doer. But sometimes I got overcommitted and felt overwhelmed. Trapped. I sensed that I couldn't possibly do everything.

When the pressure built up, my escape was to get out of things, to push them away. When I was in grad school, I took almost a double load of courses by going to two different schools, and I did well. In the middle of my second year, I added one more two-hour course, and that course became the proverbial straw that broke the camel's back. I panicked. The only way I knew to cope was to drop at least one course, which I did. I was again able to manage my overscheduled life.

Midway into my healing, I faced one of those overwhelming situations where I felt I had more work commitments than I could complete and still meet the deadlines. Panic engulfed me, and I wasn't sure what to do. I told Shirley how I felt.

"You'll get it all done," she said. "You always do."

I stared at her, and her response became one of those magic moments for me. *I could do everything to which I was committed.*

I needed to calm down and move ahead. I also realized that when I plan activities, I allow more time for getting things done than I actually need. (I don't yet understand the reason for that.) Then I finish my activities early and immediately take on more jobs. I finish everything—and usually early. That part is fine, but the negative side is that I'm often so overwhelmed at the beginning, I'm sure I'll run out of time before I finish. I'm getting better at it, but I'm not yet quite healed.

I mention these issues because they're awarenesses that came through my healing. I was learning to tackle problems and tasks differently. Because Shirley traveled with me, I was able to adjust my life, and she could do the same.

Because of her, I wasn't alone in my painful journey.

GARY

My story, however, is different from Cec's.

I know I'm healing. I know I'm not the person I used to be.

I ponder a question Cec asked: "When I'm healed, who will I be?"

I'm more eager than ever to heal. A friend's voice resonates inside my head, "Make sure you put nothing in front of your own healing. That's one of the greatest gifts you can give your family and those around you."

I'm trying to remove obstacles to my healing and pursue it fully.

I know who I *want to be* when I'm healed and whole. Here's the person I want to be:

> I live each moment, enjoying the present.
> I see things more as they truly are and not as I wish them to be.
> I am less self-conscious, able to more completely engage with
>   the person in front of me.
> I love God and those around me more fully.
> I readily see, acknowledge, and confess my faults.
> I quickly forgive others—whether they ask or not.
> I enjoy healthy, fulfilling relationships.
> I live less in fear, more in faith.
> I am peaceful inside, living with a joy that is not dependent on
>   circumstances.

And that's just the beginning.

I don't know who I'll be when I'm healed, but I look forward to the completion. I'll think and feel differently.

God is in charge of the process, so I know the results will be spectacular.

> I don't know who I'll be after I'm healed,
> but I look forward to the end result.

39

HOW I REUSE MY PAIN.

C<small>EC</small>

A book editor received my manuscript, came to Atlanta, and invited me to have lunch with him. I assumed he was going to offer me a contract.

He didn't like the book; however, he did say, "You understand people and you have the ability to get inside their heads and hearts."

That surprised me. I certainly had never thought about that ability, but he said he had seen that in my writing. "We'd like you to be a ghost-writer for our publishing house."

I knew what a ghostwriter was, of course, but I had never tried to write in someone else's point of view. I said yes.

The editor liked the results of the first project I did for them, and he sent another. And another. Over the next few years, I wrote thirty-five books for that publisher.

I did well as a ghostwriter, and it surprised me. I had no idea why I was able to get into others' frame of reference.

Eventually, I figured it out. As a kid, I had learned to observe Mr. Lee. He didn't abuse me every day, but I sensed when he wanted me. I can't explain that or give any example. As a kid, I simply knew.

Even more significant was the study of my father, who was an alcoholic. I learned to watch him and sensed when he was getting ready to beat me. I'm not sure I figured out that Thursday was the worst night. He was often sharp with us, angry, and sometimes sullen. Friday, when he got off work, he immediately headed to Slack's Tavern, a neighborhood bar, where he stayed until late and spent a large part of Saturday there as well.

Unconsciously, I learned to know when it was safe to be around my dad or Mr. Lee. As an adult, I unconsciously transferred those child-hood coping mechanisms into effective adult skills.

This isn't to say that we didn't have pain and trauma as abused children. I never want to minimize that. But that's not the end. God lovingly takes some of those coping skills we used to survive and transforms them into gifts or talents we can use to help others.

I've now met dozens of men and women who are in the helping professions for a variety of reasons. But some of them serve because they understand pain and suffering and can feel what others go through.

From a biblical perspective, this is the principle of Romans 8:28–29a: "And we know that God causes everything to work together for the good of those who love God and are called according to his purpose for them. . . . And he chose them to become like his Son."

To say it more simply, God uses the good and the bad in our lives to make us more like Jesus Christ. That means the worst things that happen in our lives become the means for grace and spiritual growth.

GARY

One thing that is consistent about God throughout the Bible is that he turns evil and disaster into redemption and healing.

Although I was severely abused by people close to me, I also believe that God protected me. The damage has been severe, but it could have been worse. I could have gone any number of directions in my life, but I ended up choosing a helping profession. My desire, even from childhood, has been to help people.

Where did that come from? I believe that in my powerlessness, I chose to protect and help the weak and downtrodden. That was God turning evil into something positive.

"God wastes nothing, especially pain," my mentor said. "If we doubt the redemptive power of pain, all we need do is think about what was accomplished through Christ's pain and suffering. And the suffering wasn't his fault. It was perpetrated on him. He willingly bore the suffering so we could be forgiven and be healed."

I've been willing to allow God to redeem my pain and suffering because I exchanged it for something that leads to freedom and healing for others. I've never felt worthy to be in full-time, vocational ministry. Yet I have been since graduating from college.

I've been drawn to those who were hurting and often neglected by others, to those who seemed the most helpless or didn't know how to reach out for that help. Without attempting to do so, I drew the hurting, wounded people. Although I can't explain it even to myself, I know that they must be aware of that yearning for help or they wouldn't respond to me.

As I've pondered who I am and the people to whom I'm attracted, it's not surprising that I have three adopted Colombian daughters who came from an abusive background.

As a professional in the church, I've started recovery ministries. At the time of this writing, I'm employed as a hospice chaplain and absolutely love what I do.

From childhood I was drawn to the story of Joseph in the Old Testament. He came from a highly dysfunctional family. His father, Jacob, was a deceiver and a thief who played favorites. Joseph was the special one, but that got him into trouble because his ten older brothers resented him. His brothers were jealous and probably had a right to feel that way.

God gave the young man dreams in which his brothers bowed down to him. That only exacerbated the conflict, and even his father rebuked him for flaunting that information.

In time, the brothers detested Joseph enough to plot to kill him. Instead, they sold him as a slave to traders going into Egypt. They tore his coat, dipped it in blood, and let their father believe that his favorite son had been killed by a wild animal.

Joseph was seventeen years old when he went from the favorite, doted-upon son to a slave with no rights, alone in a foreign country. Over the next thirteen years, Joseph was promoted in the house of his new master, falsely accused of assaulting his master's wife, and thrown into prison. He was promoted within the prison, used by God to interpret dreams, but then forgotten by one who could have spoken up for him and had him released.

When Joseph was thirty years old, God provided an amazing opportunity for him to interpret the dreams of Pharaoh, king of Egypt, with the result that Joseph became second-in-command of the most advanced civilization in the world.

Joseph must have made many serious decisions during those thirteen hard and discouraging years. He didn't become bitter or angry, and the whole time, he was able to trust God. He learned to allow God to use him where he was.

When famine struck the region, the brothers who sold him into slavery stood before Joseph (whom they didn't recognize). They were totally dependent on him for food, and the powerful man could do whatever he wanted with them.

What he decided to do was astounding: he chose to forgive. When he revealed himself to his brothers, they were terrified. But he embraced and accepted them.

After their father died, the brothers were again terrified that Joseph would seek revenge. (They assumed he had been waiting until the death of their father before taking vengeance on them.) Joseph discerned their concerns, and his response to his brothers still astounds me:

"But Joseph replied, 'Don't be afraid of me. Am I God, that I can punish you? You intended to harm me, but God intended it all for good. He brought me to this position so I could save the lives of many people. No, don't be afraid. I will continue to take care of you and your children.' So he reassured them by speaking kindly to them" (Genesis 50:19–21).

Joseph refused to punish his brothers or to seek revenge. He refused to hold a grudge. God had been at work throughout his life, turning evil into good.

I see this principle at work clearly. God turns intended evil into good. God takes suffering and rejection and uses it for tremendous blessing.

I'm challenged by Joseph. I want to be able to forgive like that. I've got a start on it. I want that same attitude. In my mind I envision myself in front of my abusers saying, "You meant it to harm me, but God used it for good. Look at what God has done."

My abusers are gone, but I'm challenged again to think deeper about my past and my pain.

Joseph's story is a cause of encouragement for me. It reminds me that God can use what happened to me for good. He has. He will.

God wants to heal my pain to bring healing to others.

40

I CAN LEARN FROM THE SERENITY PRAYER.

GARY

Most people today are familiar with what has become known as the Serenity Prayer. I thought I knew it.

I did—that is, I knew a small, slightly altered portion of the original. The Serenity Prayer was written by Reinhold Niebuhr. I discovered a number of slight variations in versions of this prayer, but here is the most authentic I can find:

> God, give us the grace to accept with serenity the things that cannot be changed, courage to change the things which should be changed, and the wisdom to distinguish the one from the other. Living one day at a time, enjoying one moment at a time, accepting hardship as a pathway to peace, taking, as Jesus did, this sinful world as it is, not as I would have it, trusting that you will make all things right, if I surrender to your will, so that I may be reasonably happy in this life, and supremely happy with you forever in the next. Amen.

Several things about this prayer I find helpful and enlightening.

> God, give us the grace to accept with serenity
> the things that cannot be changed . . .

This is the part almost everyone knows. It reminds me to ask for grace so I can deal with life in such a way that I have serenity. I like the word *serenity.* Peace. A sense of inner calm comes from trusting that God is in charge and all will work out well. I want that. I tend to be either high or low. I want to be more steady. I need that settledness of soul.

I need to accept what happened. I wish it hadn't, but it did. I used to try to keep myself from feeling the horrors of it, but the longer I did that, the more I lived in denial, trying to convince myself that it didn't really happen.

But it did. Many times.

And those abusive experiences had terrible, drastic, lifelong effects.

I accept the fact that only God can meet my primal cry for unconditional love. I didn't get what I needed from my mother; I can't make others responsible for providing what was kept from me in childhood. They can never meet that need. I was aware of that, but something kept me searching, yearning for some human to fill that void. I want God to give me *"grace to accept with serenity the things that cannot be changed."*

> Courage to change the things
> which should be changed . . .

I am *not* stuck; I can make choices. And I ask God for courage. I need supernatural courage to change the things that I can modify or amend. I can heal. I can seek healing. I can resolve to place nothing in front of my healing, but make it my highest priority, for my sake and the sake of all those attached to me.

I can't change what happened to me, but I can change myself by turning to God to correct the wrongs and to meet my needs.

> And the wisdom to distinguish
> the one from the other.

Sometimes I don't know whether to accept what's going on right now or to fight against it. I need wisdom and spiritual discernment. Solomon advises, "Getting wisdom is the wisest thing you can do! And whatever else you do, develop good judgment" (Proverbs 4:7).

> Living one day at a time,
> enjoying one moment at a time,
> accepting hardship as a pathway to peace . . .

I long to live in the moment. I'm lousy at it. I seem to live in all times but the present. I worry about what to do next. I get stuck on what happened yesterday and what it will mean for tomorrow. I seem to focus mostly on the future but feel like every thought about the future is colored by the past.

Fretting and worrying keep me from engaging in the moment with whomever I'm with, and I'm not fully aware or present. I miss important items or events. I move from one thing to the next. When I realize what I'm doing, I stop and consciously live in the moment. The contrast is striking.

When I'm strictly in the moment, a strange thing happens. A sense of connection. A deeper sense of reality. Peace. Serenity.

Godly peace comes with living in the reality of the now. It takes practice and concerted effort. And I'm amazed at how much I still live in the past/future.

If I'm in the now, I can accept hardship more readily. I was sexually abused and carry a lot of baggage. It's still getting unpacked. It's a great comfort knowing that great growth and purpose can come from serious trauma and distress. God is a turnaround artist.

> Taking, as Jesus did, this sinful world as it is,
> not as I would have it . . .

This part of the prayer grabs me each time. Although sexual abuse touches every part of our lives, too often, I've chosen to think things were better than they were. I would interpret actions and words as positively as possible. Even though great evil has been perpetrated in my life, I'm still honestly shocked when I see or hear about evil being done.

No one except God sees reality exactly as it is; however, I'm amazed at how blind I can be. Rather than continually interpreting events, I want to see things as they are. If I give up my need to seek unconditional love from others, it seems to help. I see things more clearly because my vision is less clouded by the silent, unconscious drivenness to meet that need.

Words, behavior, and relationships are what they are. I could wish that certain people or circumstances were different, but that doesn't change the facts. I want to see the world as it is and engage with it.

> Trusting that you will make things right,
> if I surrender to your will,
> so that I may be reasonably happy in this life,
> and supremely happy with you forever in the next.

I can choose to surrender to God because it's the only way I can be "reasonably happy" in my day-to-day living. I also remind myself, as many do, that I'm a Christian under construction. God is still building, changing, and correcting my life. And in the process, I'm transformed by divine grace.

I'm not in charge of my life even though I sometimes act that way. I can influence others and work hard, but I'm not in control of much. The best I can do (and even that not perfectly) is take control of myself. That means I need to stop trying to manage and fix people and situations and instead exercise what the Bible calls self-control.

It's up to God to do what he wants. He planned me, created me, and included me in his love story. Yet I'm reluctant to surrender because full trust is still difficult for me. As I witness the Holy Spirit at work in my daily life, thank him, and appreciate what he's doing, it's getting easier to trust.

Once in a while—and less often than before—a lurking fear whispers, "If you can no longer protect yourself, more abuse might occur."

A counselor friend said, "Self-protection comes from not being or feeling loved. Self-protection leads to an unhealthy self-reliance, and self-reliance moves us away from God."

I see this in my life all the time. As I allow God to meet my primal need for unconditional mother-love, my need to protect myself will diminish. I want to surrender, fully and completely.

God still has to do healing work for that to happen. But I believe he is doing it now, as I type. I want to surrender. I want to heal and live life with more peace and joy. I want this for myself and for all those with whom I come in contact. Happy? That's a word that, if I'm honest, I don't allow myself to think of too often.

If happy means pleased, content, joyful, and peaceful, I long for happiness. I get tastes of it from time to time—just enough so that I'm not satisfied and I want more.

I want

> more freedom to be myself;
> more love and to feel more loved;
> to be more loving, kind, and tender toward others;
> to be transparently real; and
> to surrender fully, completely to God.

I'm definitely not quite healed. Some days, I feel far from my goal. When that happens, I pluck and chew the leaves of my artichoke and discover the unhealed parts.

Most of all, I remind myself that healing is a process, not a destination. The silence has been shattered. The light is shining.

> Because I seek divine wisdom,
> I will receive it, and I will grow.

I hurt for a long time because of childhood sexual abuse, and I wanted to provide a safe place where hurting men could connect with other survivors of sexual abuse. Visit www.menshatteringthesilence.blogspot.com.

CEC

At the end of each chapter, I wrote self-affirming truth statements. I'm reprinting them here with a number corresponding to the chapter in which the truth was presented. You might choose to copy them or say one or more daily.

1. I'm not quite healed, but I am being healed.
2. I am not quite healed; I am a healing-in-progress.
3. I was a needy, innocent child; someone took advantage of me. I wasn't bad; something bad was done to me.
4. I matter to God—the one who has the power to heal me.
5. Because I'm being healed, I continue to gain new insights into my behavior.
6. It hurts to learn more about myself, but the pain assures me that I am learning. And growing.
7. I will avoid using code words for my failure. I confess my wrongdoing, ask God to help me not to do it again, and take more steps down the healing path.
8. Pornography is a substitute for intimacy. I choose to strive for the real thing.
9. Despite my attractions and desires, I don't have to give in to any wrong impulses.
10. Others may not like who I am, and that's all right. For a long time I didn't like me either.
11. The need to feel responsible as an adult comes from my powerlessness as a child.
12. God gave me emotions; the more I heal, the more aware I become of what I feel.

13. Life's paradoxes can be confusing, but the more honest I'm willing to be, the less often contradictions trouble me.

14. I may feel lonely, but I am never alone; God is with me.

15. When I speak aloud about my abuse, I am healing my shame and empowering myself.

16. I'll never be fully healed if I hide the secrets of my past. A big step—and a difficult one—is to move out of darkness into light.

17. I don't like to feel the pain again, but the only way out of the pain is to go through it again.

18. Grief is not my enemy; it testifies that what happened really does matter.

19. That which seems the most intimate and private, when expressed well, becomes the most universal.

20. I can turn from the lies I believed; I can embrace the truth because the truth sets me free.

21. The lies are many, and I believed them. The truth is simple, but I'm often slow to accept wonderful, loving messages about myself.

22. I don't deserve your love. I can't earn it. Thank you, God, that I can accept it.

23. I can be—and will be—compassionate toward myself.

24. God not only forgives sin; God loves the sinners. That's the example I want to follow.

25. Forgiveness is difficult for me, but it's simple for God. He's the expert, and he teaches me how to forgive.

26. Our perpetrators did wrong. Our best revenge is to extend compassion.

27. Accountability is the first step toward livability.

28. Admitting I need help is a sign of humility, not weakness. Reaching out for help is a sign of courage.

29. The tools that helped me survive as a child are no longer the

tools I need to enjoy my adult life. Now I can consciously choose my tools.

30. Because of my abuse, I have a hurting soul and an injured body. But I am healing in both soul and body.

31. My childhood was stolen from me, but I can rescue my inner child and become whole.

32. I don't have to keep listening to the same words inside my head. I have the power to change them.

33. I can't change the past, but I can pick up the painful pieces of my past and become whole.

34. What do I really want? It's a question I'm learning to answer for myself. As I face my desires, I continue to heal.

35. I give to others what I want to receive. That's part of my quest for wholeness.

36. When I give of myself to those in pain, I fulfill my calling as God's hero. I complete the circle.

37. I am becoming different. And I like the new me.

38. I don't know who I'll be after I'm healed, but I look forward to the end result.

39. God wants to heal my pain to bring healing to others.

40. Because I seek divine wisdom, I will receive it, and I will grow.

— *Acknowledgments* —

Special words of love from Cec to Shirley and his supportive family.

Many thanks to Steve Barclift and the fine people at Kregel Publications for having the courage to publish this book as well as my previous book, *When a Man You Love Was Abused.*

Both of us want to express appreciation for our agent, Deidre Knight, of the Knight Agency.

Special gratitude from Gary to the Wills family for their incredible support and to counselor Paul Casale for his crucial role in Gary's healing journey.